I0727961

富士山

八十八景

Eighty-eight views of Mt. Fuji

PIE INTERNATIONAL

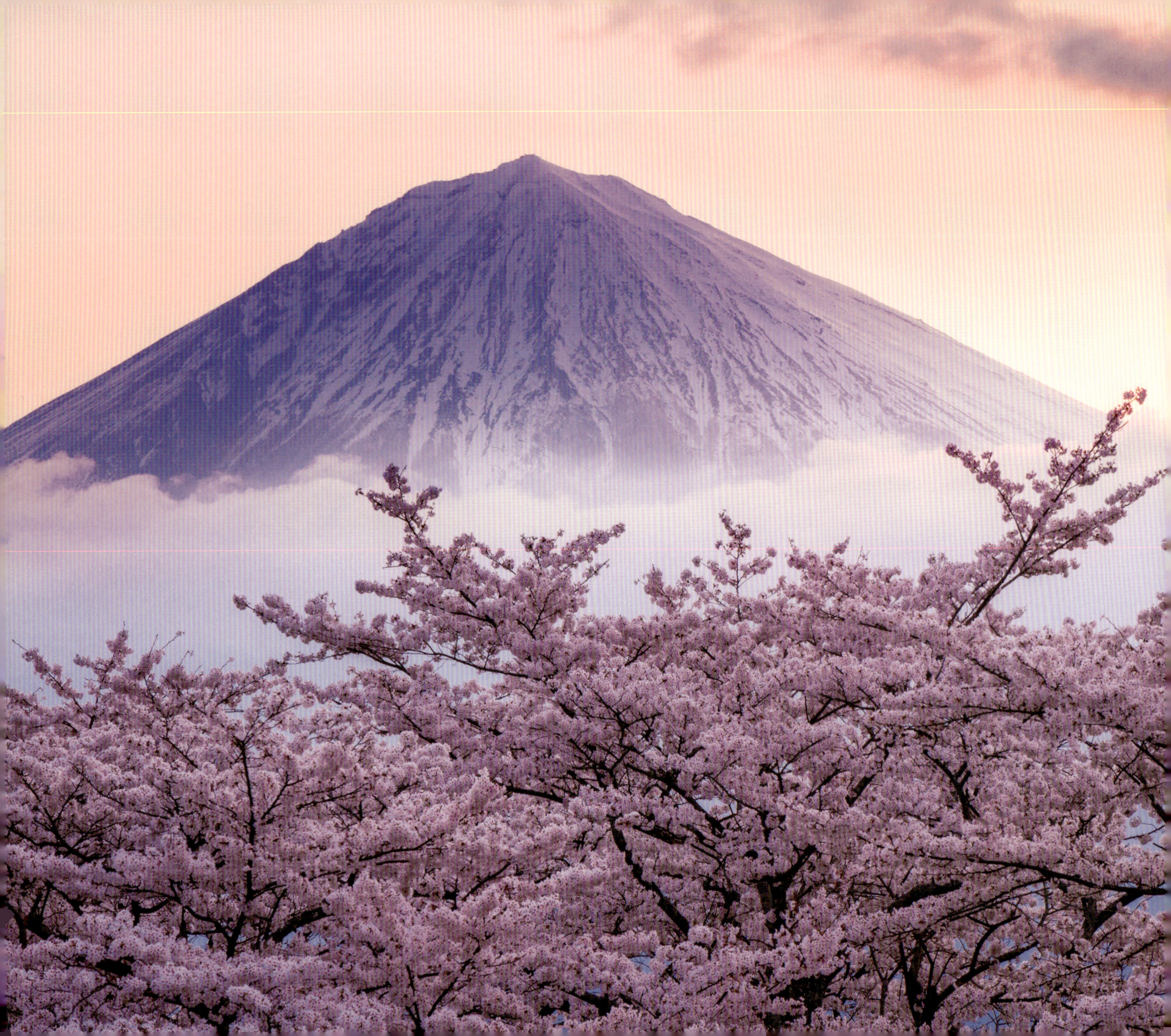

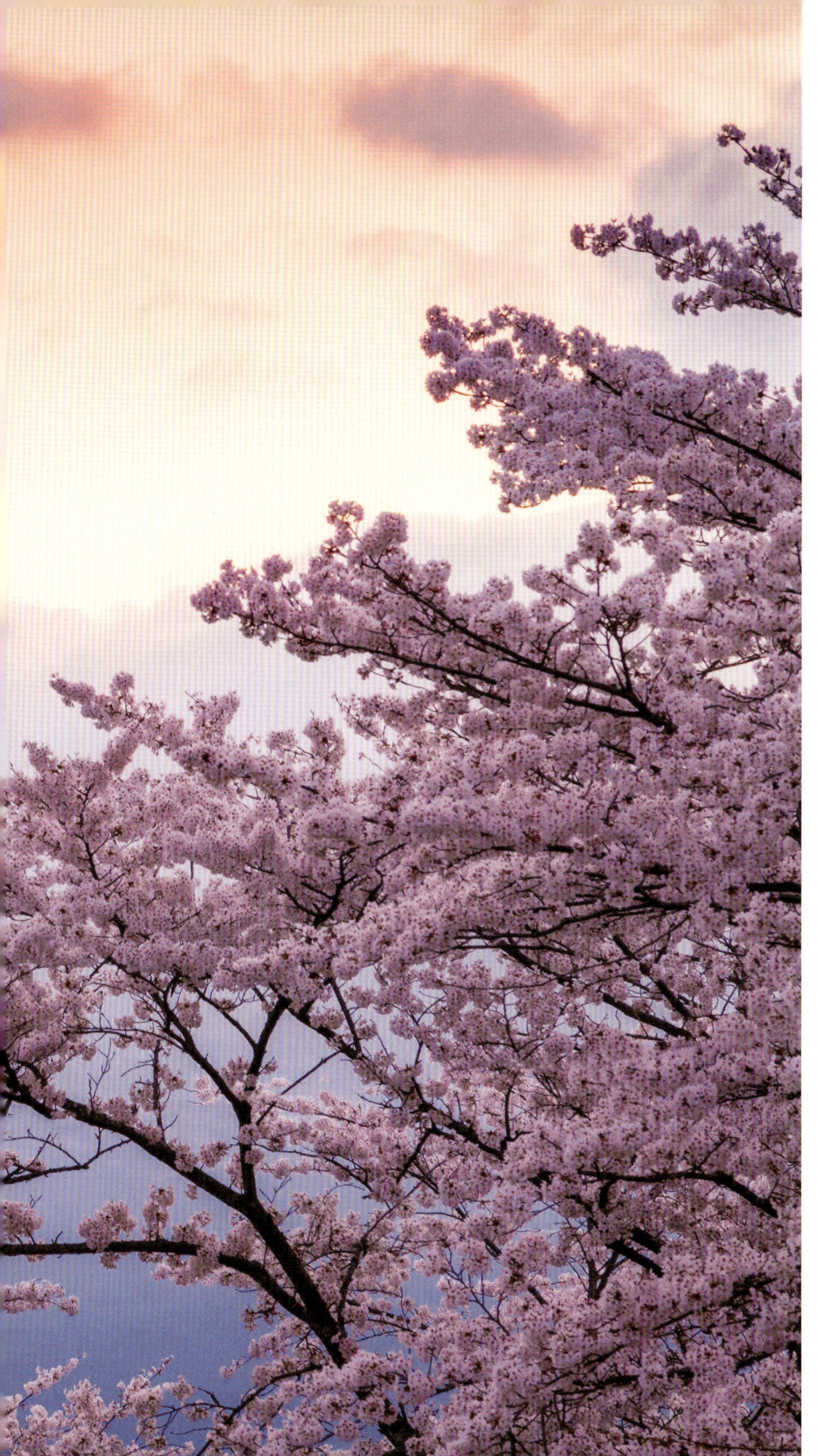

01　朝焼けの富士山と桜　　　　　高椋俊樹

山麓に湧いた雲から、突き抜けた富士山が、朝焼けによって神秘的な雰囲気を纏っていた。富士山は桜がよく似合う。（静岡県富士宮市）

Mt. Fuji and cherry blossoms at sunrise

Sunrise suffuses Mt. Fuji with an aura of mystery, as it pierces through the clouds at its base. Cherry blossoms pair to perfection with Fuji. (Fujinomiya, Shizuoka)

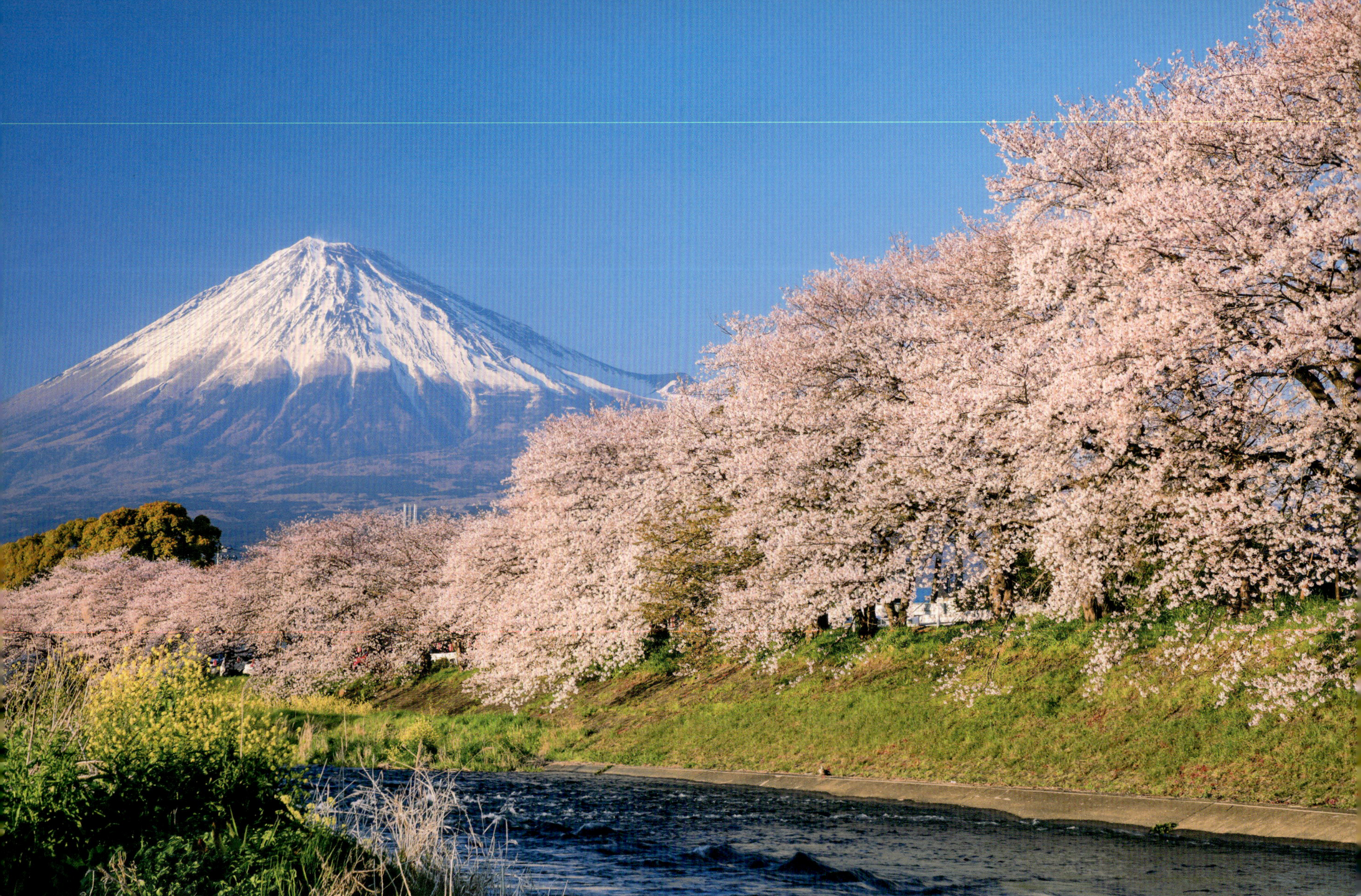

02　夕日を浴びる龍巌淵の桜と富士山　　縄手英樹

潤井川（うるいがわ）沿いに咲く龍巌淵（りゅうがんぶち）の桜並木
は、夕日がしっかりと当たるので、夕暮れ時はオレンジ色に染まる。
花見客も日が暮れるのを待って帰っていく。（静岡県富士市）

Cherry blossoms of Ryuganbuchi at sunset and Mt. Fuji

The stretch of cherry trees blooming along the Urui River at Ryuganbuchi
is tinged orange by the rays of the setting sun. Cherry blossom viewers
also await this spectacle, before returning home. (Fuji, Shizuoka)

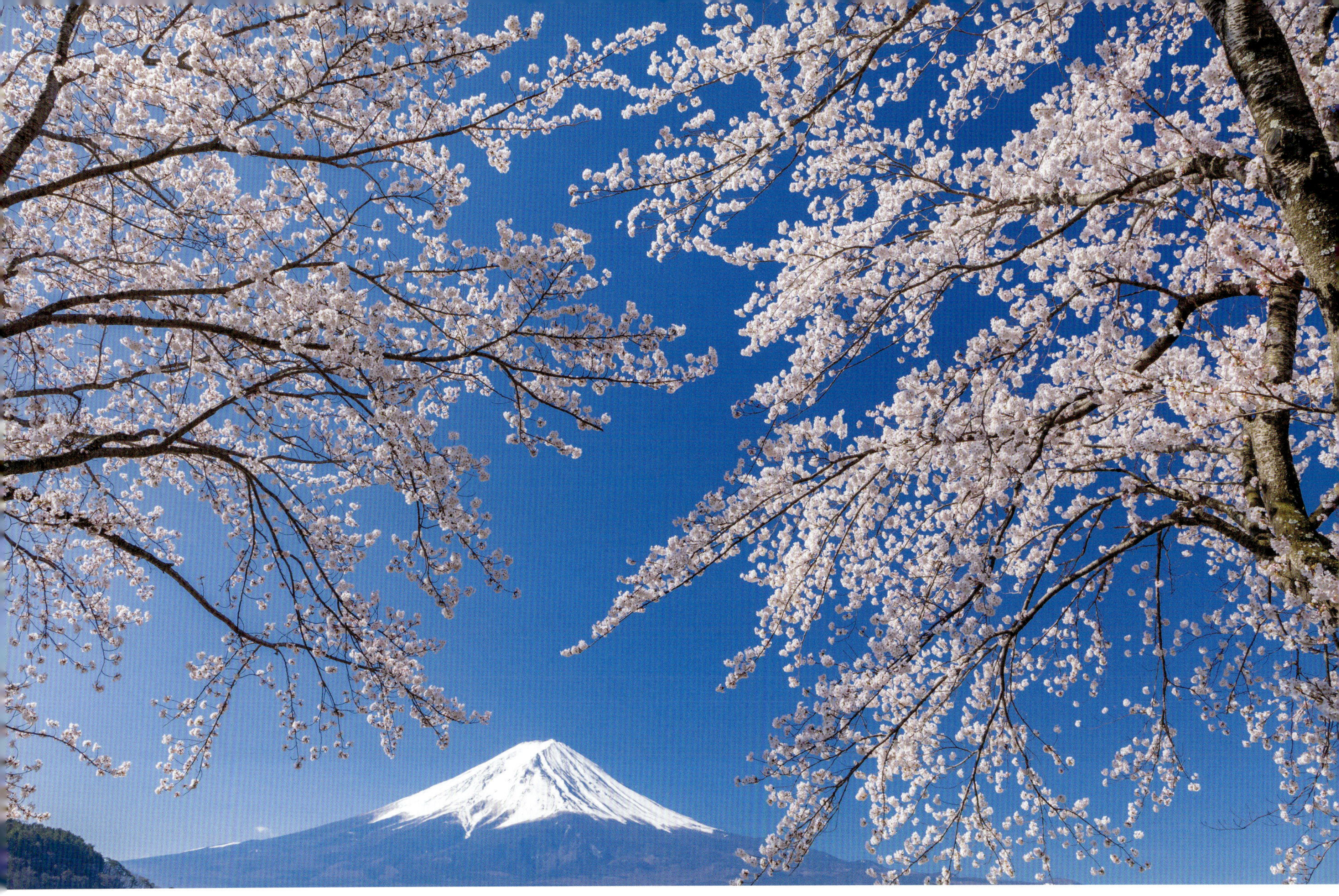

03 河口湖の桜と富士山　　　　　　　　　　　　　　山梨勝弘

日本を代表する富士と桜は実によく似合う。河口湖畔の桜の時期に
は国内外から多くの観光客が押し寄せる。人波をカットしての撮影
となった。(山梨県南都留郡富士河口湖町 / 河口湖)

Cherry blossoms at Lake Kawaguchi and Mt. Fuji

Symbol-of-Japan Mt. Fuji pairs exquisitely with cherry blossoms.
People flock from near and far to see the Kawaguchi lakeside cherry
trees in bloom, making careful cropping a must in order to exorcise
their presence. (Fujikawaguchiko, Yamanashi / Lake Kawaguchi)

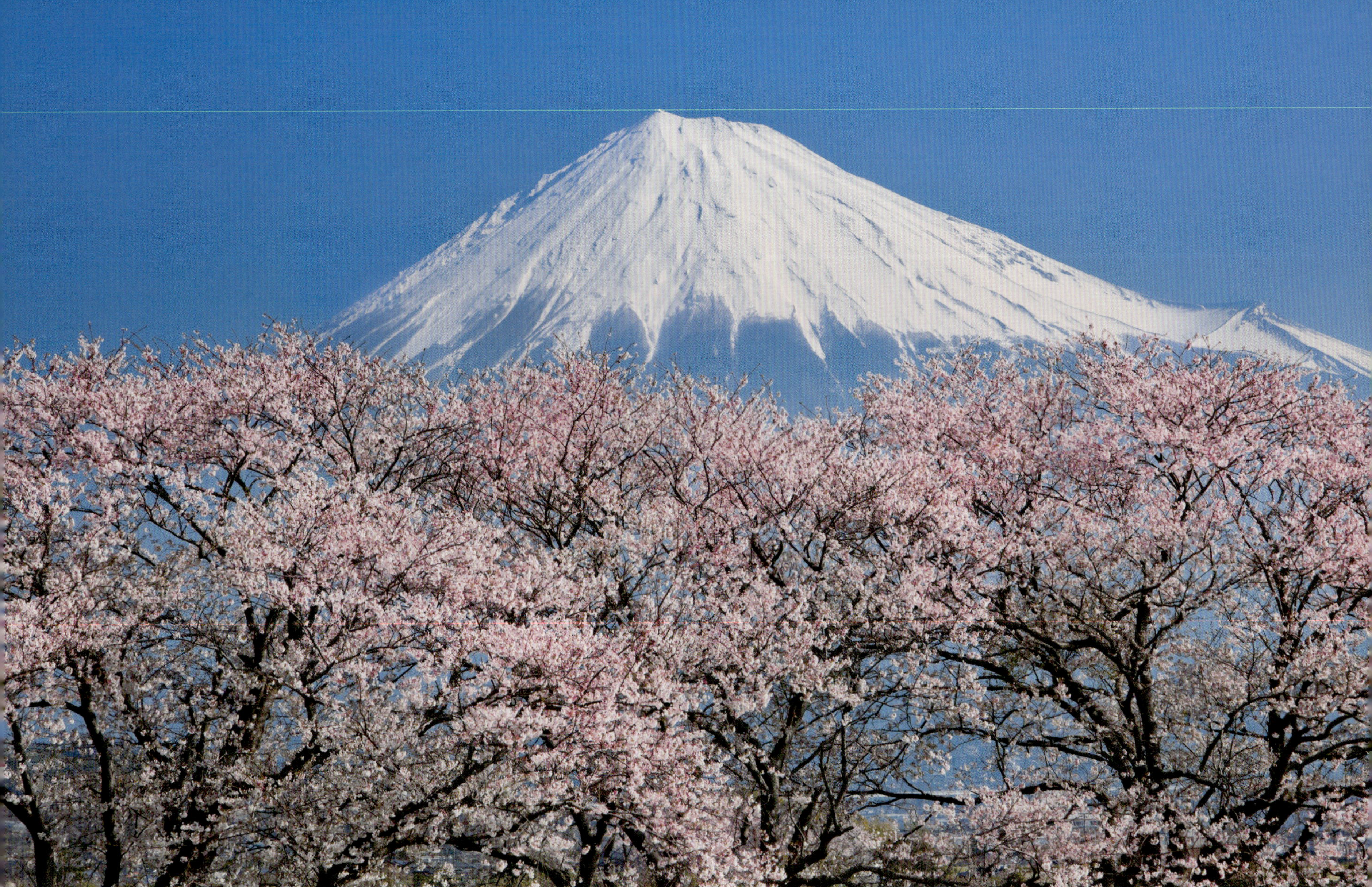

04 **かりがね堤の桜と富士山**　山梨勝弘

富士川沿いの2キロに及ぶかりがね堤には芝生広場が広がる。約120本のソメイヨシノは3月下旬から4月上旬に見頃を迎える。（静岡県富士市／かりがね堤）

Cherry blossoms at Karigane Zutsumi and Mt. Fuji

Cherry blossoms stretch for two kilometers along the Fuji River at the Karigane Zutsumi green. There, some 120 Somei Yoshino, the king of cherry trees, come into full bloom from late March to early April. (Fuji, Shizuoka / Karigane embankment)

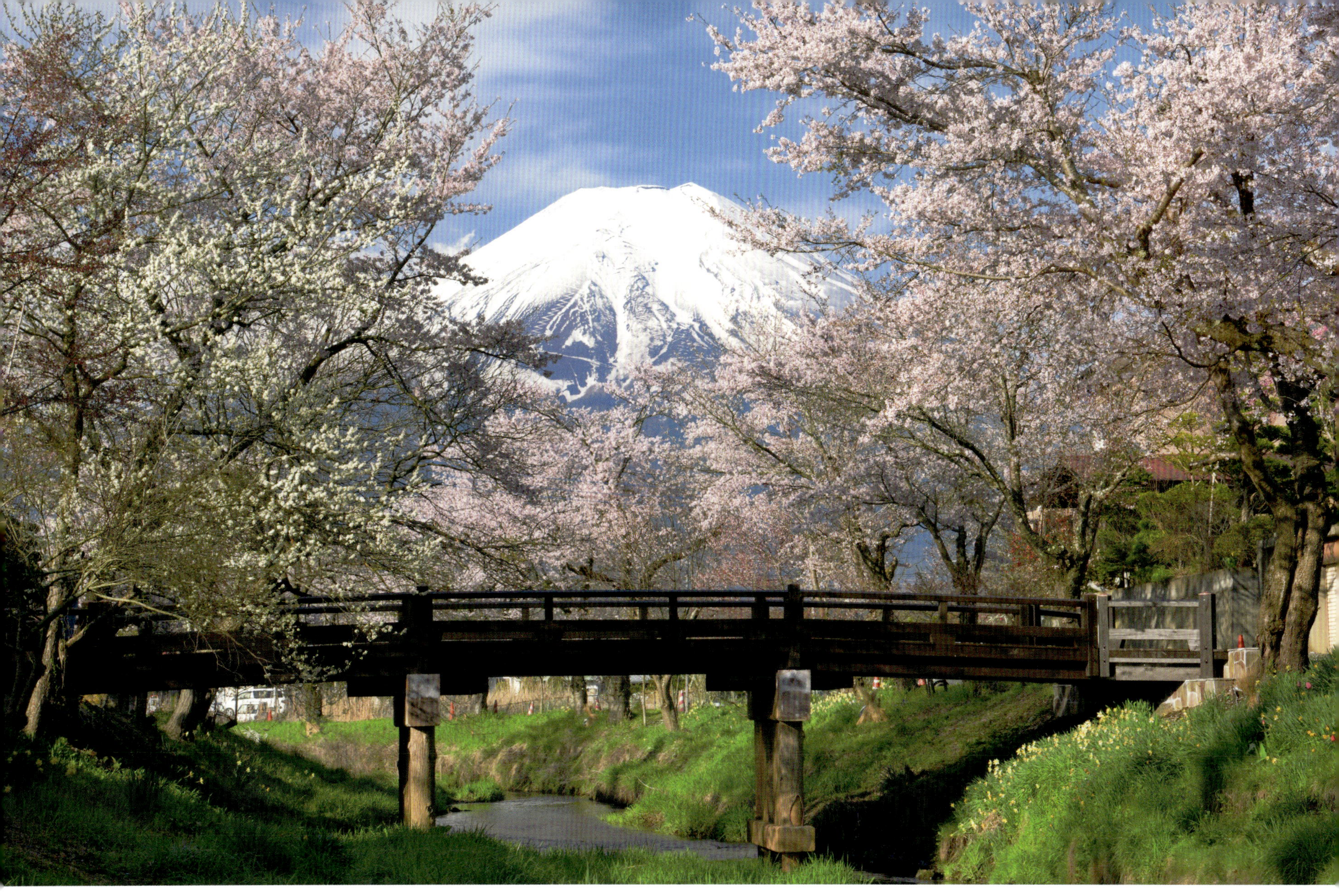

05 新名庄川の桜並木と富士山　　深澤武

新名庄川に架かるお宮橋は桜並木と富士山を見渡せる絶好の
ビュースポット。小川沿いにはスイセンなどの花々が咲いており、忍
野らしい春の風景を楽しむことができた。（山梨県南都留郡忍野村）

Cherry trees along the Shinnasho River and Mt. Fuji

This bridge spanning the Shinnasho River offers a splendid lookout over the cherry trees lining the riverbanks and Mt. Fuji beyond. Narcissus and other flowers in bloom along the stream enhanced this delightful spring scene in Oshino. (Oshino, Yamanashi)

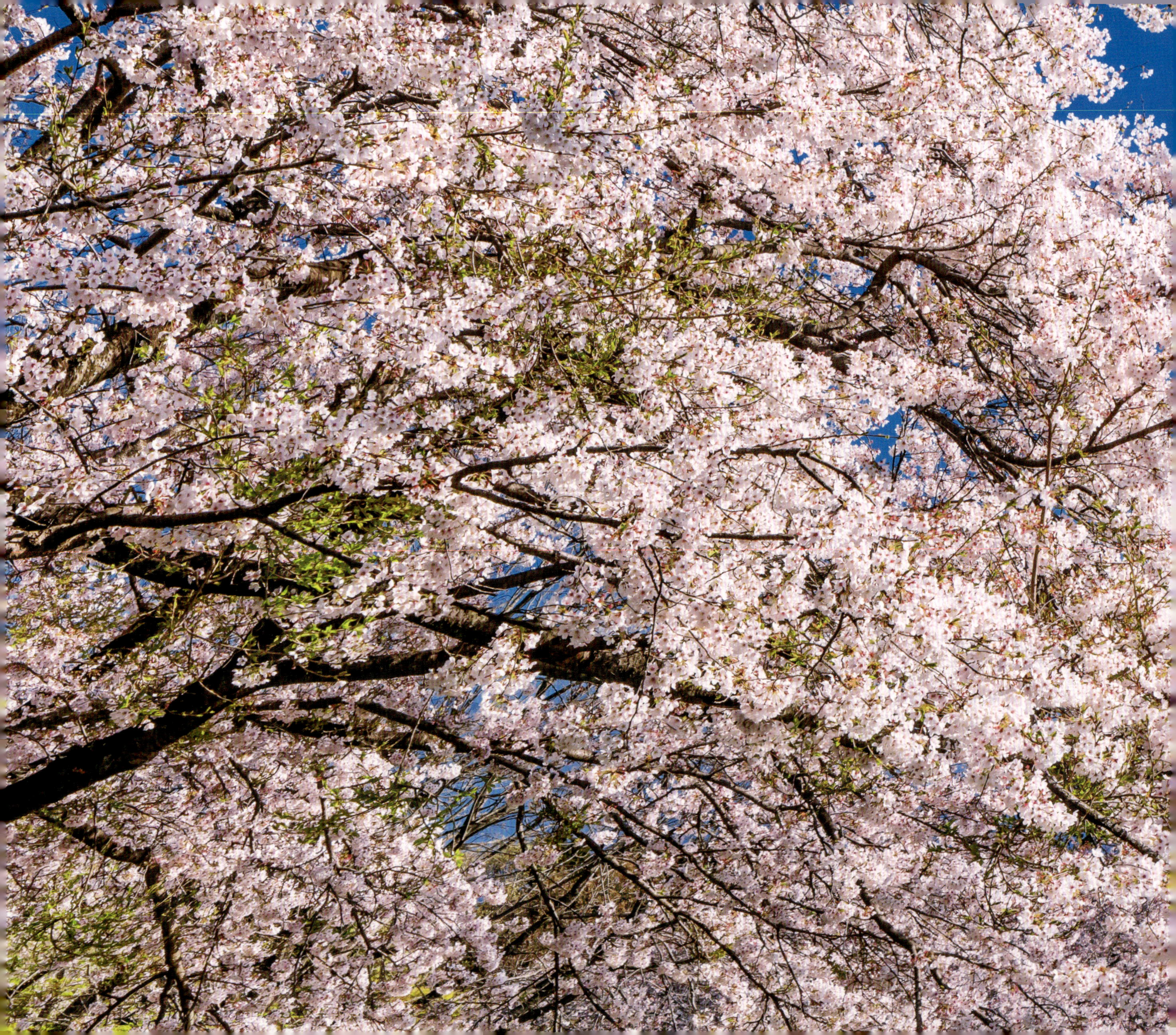

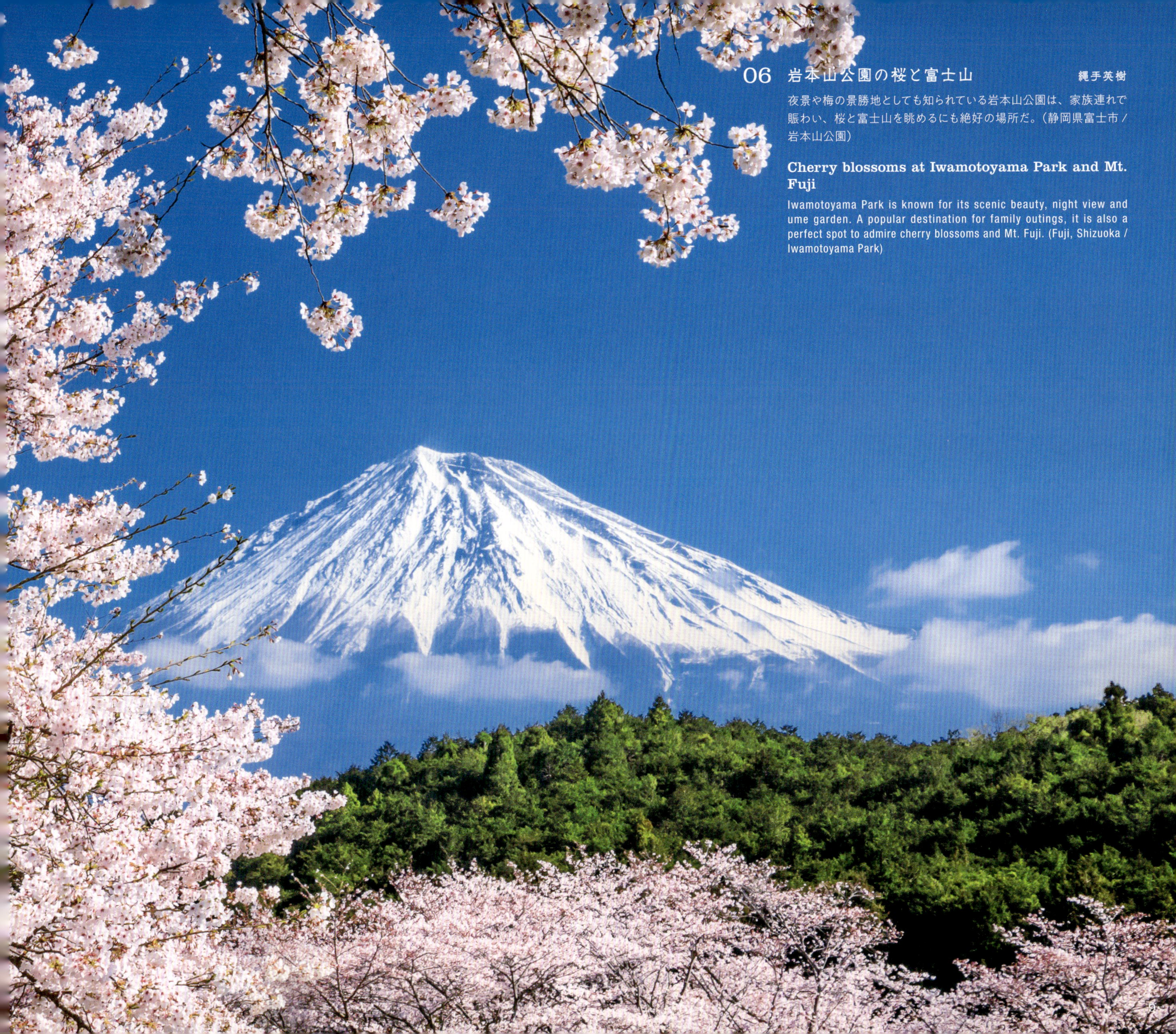

06 岩本山公園の桜と富士山
縄手英樹
夜景や梅の景勝地としても知られている岩本山公園は、家族連れで賑わい、桜と富士山を眺めるにも絶好の場所だ。（静岡県富士市／岩本山公園）

Cherry blossoms at Iwamotoyama Park and Mt. Fuji

Iwamotoyama Park is known for its scenic beauty, night view and ume garden. A popular destination for family outings, it is also a perfect spot to admire cherry blossoms and Mt. Fuji. (Fuji, Shizuoka / Iwamotoyama Park)

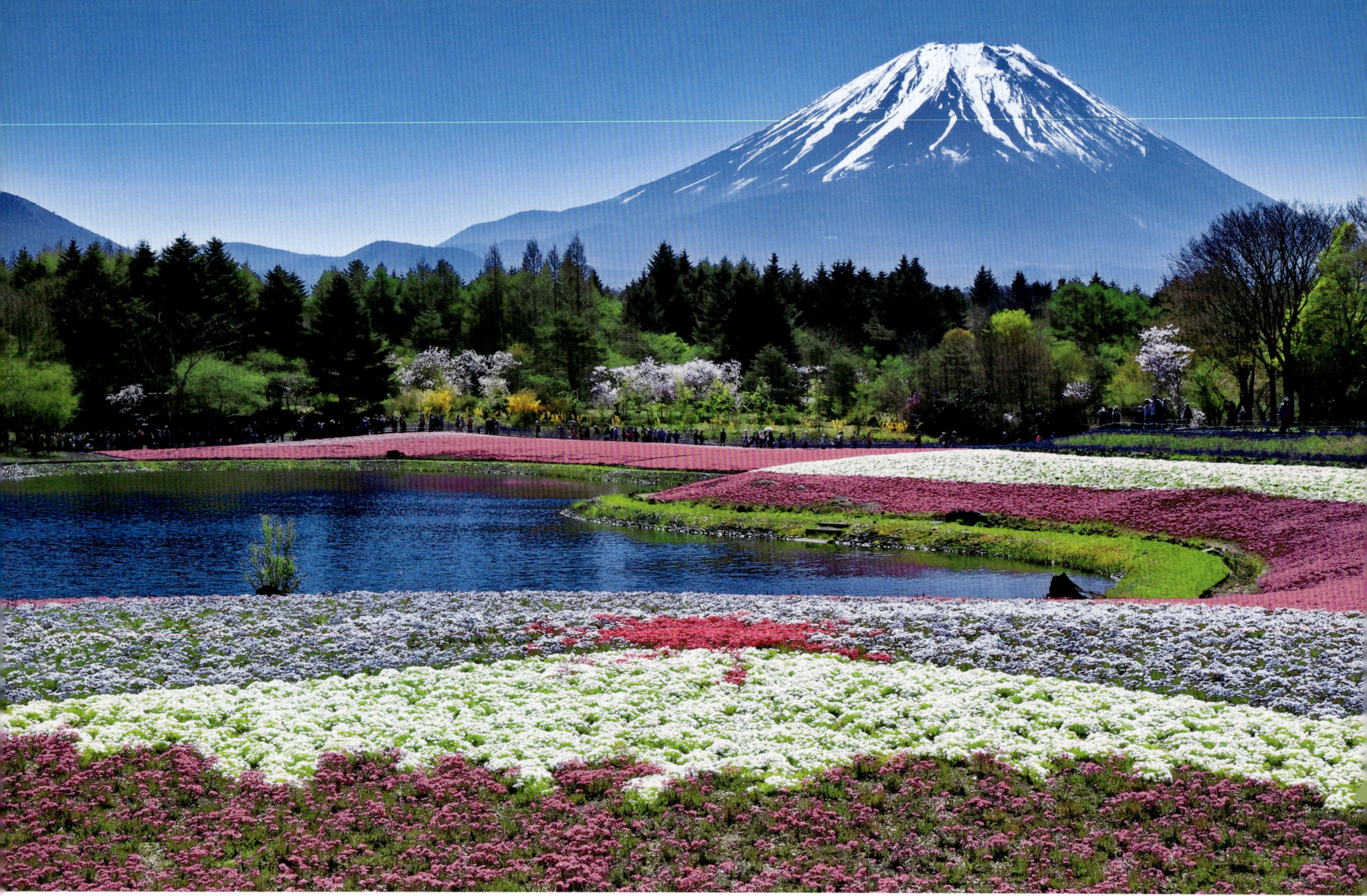

　富士本栖湖リゾートの芝桜　　　　米原敬太郎

芝桜が満開になると、交通が麻痺するくらいに人が押し寄せる。家
族での行楽にぴったりの楽し気な富士山の姿だ。（山梨県南都留郡
富士河口湖町）

Moss pinks at Fuji Motosuko Resort

Local roads are paralyzed as people throng to see this carpet of moss
pinks in bloom. Set against Mt. Fuji as a backdrop, this resort makes
for a delightful family outing. (Fujikakoko, Yamanashi)

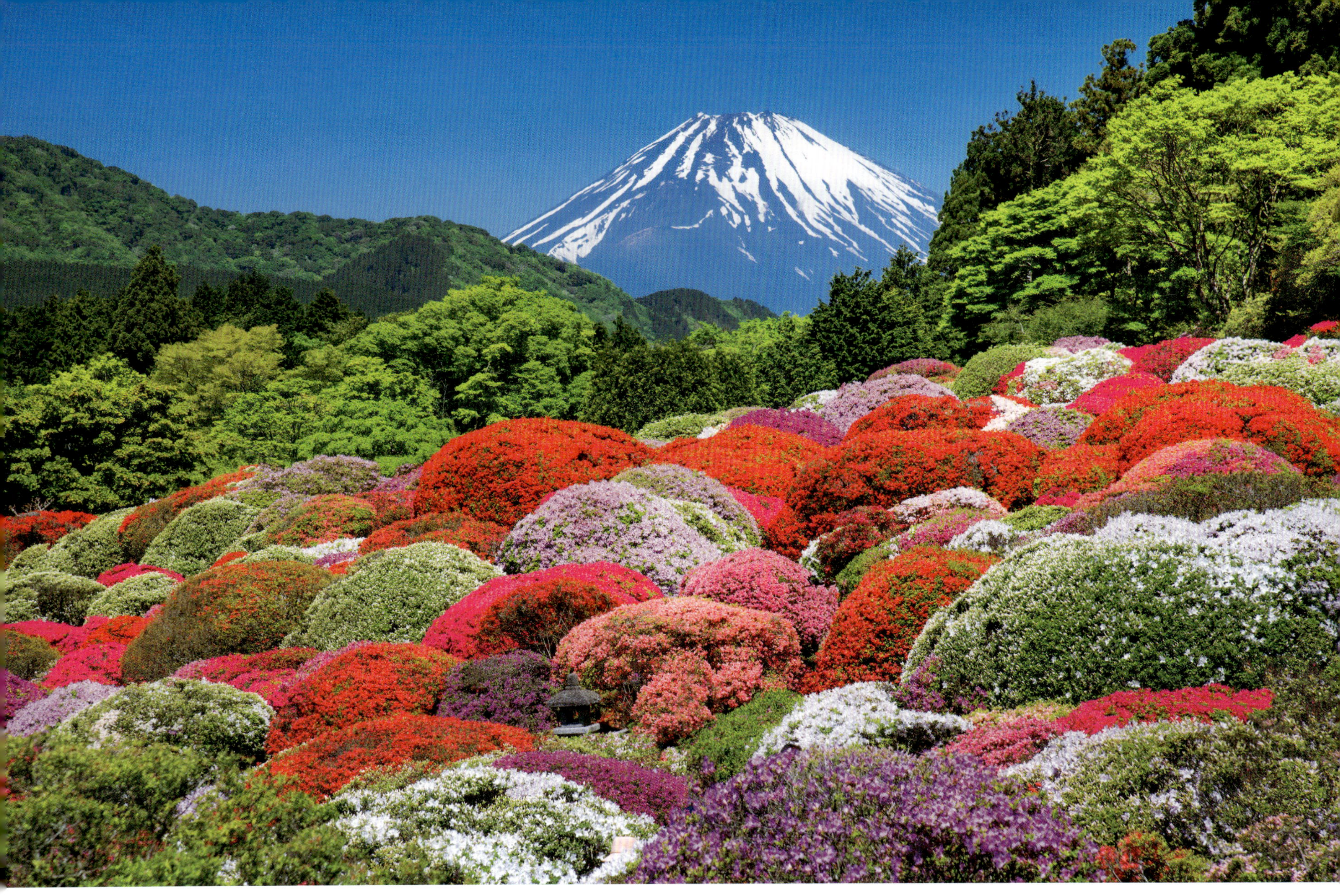

08 ツツジと富士山　　　　　　　　　　片岡巌

箱根芦ノ湖畔にある「小田急 山のホテル」の庭園で5月中旬になると、富士山を背景に色とりどりのツツジやシャクナゲが咲き誇る。（神奈川県足柄下郡箱根町）

Azaleas and Mt. Fuji

Azaleas and rhododendrons of various colors bloom in mid-May, against Mt. Fuji in the background, in the garden of the Odakyu Yamano Hotel located at Lake Ashino in Hakone. (Hakone, Kanagawa)

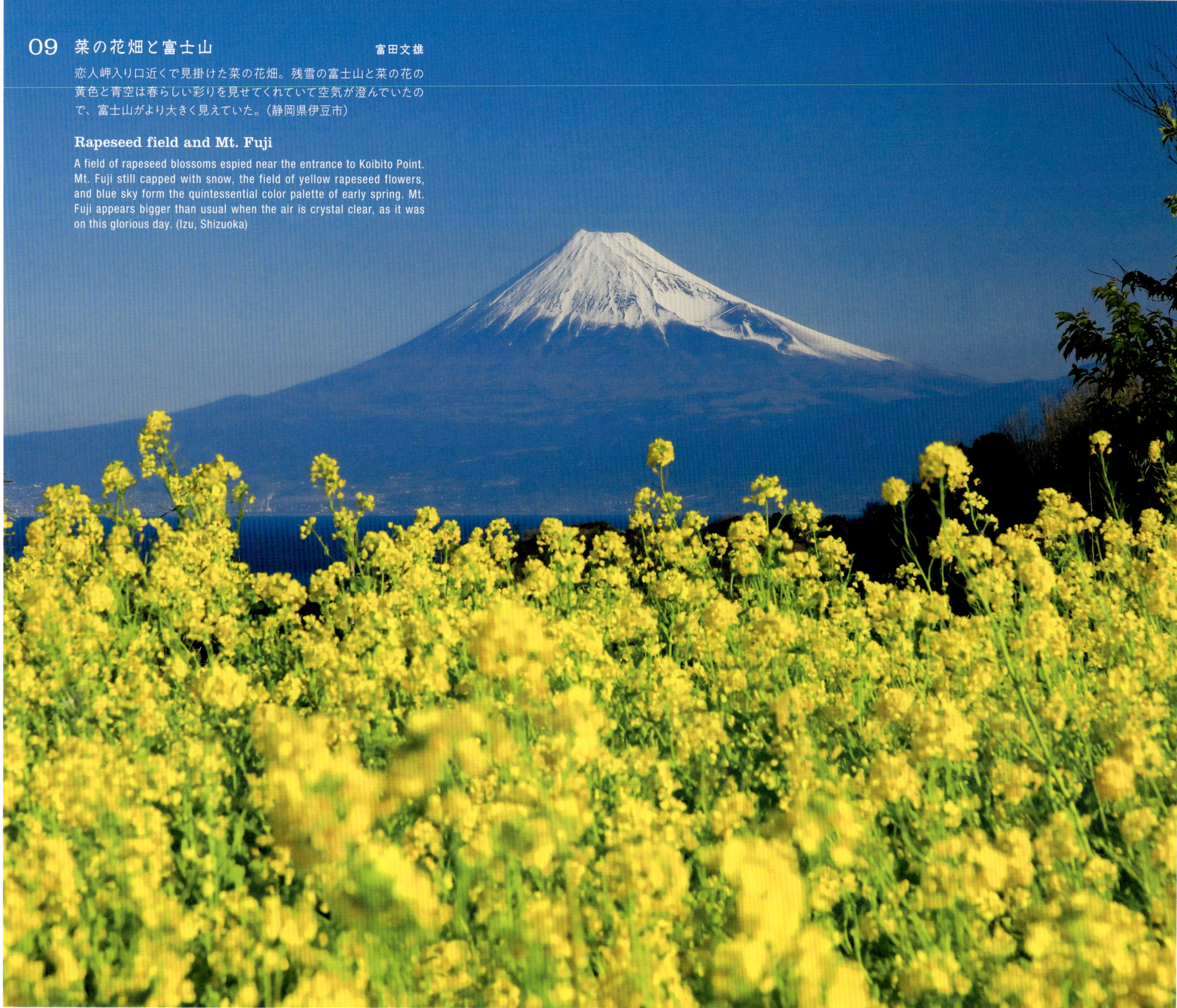

09　菜の花畑と富士山　　富田文雄

恋人岬入り口近くで見掛けた菜の花畑。残雪の富士山と菜の花の
黄色と青空は春らしい彩りを見せてくれていて空気が澄んでいたの
で、富士山がより大きく見えていた。(静岡県伊豆市)

Rapeseed field and Mt. Fuji

A field of rapeseed blossoms espied near the entrance to Koibito Point.
Mt. Fuji still capped with snow, the field of yellow rapeseed flowers,
and blue sky form the quintessential color palette of early spring. Mt.
Fuji appears bigger than usual when the air is crystal clear, as it was
on this glorious day. (Izu, Shizuoka)

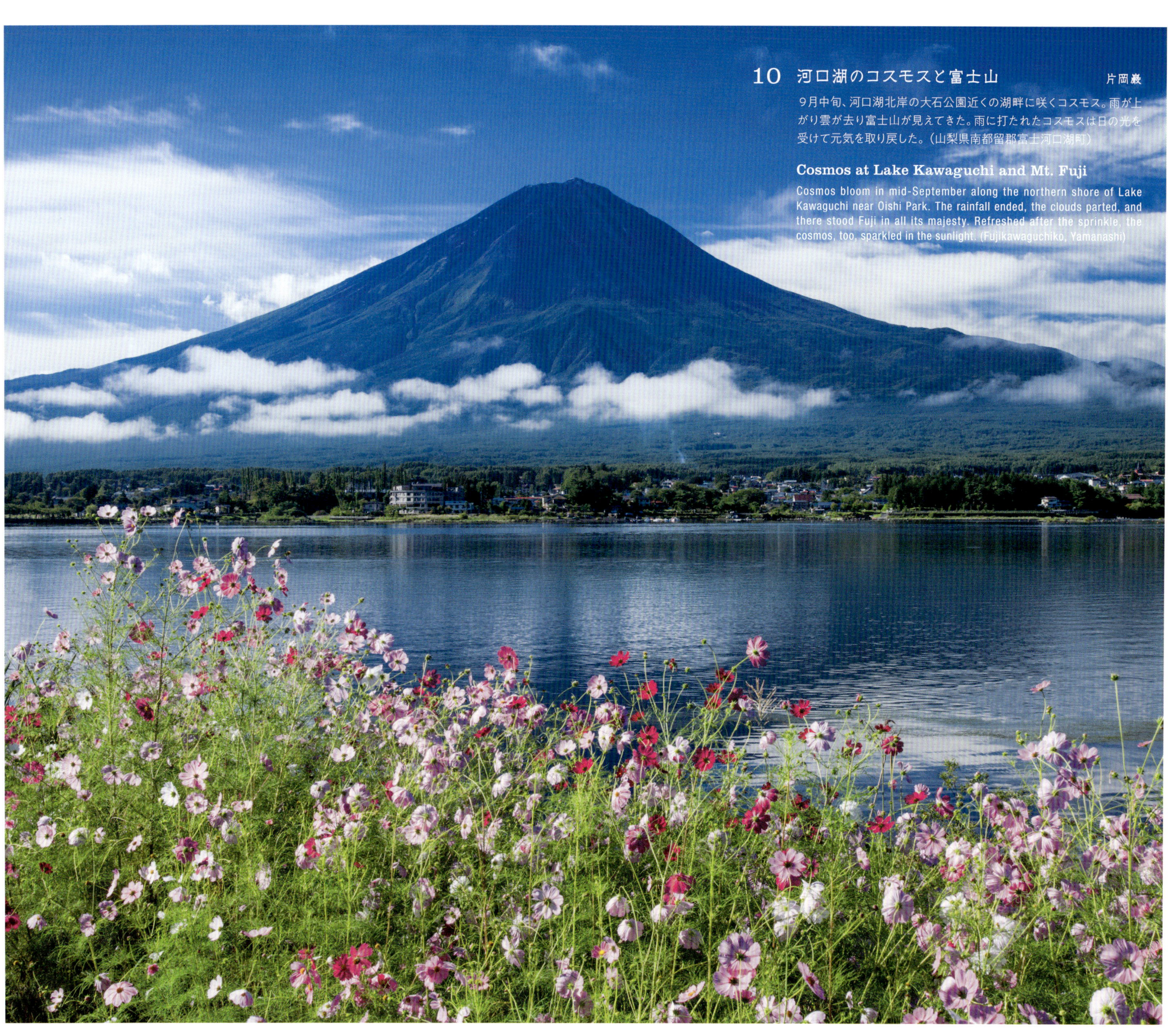

9月中旬、河口湖北岸の大石公園近くの湖畔に咲くコスモス。雨が上がり雲が去り富士山が見えてきた。雨に打たれたコスモスは日の光を受けて元気を取り戻した。（山梨県南都留郡富士河口湖町）

Cosmos at Lake Kawaguchi and Mt. Fuji

Cosmos bloom in mid-September along the northern shore of Lake Kawaguchi near Oishi Park. The rainfall ended, the clouds parted, and there stood Fuji in all its majesty. Refreshed after the sprinkle, the cosmos, too, sparkled in the sunlight. (Fujikawaguchiko, Yamanashi)

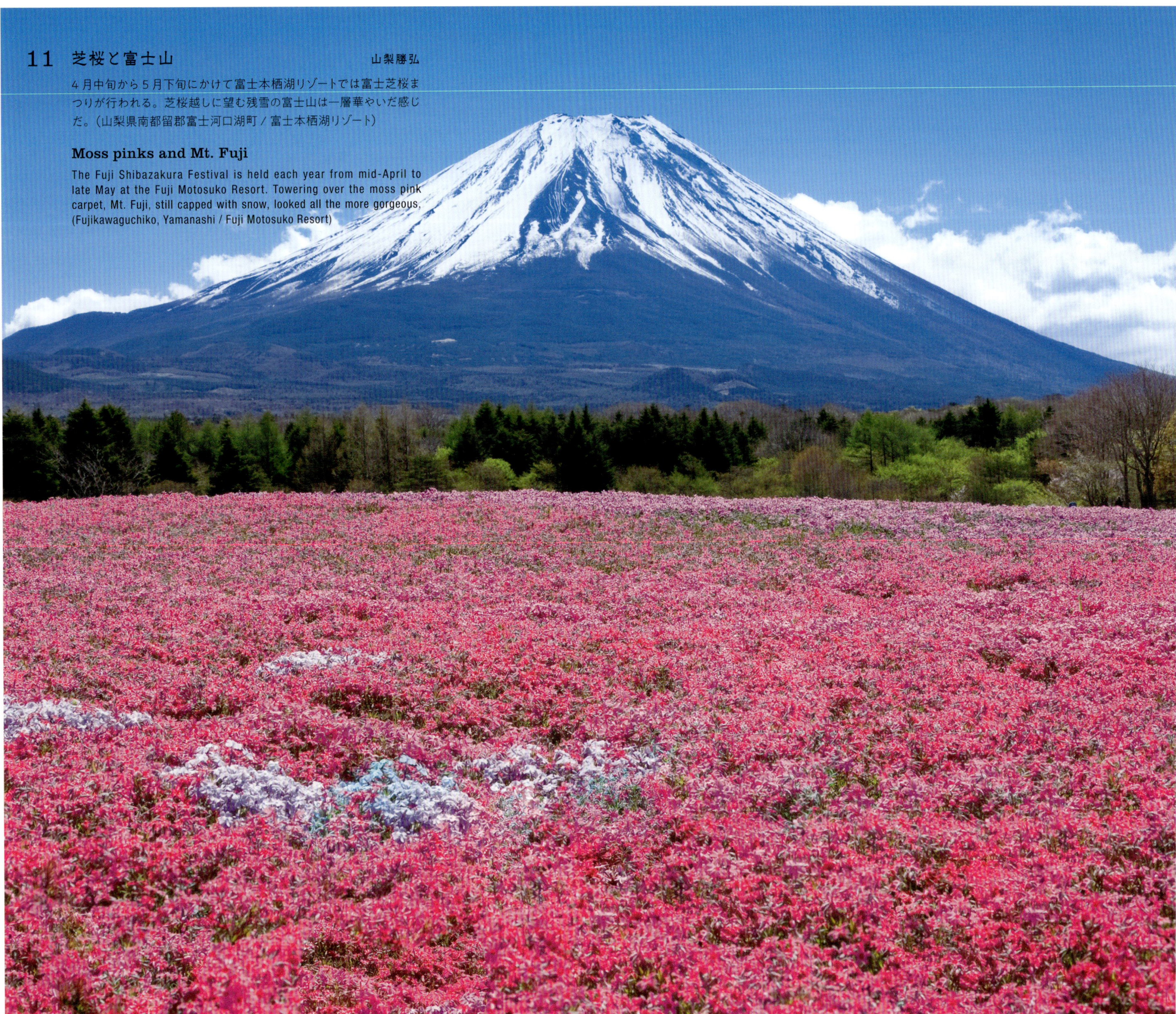

11　芝桜と富士山　　　　　　　　　　　　　　山梨勝弘
４月中旬から５月下旬にかけて富士本栖湖リゾートでは富士芝桜ま
つりが行われる。芝桜越しに望む残雪の富士山は一層華やいだ感じ
だ。（山梨県南都留郡富士河口湖町／富士本栖湖リゾート）

Moss pinks and Mt. Fuji
The Fuji Shibazakura Festival is held each year from mid-April to
late May at the Fuji Motosuko Resort. Towering over the moss pink
carpet, Mt. Fuji, still capped with snow, looked all the more gorgeous.
(Fujikawaguchiko, Yamanashi / Fuji Motosuko Resort)

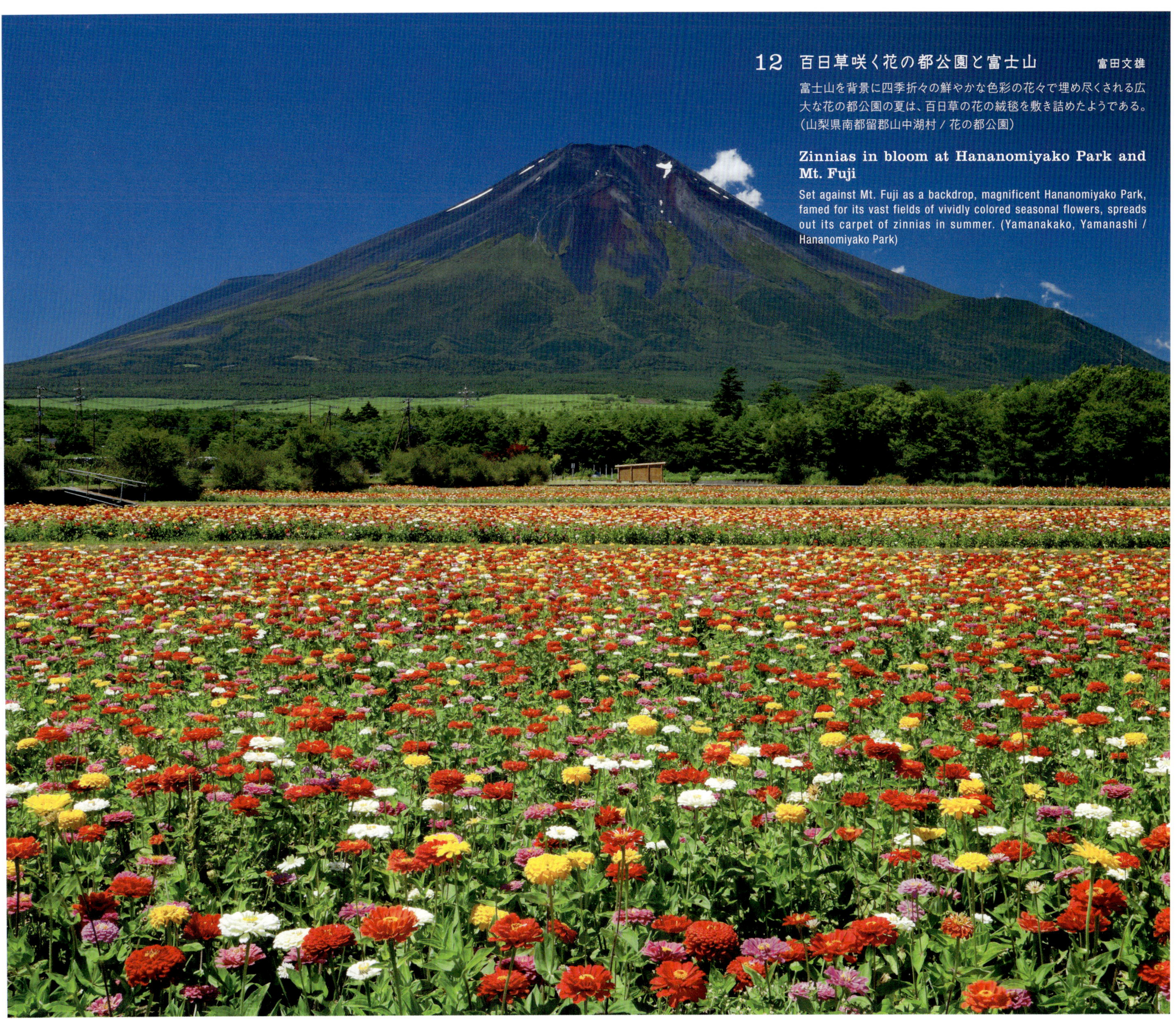

12　百日草咲く花の都公園と富士山　　富田文雄

富士山を背景に四季折々の鮮やかな色彩の花々で埋め尽くされる広大な花の都公園の夏は、百日草の花の絨毯を敷き詰めたようである。（山梨県南都留郡山中湖村／花の都公園）

Zinnias in bloom at Hananomiyako Park and Mt. Fuji

Set against Mt. Fuji as a backdrop, magnificent Hananomiyako Park, famed for its vast fields of vividly colored seasonal flowers, spreads out its carpet of zinnias in summer. (Yamanakako, Yamanashi / Hananomiyako Park)

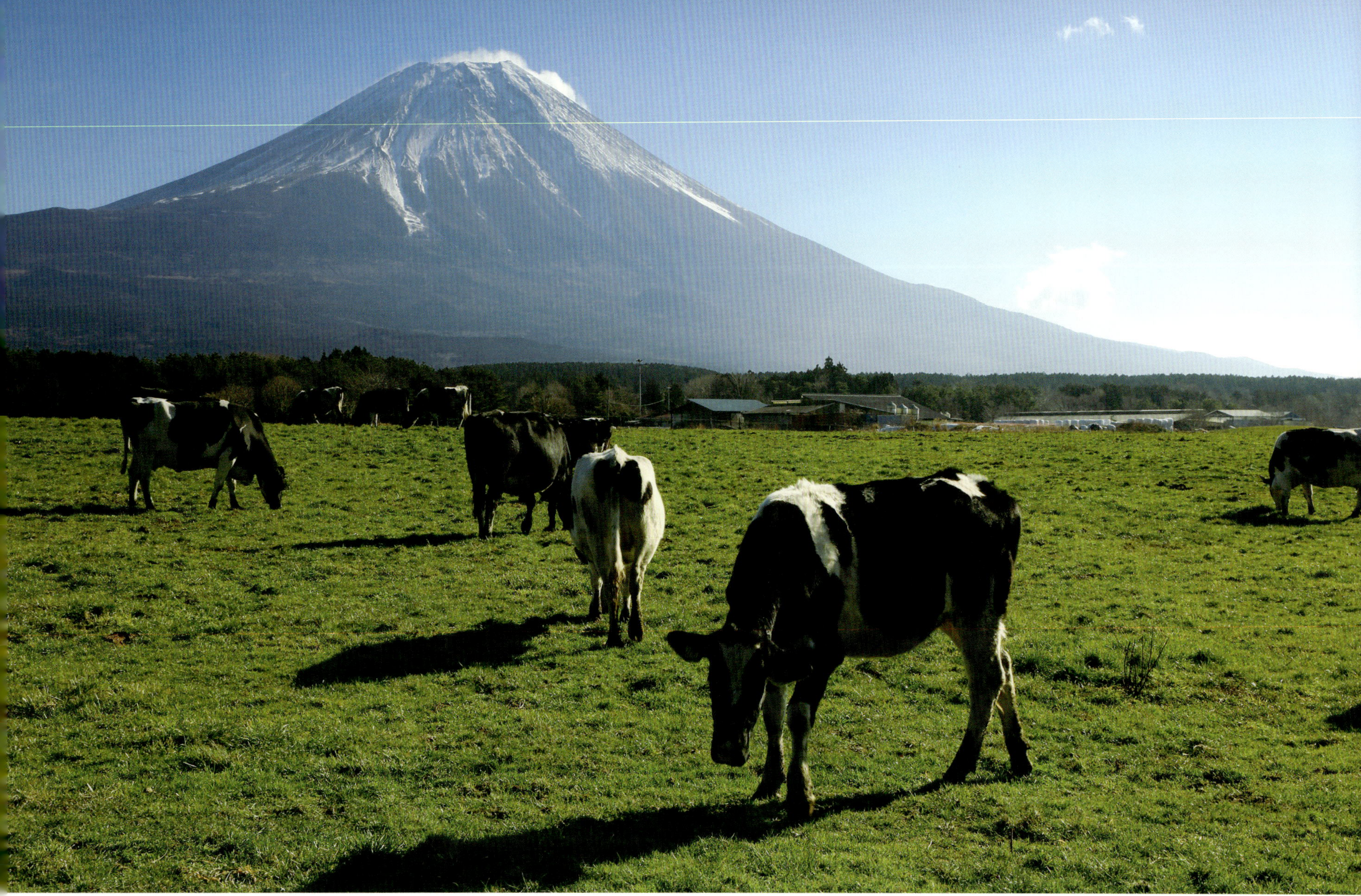

13　放し飼いの乳牛

竹内トキ子

「道の駅 朝霧公園」を少し過ぎた国道 139 号線沿いに開けた牧草地があり、よく晴れた日は乳牛を遊ばせている。車を走らせていると、思わず車をとめて見たくなる。(静岡県富士宮市)

Free range dairy cows

A stretch of open pasture along National Route 139, just past the Asagiri Kogen rest area, where dairy cows were out grazing on a sunny day. Espied as I was driving past, I stopped without giving it a thought to take in the scene. (Fujinomiya, Shizuoka)

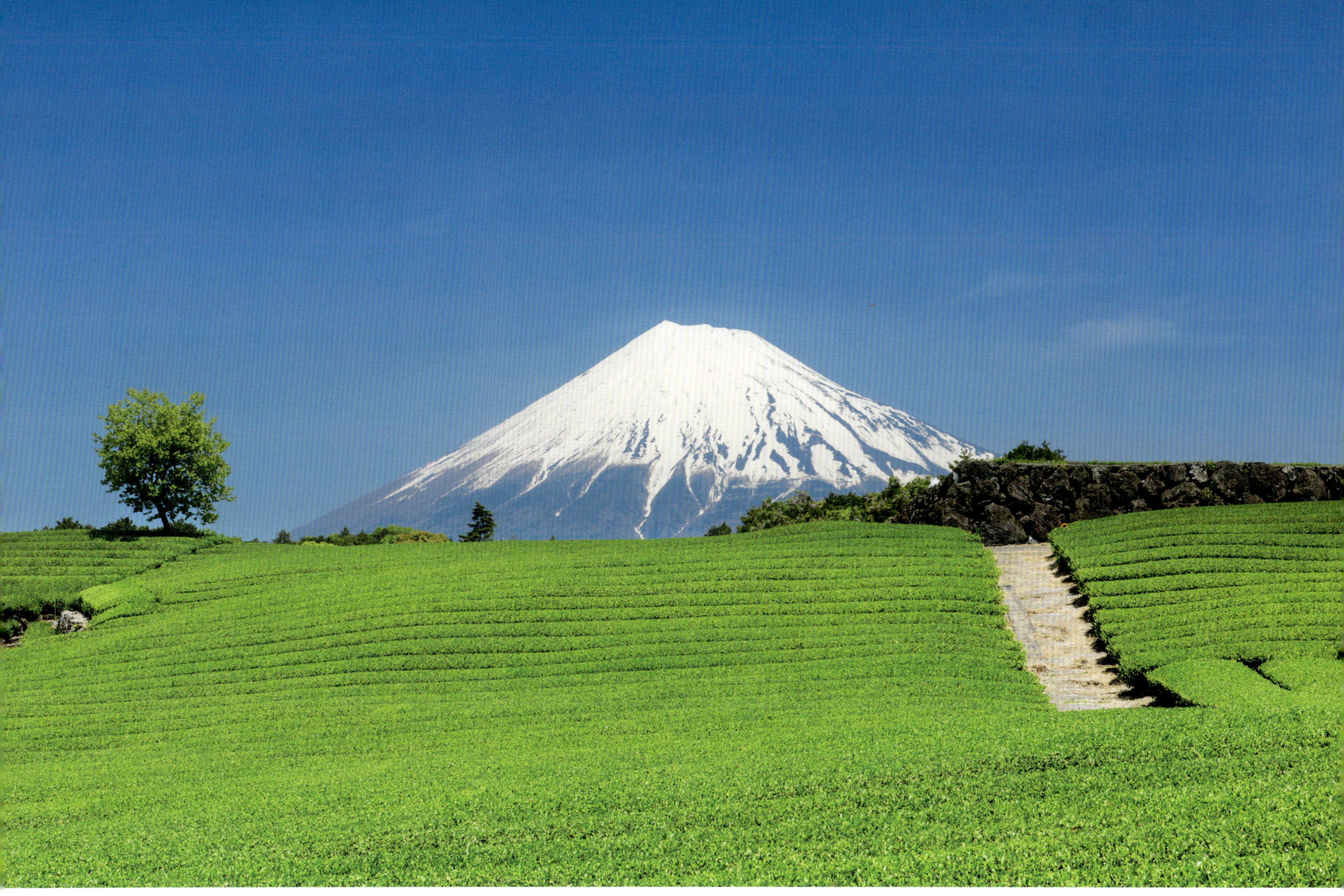

14　茶畑から望む富士山　　　　　　　　　　　　館野二朗

新緑の茶葉が美しい大淵笹場。畑の奥には雪の残る富士山が顔を出
して、静岡らしい風景が広がっている。（静岡県富士市／大淵笹場）

Mt. Fuji seen from a tea plantation

Obuchi-Sasaba, where the fields of young green tea leaves are simply
beautiful. A still snow-capped Mt. Fuji, looming in the background,
creates a scene characteristic of Shizuoka. (Fuji, Shizuoka / Obuchi-
Sasaba)

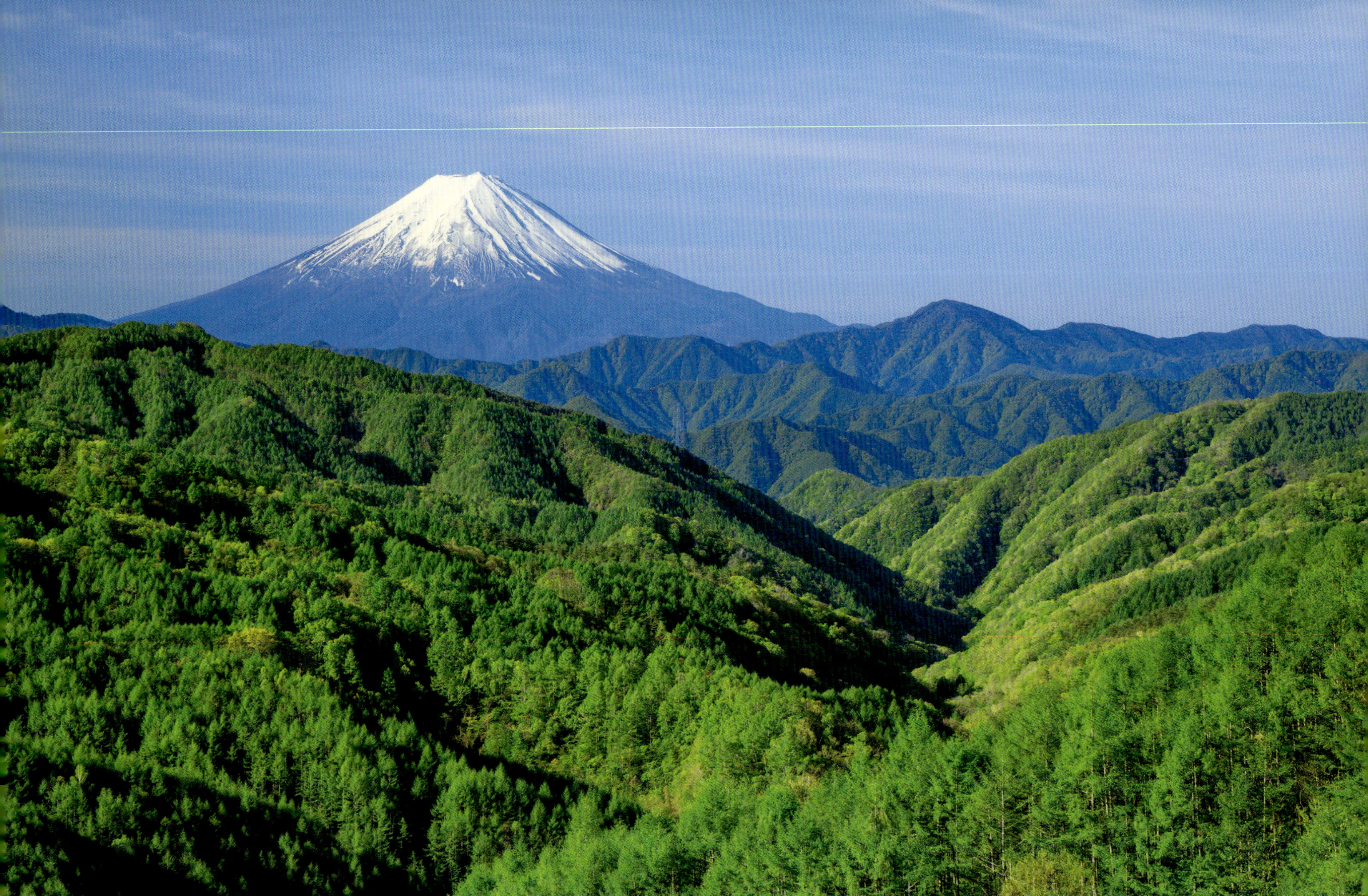

15　新緑に覆われた甲州の山並み　　縄手英樹

山奥の林道をバイクで走っていて、偶然見つけた撮影地。誰もいない朝の清々しい空気に包まれながらの撮影となった。(山梨県甲州市)

Koshu mountains dressed in fresh green

A picture-perfect scene discovered by chance while riding my motorbike on a forestry road in the mountains. I took this shot, enveloped in fresh morning air, not another soul in sight. (Koshu, Yamanashi)

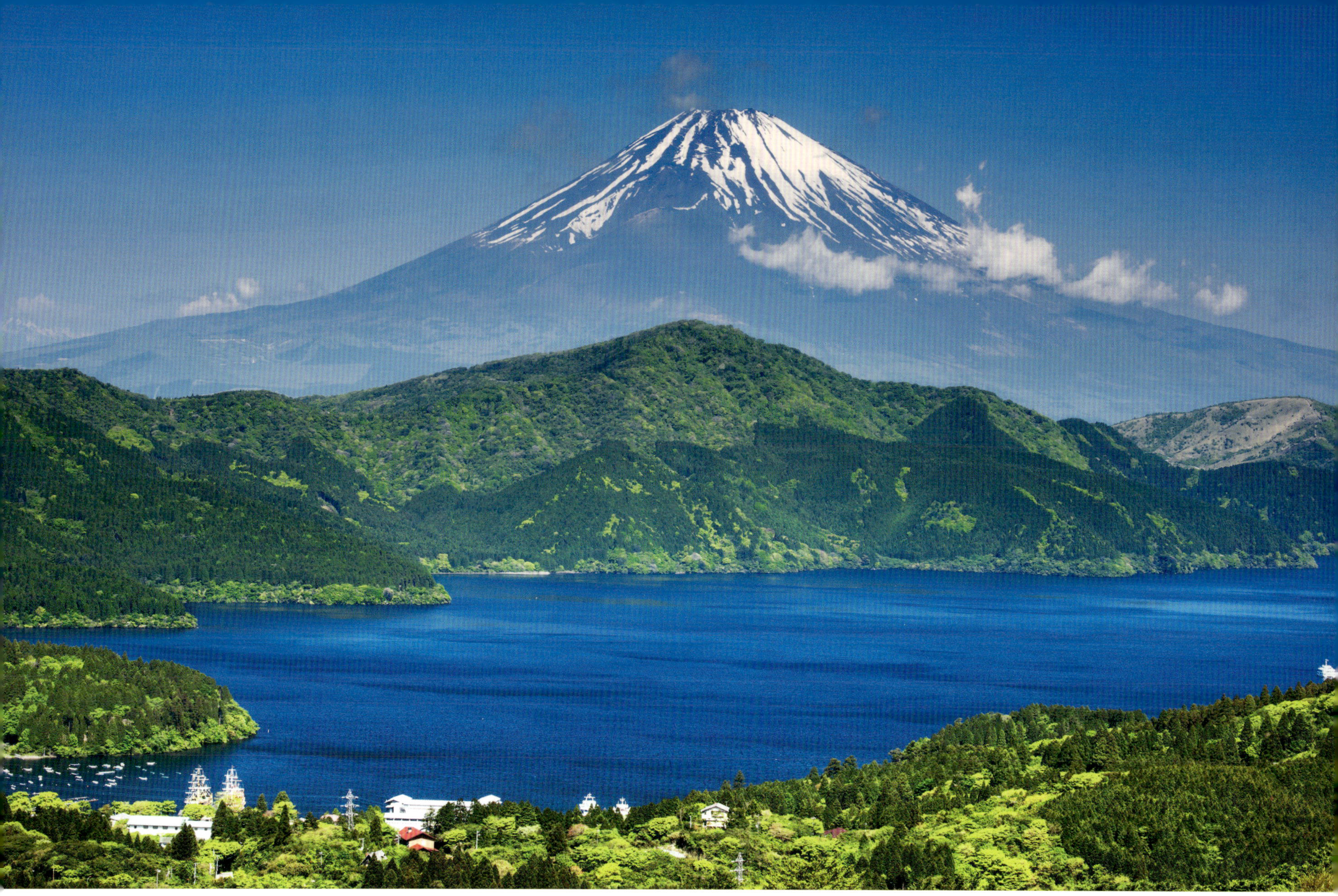

16　芦ノ湖より望む富士

片岡嚴

大観山（たいかんざん）からは、朝焼け、雲海、星空、月など、四季を
通して様々な富士山と芦ノ湖の絶景を見られる。青い湖と空と新緑に
囲まれた初夏の富士は眩しいほどだ。(神奈川県足柄下郡箱根町)

Mt. Fuji seen from Lake Ashi

Mt. Taikan affords spectacular views of Mt. Fuji and Lake Ashi
throughout the seasons, with the glow of dawn, a sea of clouds, or a
starry sky and the moon. Surrounded by the blue lake and sky and fresh
greenery of early summer, Fuji is utterly dazzling. (Hakone, Kanagawa)

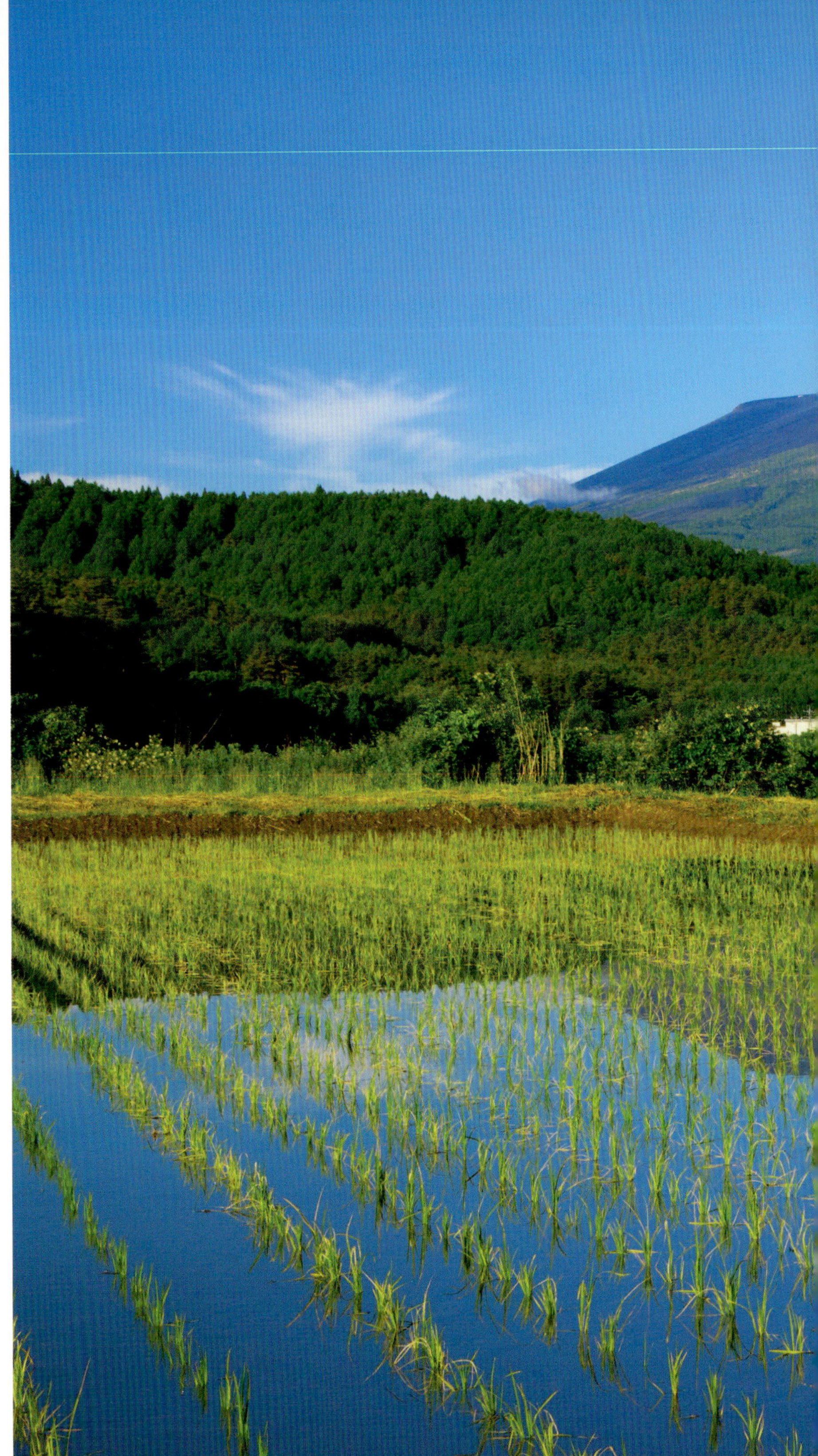

17　水田に映える富士

高椋俊樹

田植えを終えた水田の水鏡に映る富士山は、とても優しい表情を見せてくれる。朝の晴れた空と白い雲が清々しく素晴らしい。（山梨県南都留郡忍野村）

Mt. Fuji reflected in the paddy fields

Mirrored on the surface of the flooded paddy fields after rice planting, Fuji shows a subdued visage. The clear morning sky and wisps of white cloud add to the refreshing sense of splendor. (Oshino, Yamanashi)

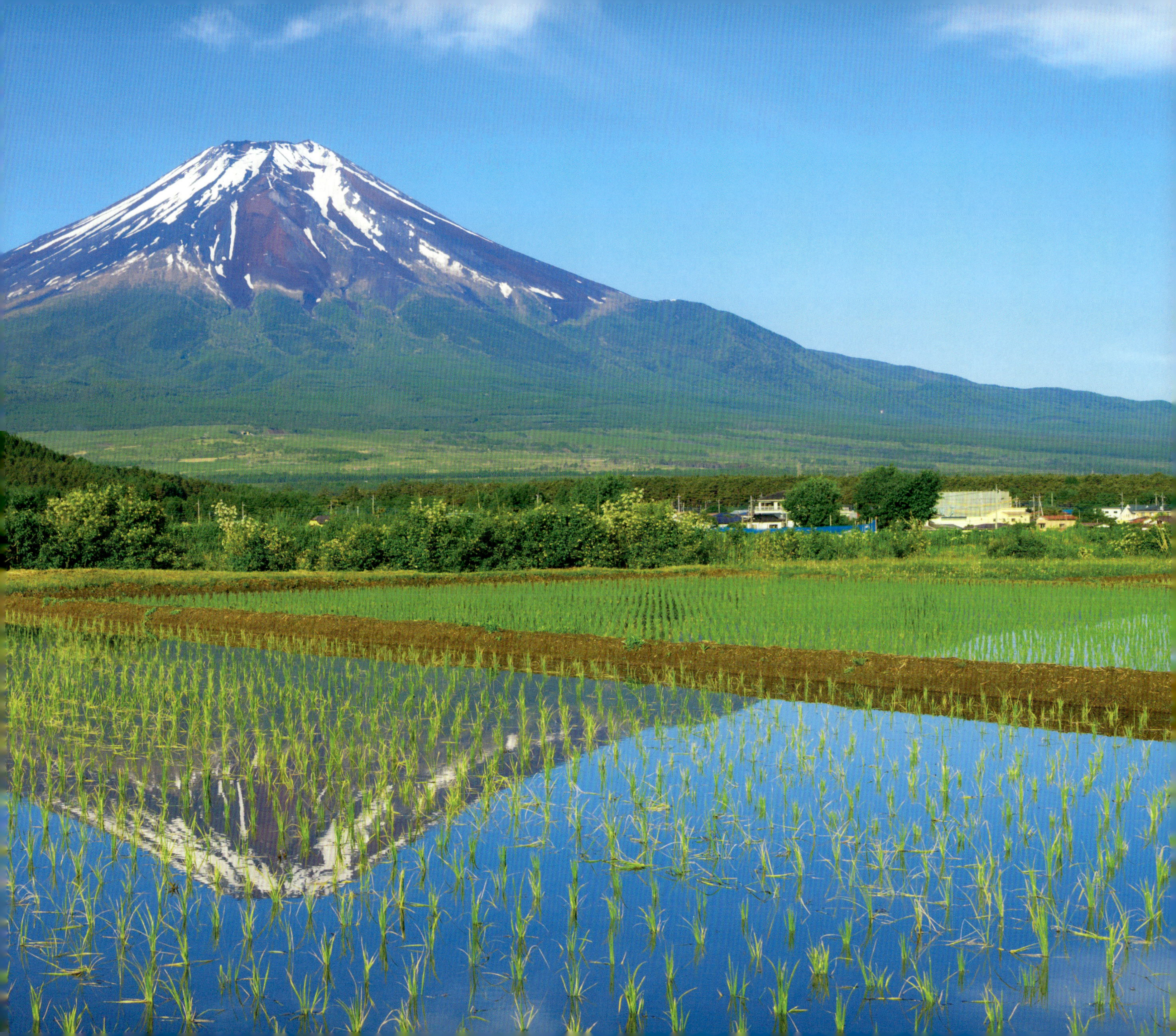

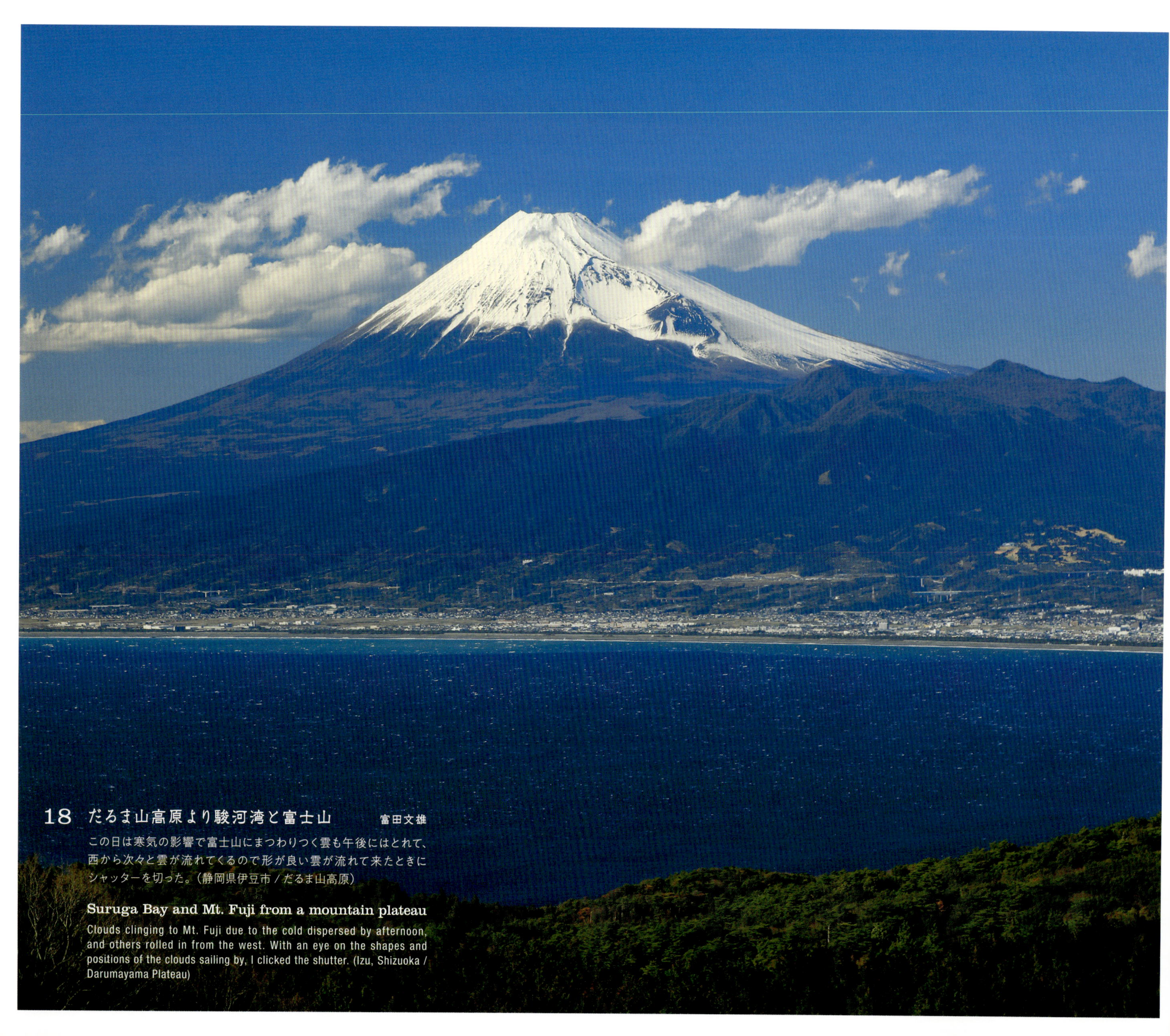

18 だるま山高原より駿河湾と富士山　　富田文雄

この日は寒気の影響で富士山にまつわりつく雲も午後にはとれて、
西から次々と雲が流れてくるので形が良い雲が流れて来たときに
シャッターを切った。（静岡県伊豆市／だるま山高原）

Suruga Bay and Mt. Fuji from a mountain plateau

Clouds clinging to Mt. Fuji due to the cold dispersed by afternoon,
and others rolled in from the west. With an eye on the shapes and
positions of the clouds sailing by, I clicked the shutter. (Izu, Shizuoka /
Darumayama Plateau)

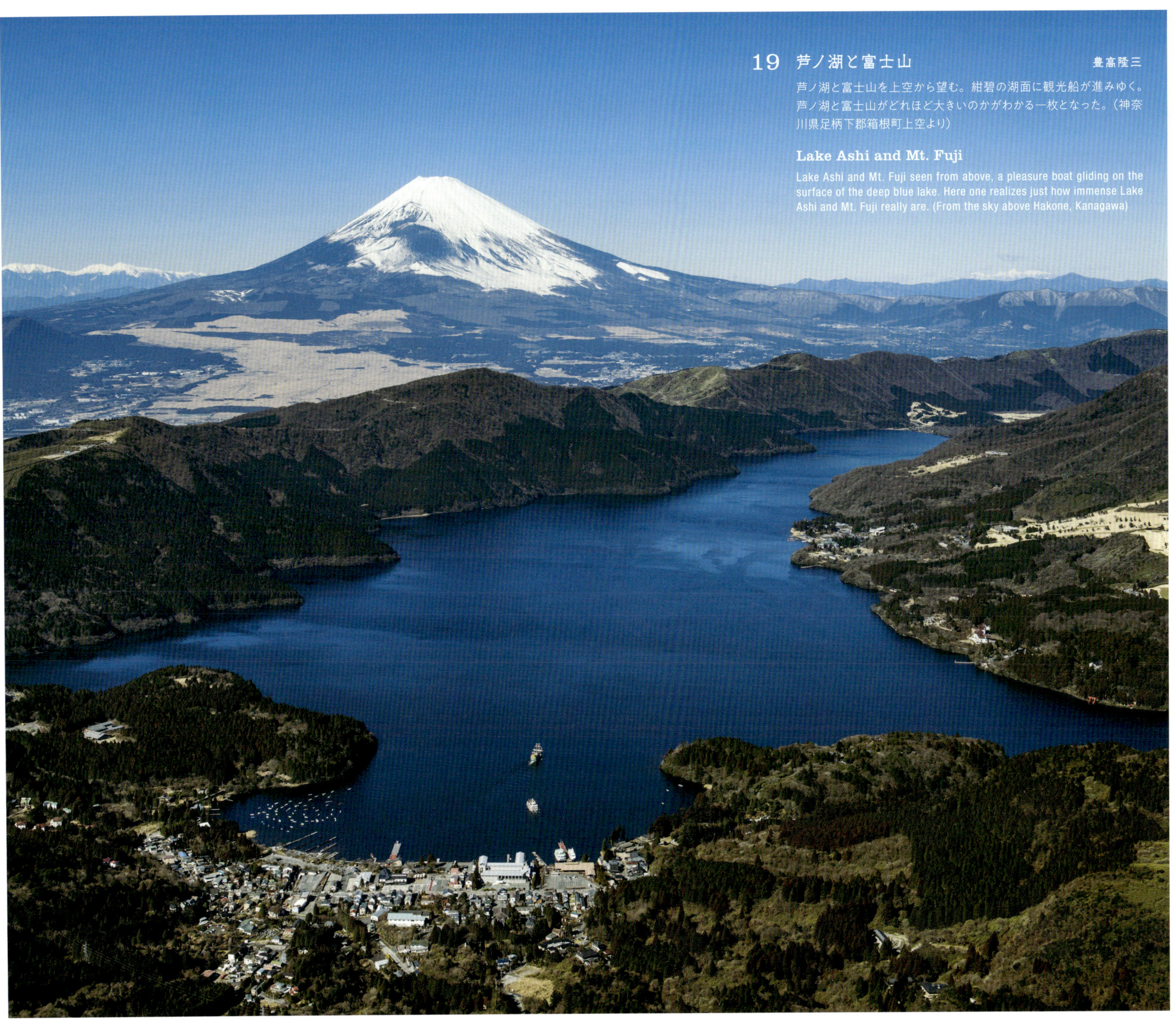

19　芦ノ湖と富士山　　　　　　　　　　豊高隆三

芦ノ湖と富士山を上空から望む。紺碧の湖面に観光船が進みゆく。芦ノ湖と富士山がどれほど大きいのかがわかる一枚となった。（神奈川県足柄下郡箱根町上空より）

Lake Ashi and Mt. Fuji

Lake Ashi and Mt. Fuji seen from above, a pleasure boat gliding on the surface of the deep blue lake. Here one realizes just how immense Lake Ashi and Mt. Fuji really are. (From the sky above Hakone, Kanagawa)

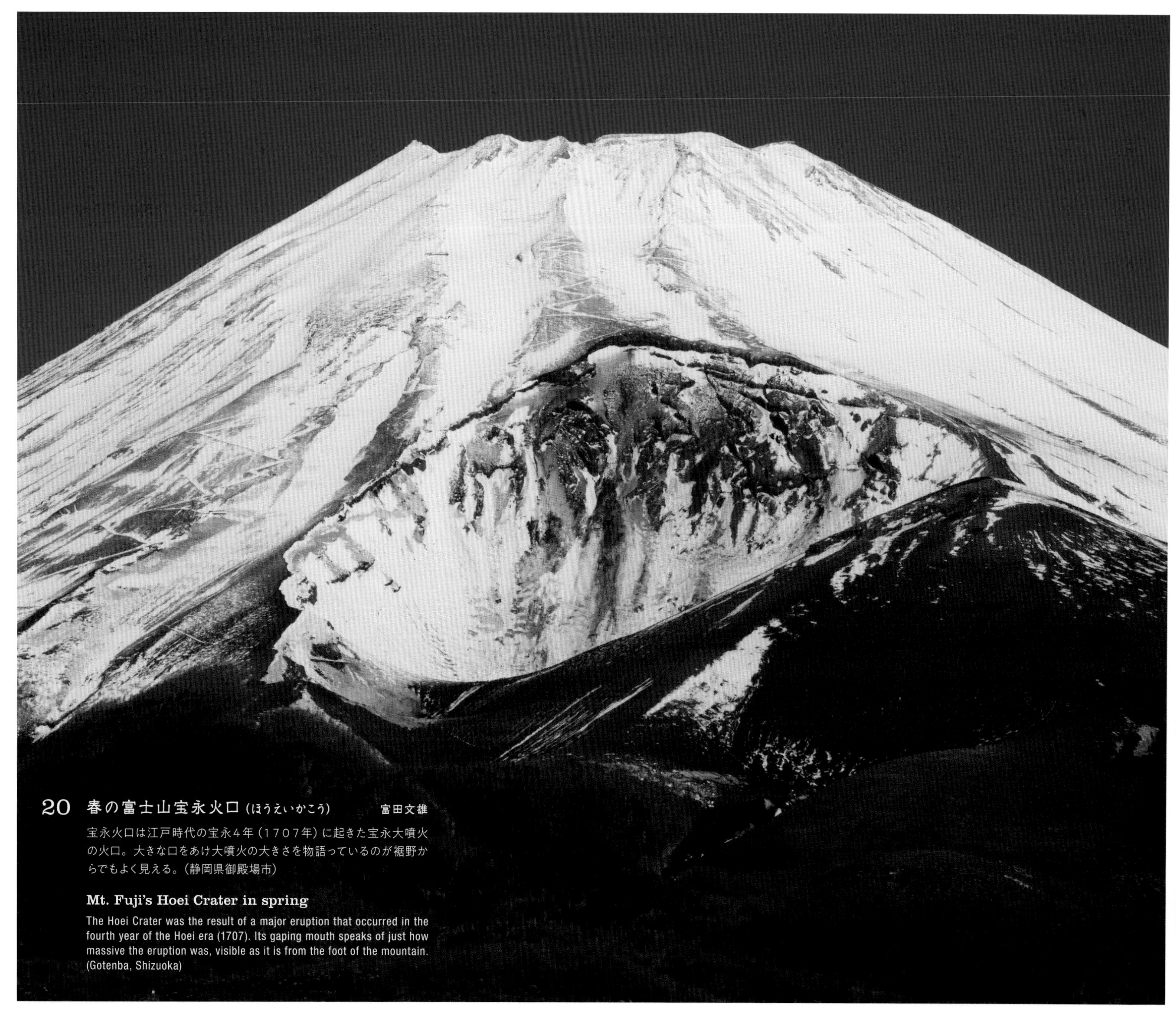

20　春の富士山宝永火口 (ほうえいかこう)　　富田文雄

宝永火口は江戸時代の宝永4年 (1707年) に起きた宝永大噴火の火口。大きな口をあけ大噴火の大きさを物語っているのが裾野からでもよく見える。(静岡県御殿場市)

Mt. Fuji's Hoei Crater in spring

The Hoei Crater was the result of a major eruption that occurred in the fourth year of the Hoei era (1707). Its gaping mouth speaks of just how massive the eruption was, visible as it is from the foot of the mountain. (Gotenba, Shizuoka)

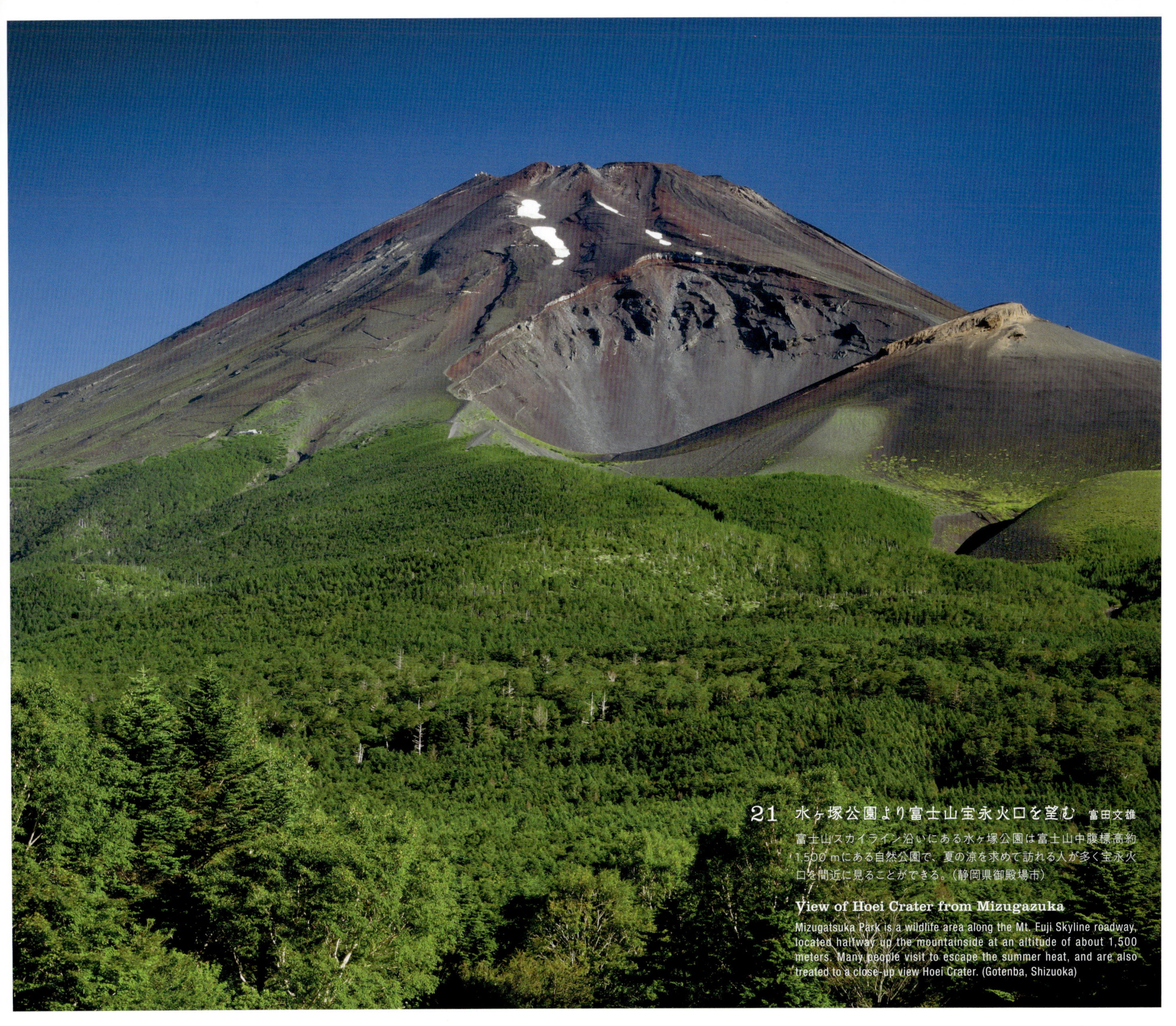

21　水ヶ塚公園より富士山宝永火口を望む　富田文雄

富士山スカイライン沿いにある水ヶ塚公園は富士山中腹標高約1,500ｍにある自然公園で、夏の涼を求めて訪れる人が多く宝永火口を間近に見ることができる。（静岡県御殿場市）

View of Hoei Crater from Mizugazuka

Mizugatsuka Park is a wildlife area along the Mt. Fuji Skyline roadway, located halfway up the mountainside at an altitude of about 1,500 meters. Many people visit to escape the summer heat, and are also treated to a close-up view Hoei Crater. (Gotenba, Shizuoka)

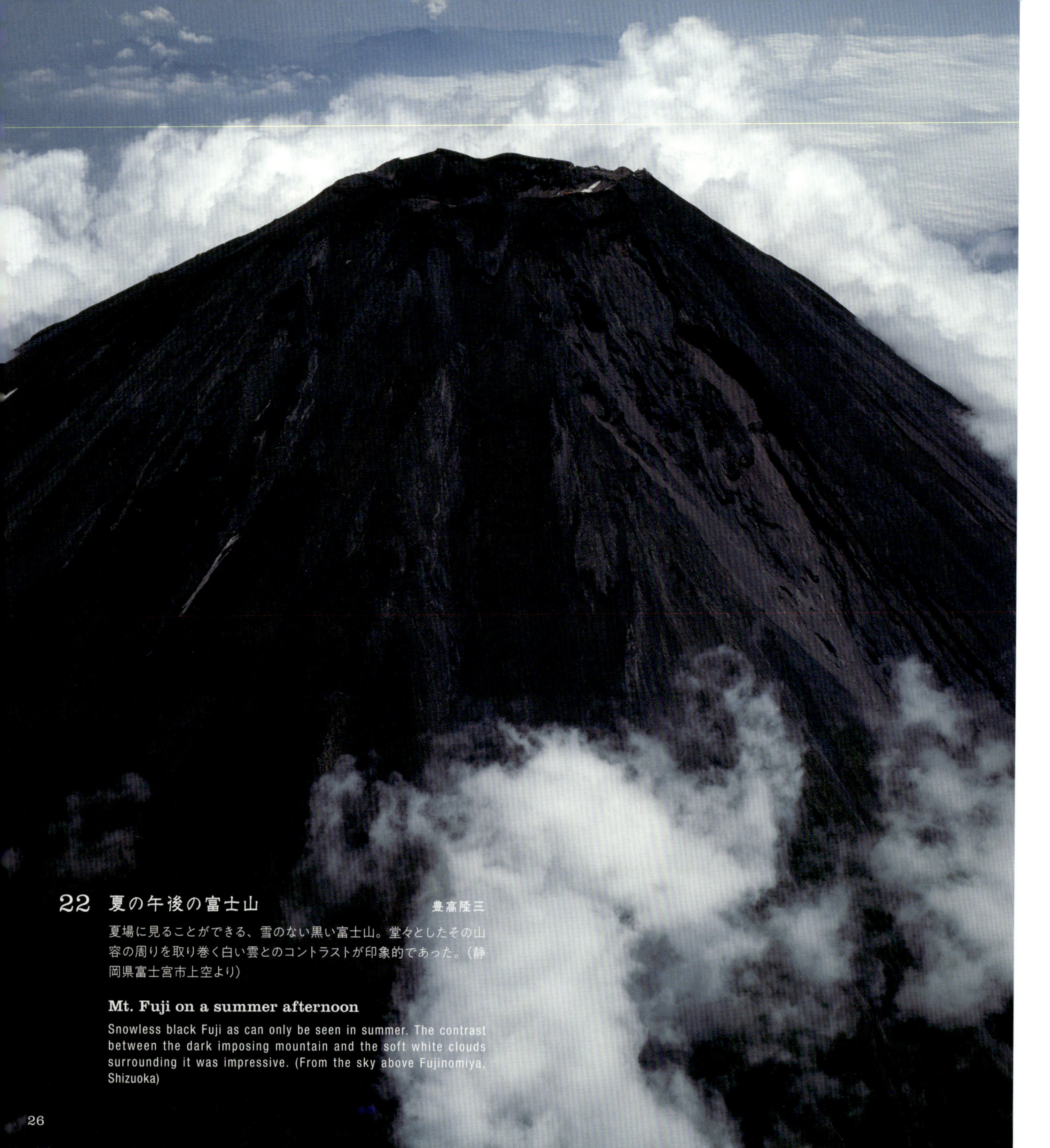

22　夏の午後の富士山　　　　　豊高隆三

夏場に見ることができる、雪のない黒い富士山。堂々としたその山容の周りを取り巻く白い雲とのコントラストが印象的であった。（静岡県富士宮市上空より）

Mt. Fuji on a summer afternoon

Snowless black Fuji as can only be seen in summer. The contrast between the dark imposing mountain and the soft white clouds surrounding it was impressive. (From the sky above Fujinomiya, Shizuoka)

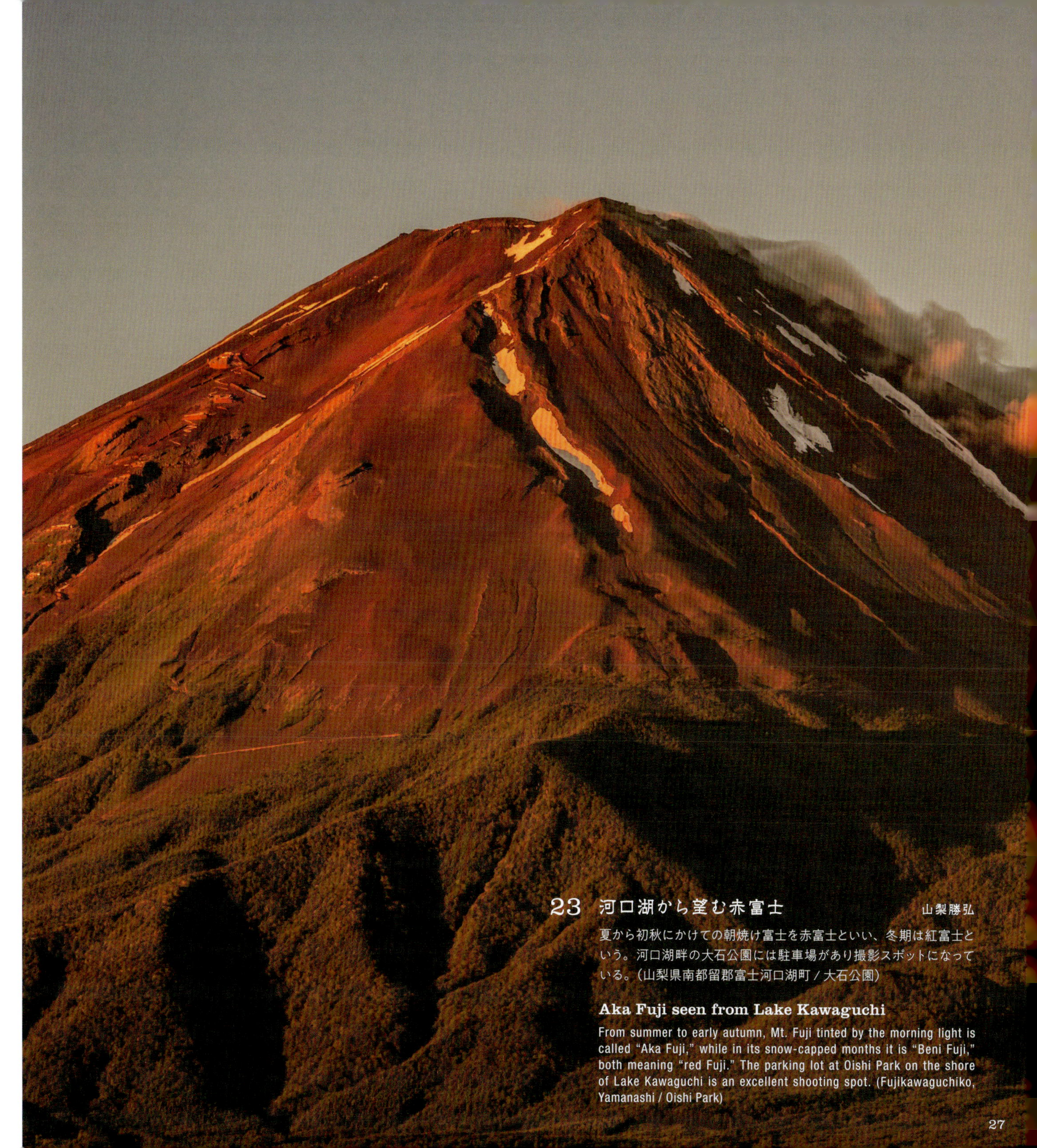

23 河口湖から望む赤富士　　　　　　　　山梨勝弘

夏から初秋にかけての朝焼け富士を赤富士といい、冬期は紅富士という。河口湖畔の大石公園には駐車場があり撮影スポットになっている。(山梨県南都留郡富士河口湖町／大石公園)

Aka Fuji seen from Lake Kawaguchi

From summer to early autumn, Mt. Fuji tinted by the morning light is called "Aka Fuji," while in its snow-capped months it is "Beni Fuji," both meaning "red Fuji." The parking lot at Oishi Park on the shore of Lake Kawaguchi is an excellent shooting spot. (Fujikawaguchiko, Yamanashi / Oishi Park)

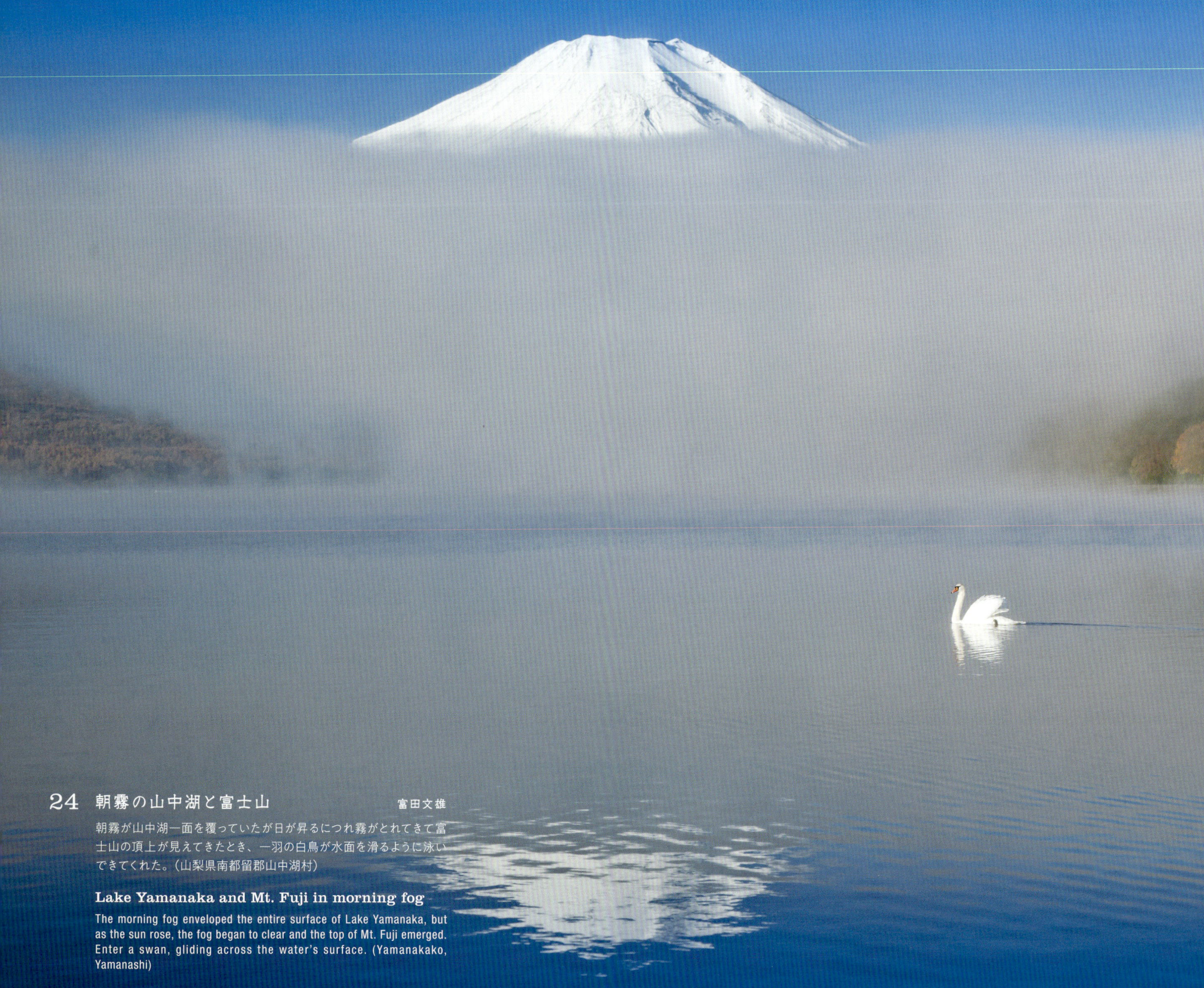

24　朝霧の山中湖と富士山　　　富田文雄

朝霧が山中湖一面を覆っていたが日が昇るにつれ霧がとれてきて富士山の頂上が見えてきたとき、一羽の白鳥が水面を滑るように泳いできてくれた。（山梨県南都留郡山中湖村）

Lake Yamanaka and Mt. Fuji in morning fog

The morning fog enveloped the entire surface of Lake Yamanaka, but as the sun rose, the fog began to clear and the top of Mt. Fuji emerged. Enter a swan, gliding across the water's surface. (Yamanakako, Yamanashi)

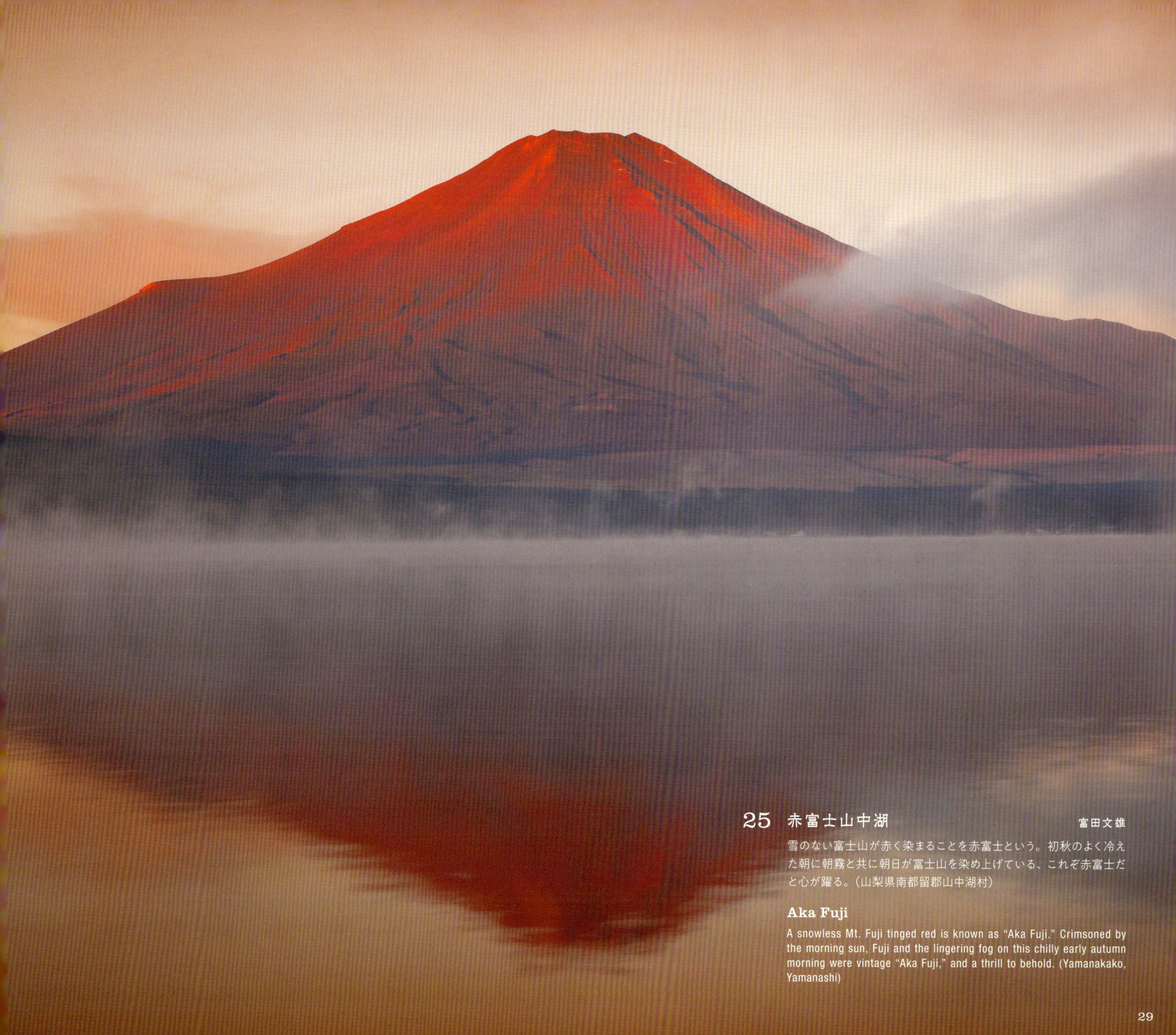

25　赤富士山中湖　　　　　　　　　　　　　　　富田文雄

雪のない富士山が赤く染まることを赤富士という。初秋のよく冷え
た朝に朝霧と共に朝日が富士山を染め上げている、これぞ赤富士だ
と心が躍る。（山梨県南都留郡山中湖村）

Aka Fuji

A snowless Mt. Fuji tinged red is known as "Aka Fuji." Crimsoned by
the morning sun, Fuji and the lingering fog on this chilly early autumn
morning were vintage "Aka Fuji," and a thrill to behold. (Yamanakako,
Yamanashi)

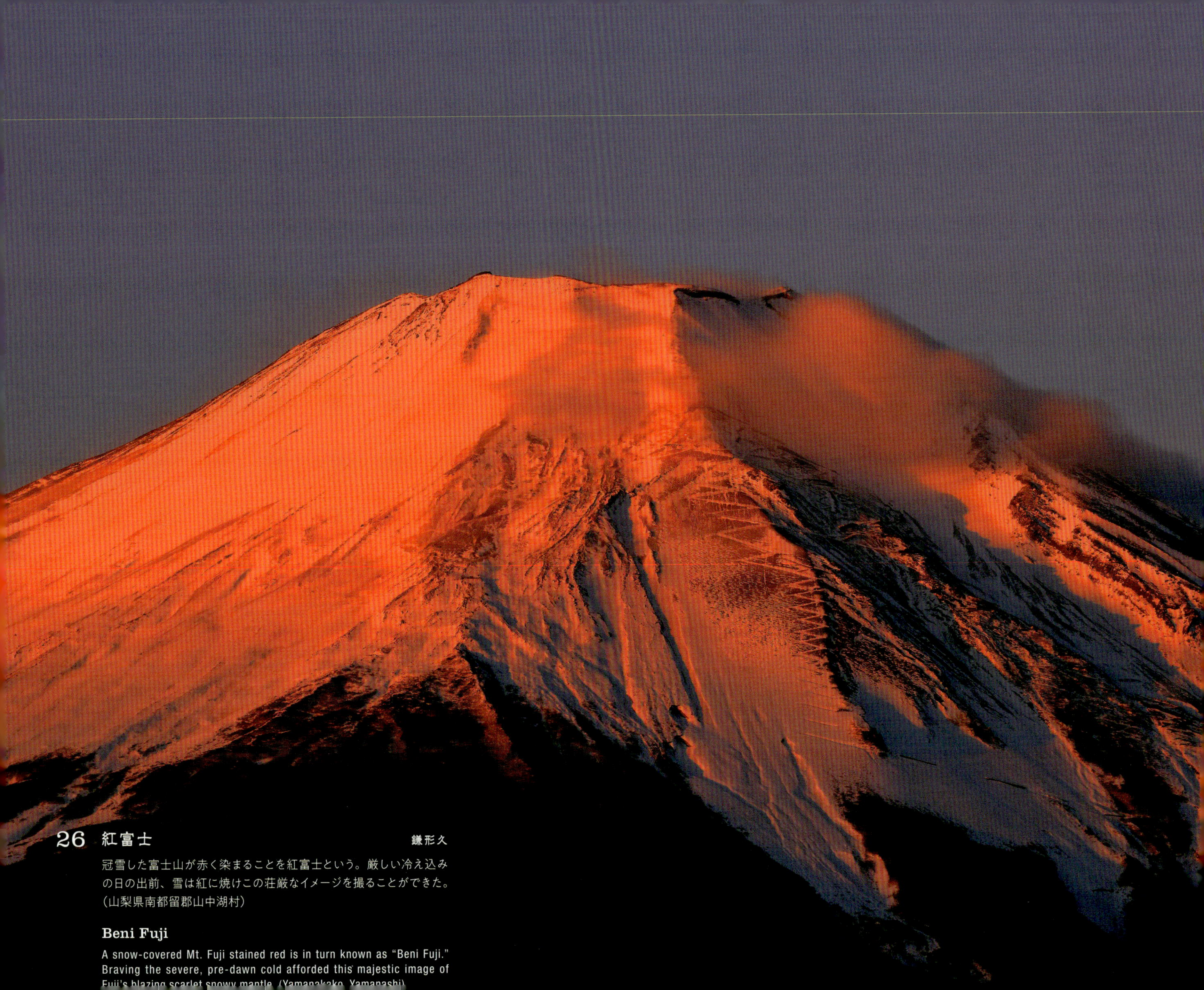

26　紅富士　　　　　　　　　　　　　　鎌形久

冠雪した富士山が赤く染まることを紅富士という。厳しい冷え込み
の日の出前、雪は紅に焼けこの荘厳なイメージを撮ることができた。
（山梨県南都留郡山中湖村）

Beni Fuji

A snow-covered Mt. Fuji stained red is in turn known as "Beni Fuji."
Braving the severe, pre-dawn cold afforded this majestic image of
Fuji's blazing scarlet snowy mantle. (Yamanakako, Yamanashi)

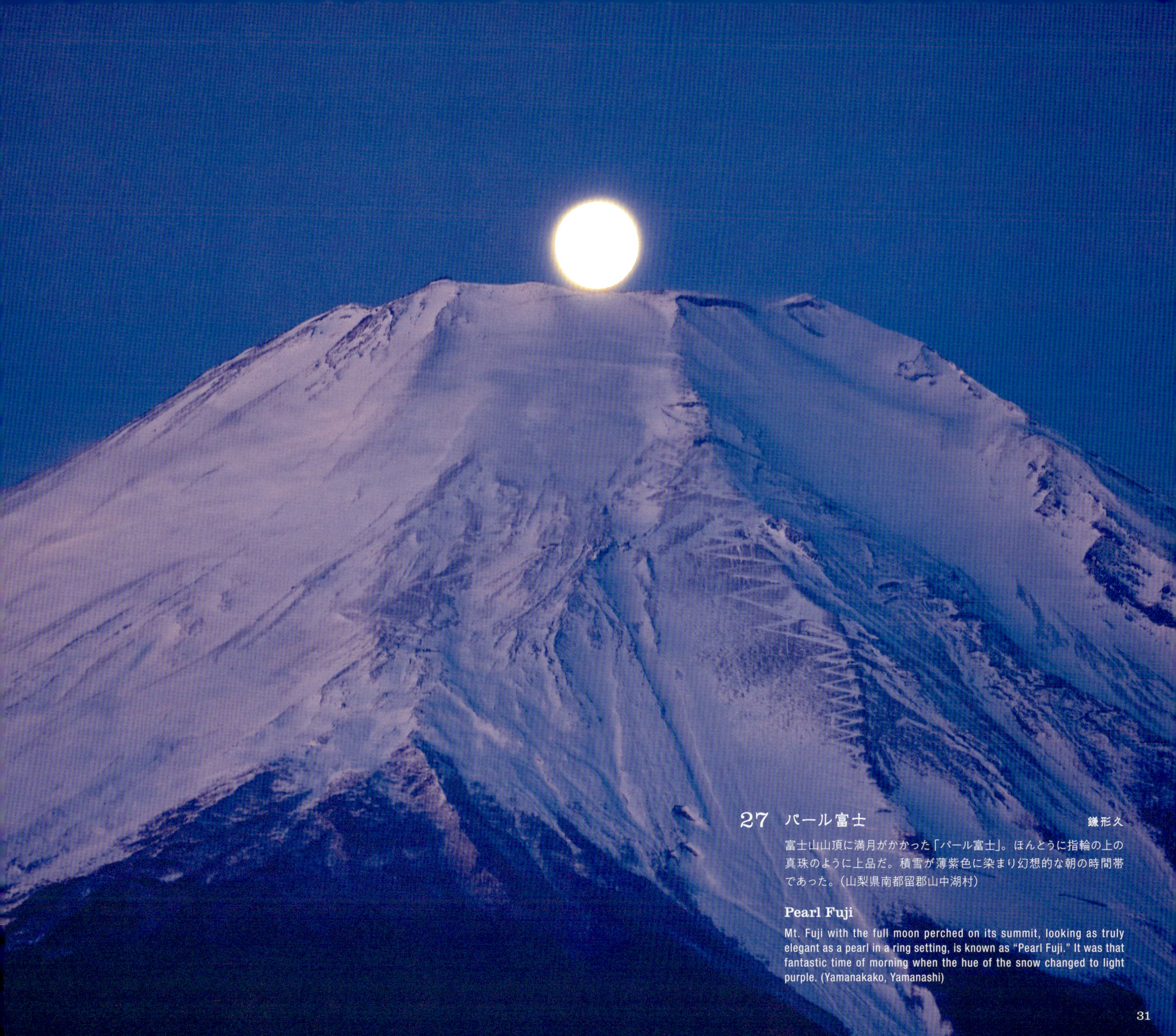

27　パール富士　　　　　　　　　　　　鎌形久

富士山山頂に満月がかかった「パール富士」。ほんとうに指輪の上の
真珠のように上品だ。積雪が薄紫色に染まり幻想的な朝の時間帯
であった。（山梨県南都留郡山中湖村）

Pearl Fuji

Mt. Fuji with the full moon perched on its summit, looking as truly
elegant as a pearl in a ring setting, is known as "Pearl Fuji." It was that
fantastic time of morning when the hue of the snow changed to light
purple. (Yamanakako, Yamanashi)

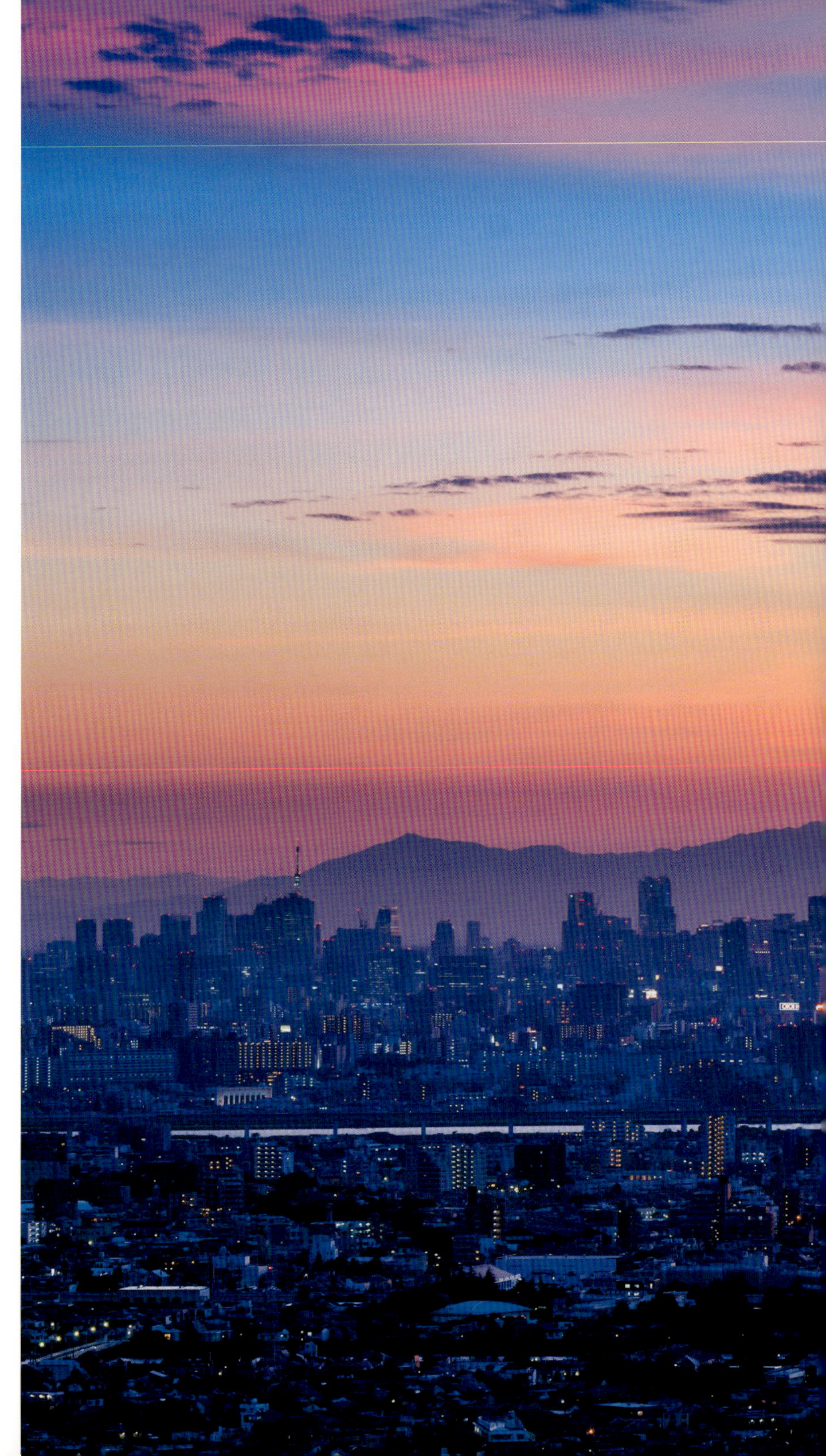

28 夕暮れの東京スカイツリーと富士山　　山梨将典

市川駅に隣接しているアイ・リンクタウンには展望施設がある。この日は朝から夕方までよい天気が続き、真夏では珍しく美しい富士山の姿が広がった。（千葉県市川市／アイ・リンクタウン）

Tokyo Skytree and Mt. Fuji at dusk

There is an observation deck in I-link Town, adjacent to Ichikawa Station, from which clear skies morning to evening afforded this view of these two towering beauties, a rarity in midsummer. (Ichikawa, Chiba / I-link Town)

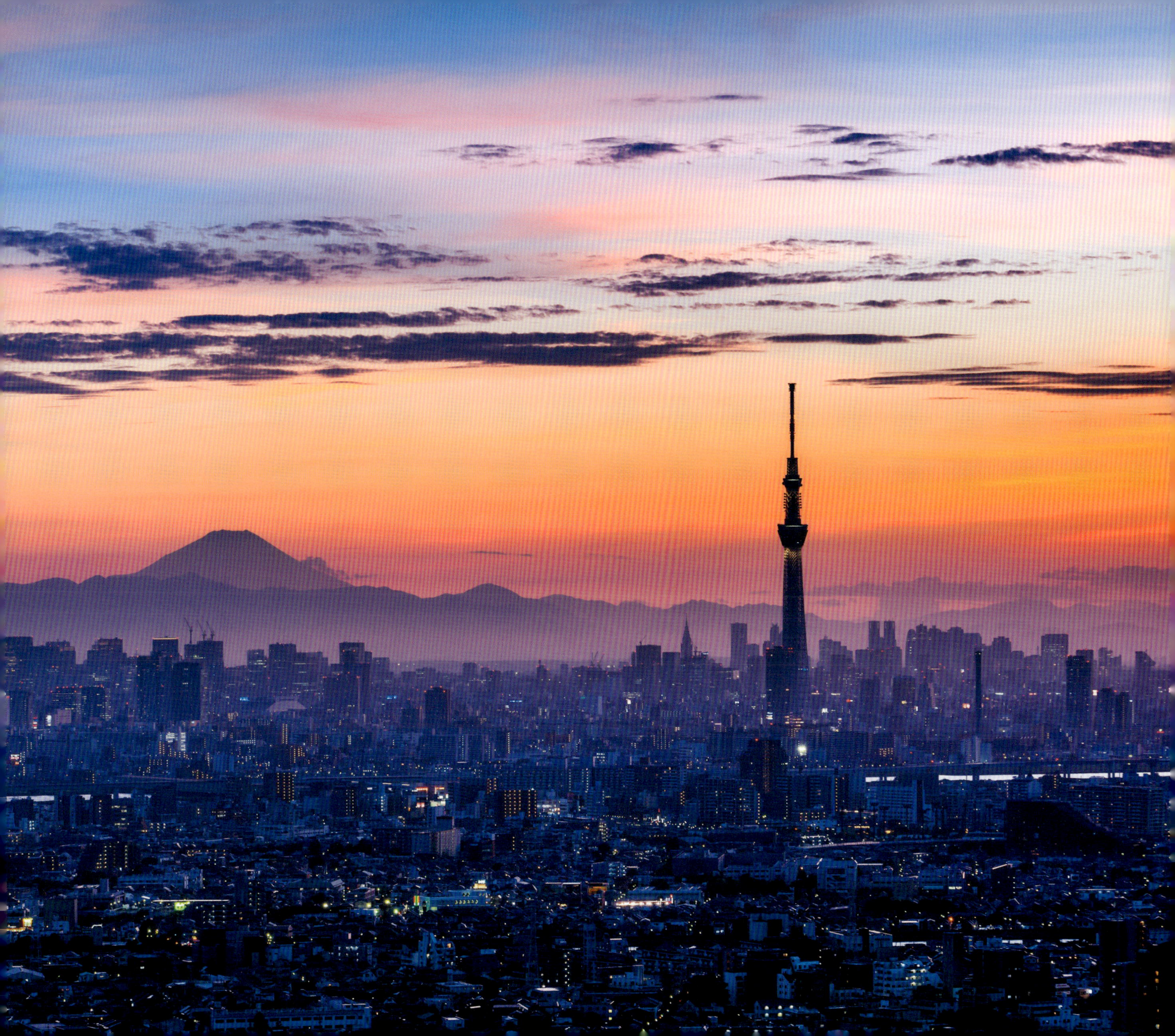

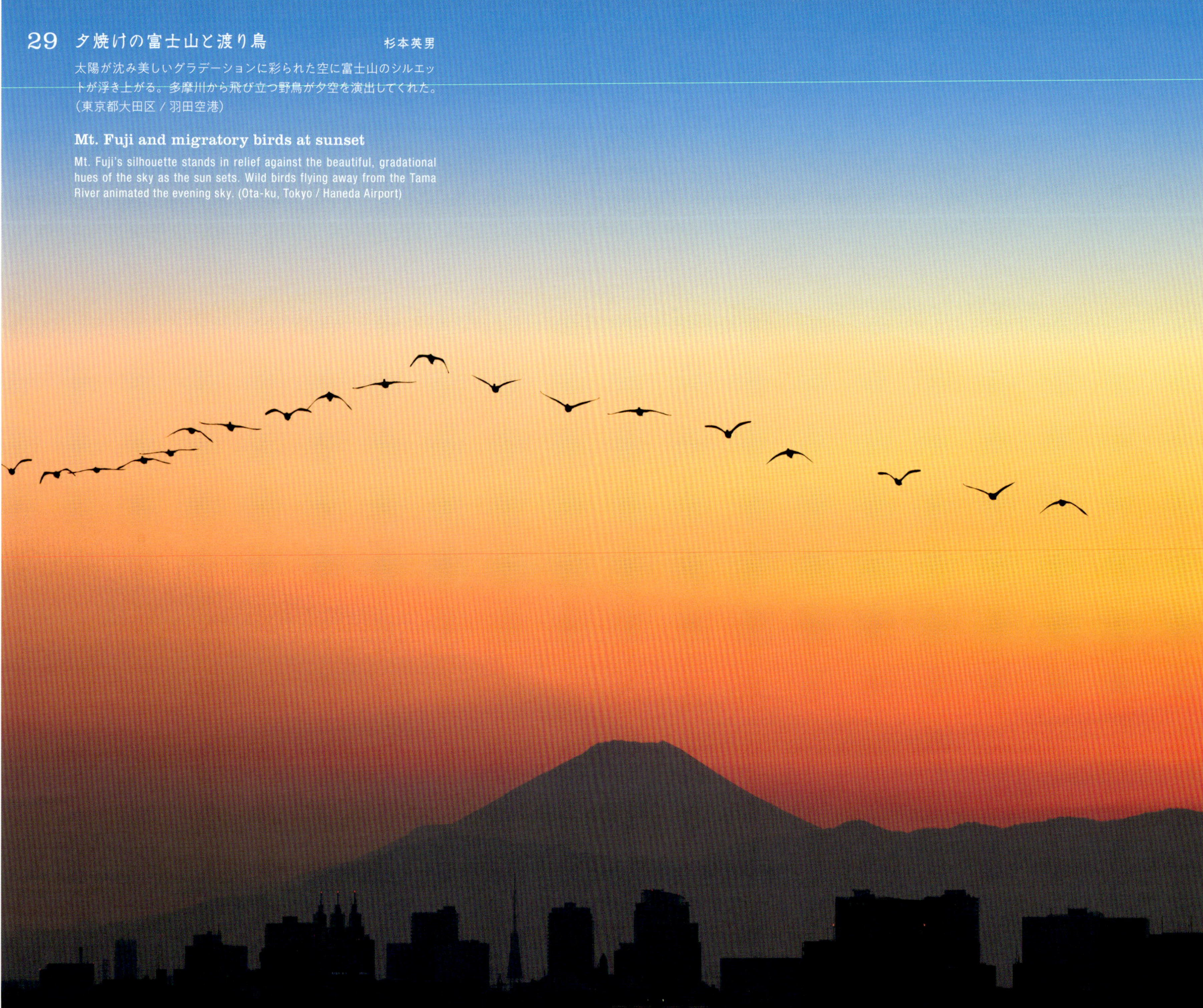

29　夕焼けの富士山と渡り鳥　　　　杉本英男
太陽が沈み美しいグラデーションに彩られた空に富士山のシルエッ
トが浮き上がる。多摩川から飛び立つ野鳥が夕空を演出してくれた。
（東京都大田区 / 羽田空港）

Mt. Fuji and migratory birds at sunset
Mt. Fuji's silhouette stands in relief against the beautiful, gradational
hues of the sky as the sun sets. Wild birds flying away from the Tama
River animated the evening sky. (Ota-ku, Tokyo / Haneda Airport)

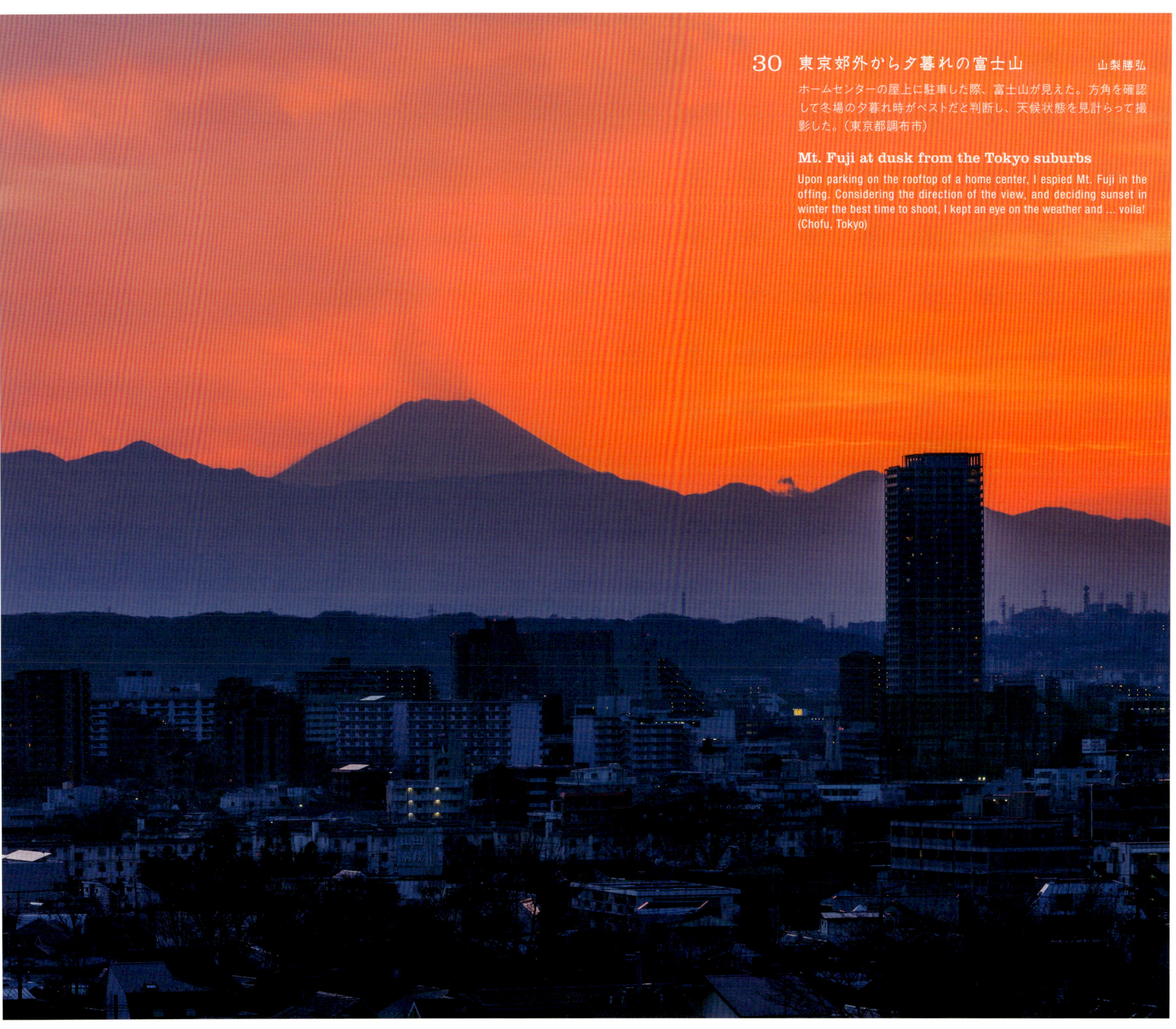

30　東京郊外から夕暮れの富士山　　　山梨勝弘
ホームセンターの屋上に駐車した際、富士山が見えた。方角を確認して冬場の夕暮れ時がベストだと判断し、天候状態を見計らって撮影した。（東京都調布市）

Mt. Fuji at dusk from the Tokyo suburbs
Upon parking on the rooftop of a home center, I espied Mt. Fuji in the offing. Considering the direction of the view, and deciding sunset in winter the best time to shoot, I kept an eye on the weather and ... voila! (Chofu, Tokyo)

31　朝の横浜から見た富士山　　　　　　　　　山梨将典

大黒ふ頭にかかる大黒大橋はみなとみらいの高層ビル群と富士山が
見えて、夜景のスポットでも有名である。初日の出に照らされた富
士山が縁起よく赤く染まっていた。（神奈川県横浜市／大黒大橋）

Mt. Fuji seen from Yokohama in morning

Daikoku Ohashi, the bridge leading to the Daikoku pier in the center of
Yokohama Port, is famed for its nighttime view of the skyscrapers of
Minatomirai, and of Mt. Fuji, here illuminated by the first sunrise of the
New Year, and tinged the auspicious color red. (Yokohama, Kanagawa /
Daikoku Ohashi)

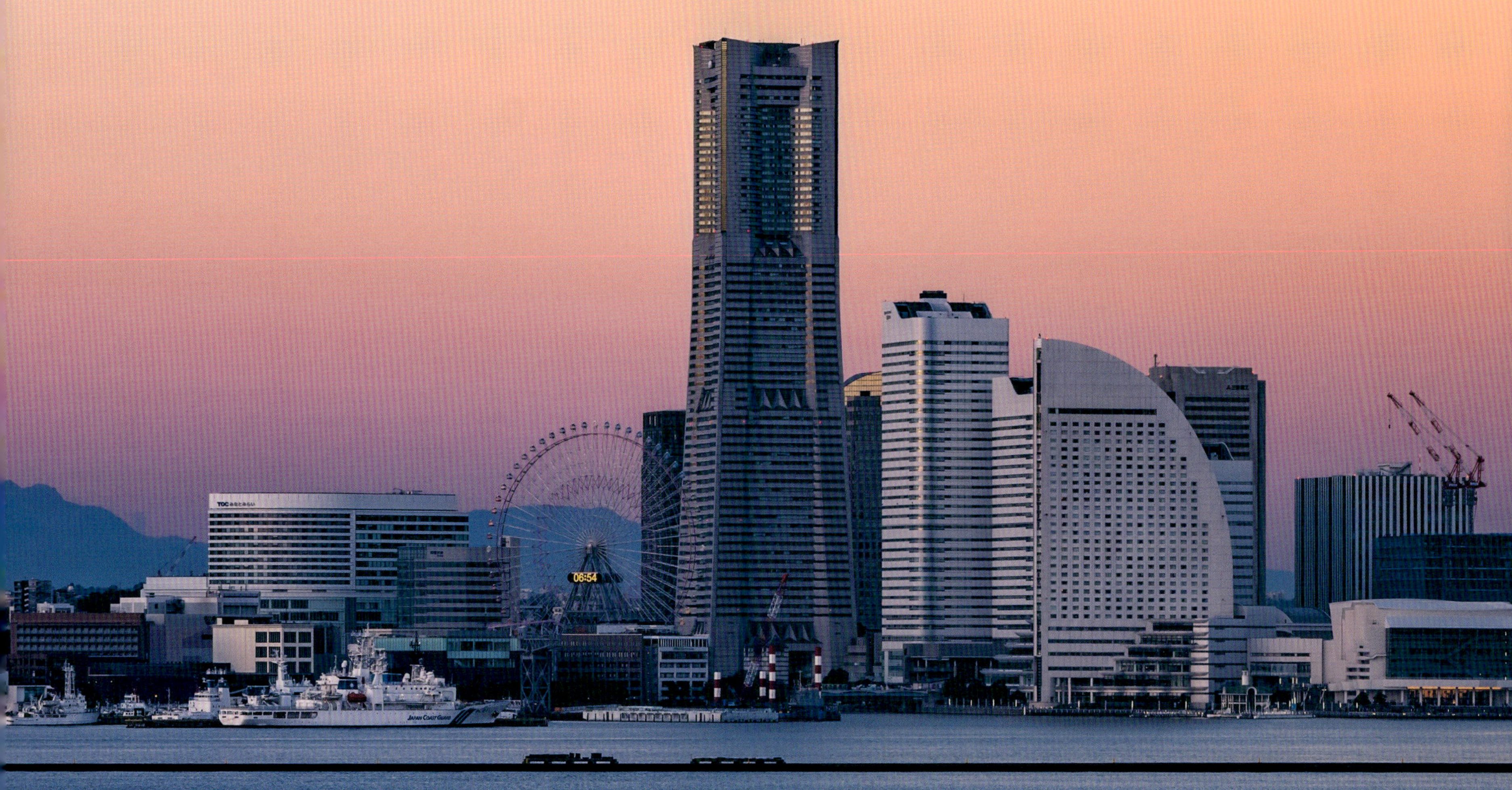

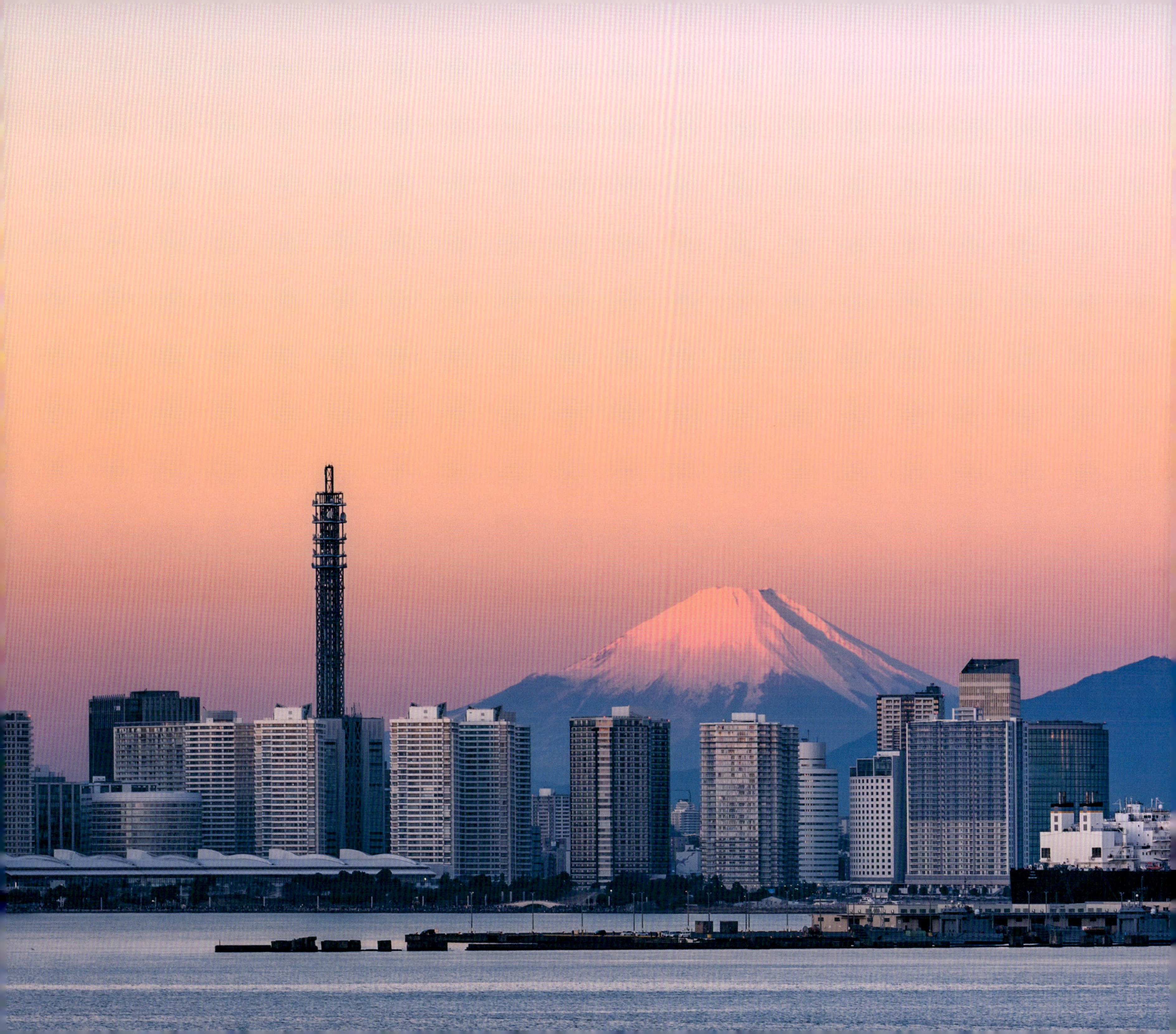

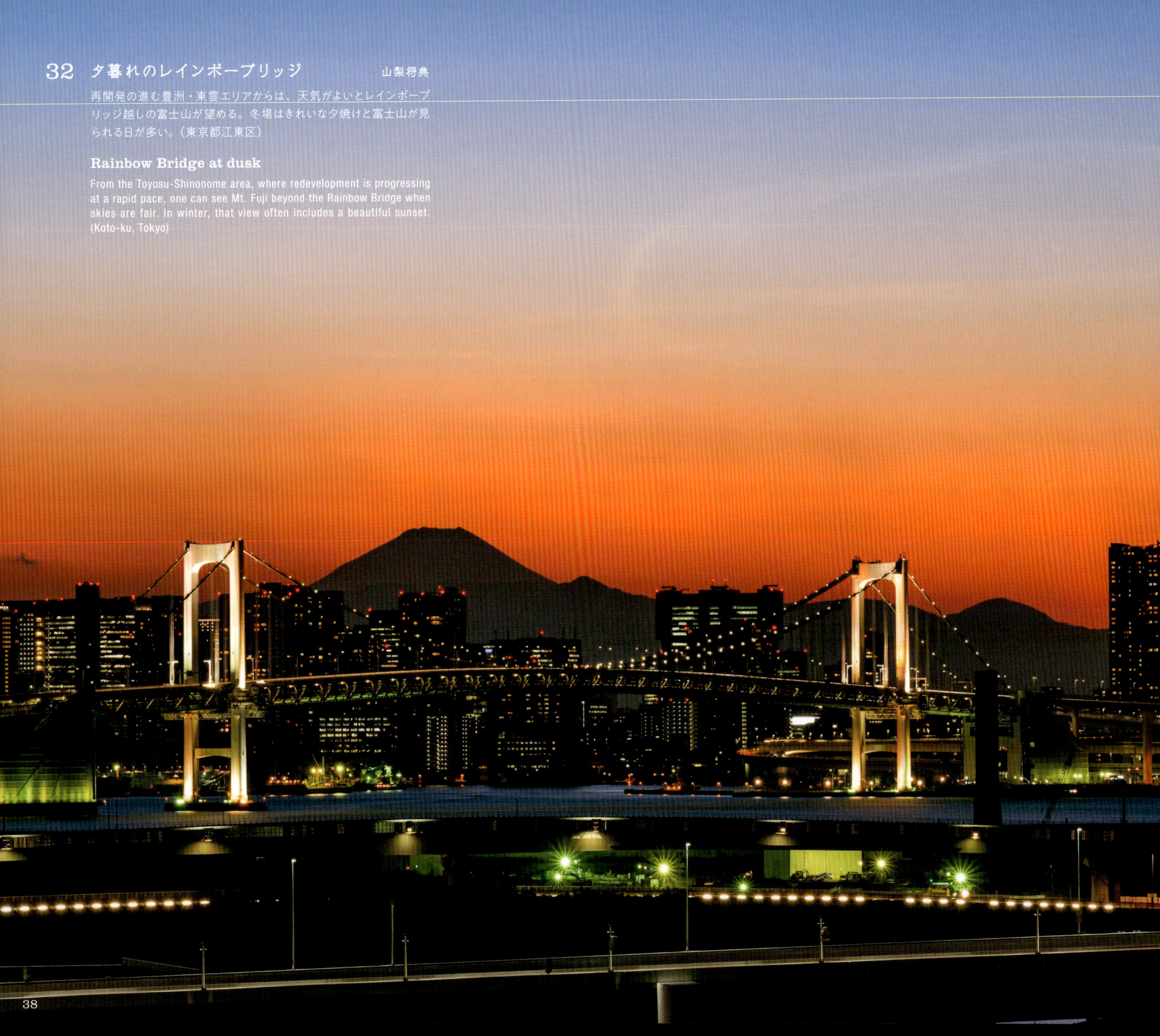

再開発の進む豊洲・東雲エリアからは、天気がよいとレインボーブリッジ越しの富士山が望める。冬場はきれいな夕焼けと富士山が見られる日が多い。（東京都江東区）

Rainbow Bridge at dusk

From the Toyosu-Shinonome area, where redevelopment is progressing at a rapid pace, one can see Mt. Fuji beyond the Rainbow Bridge when skies are fair. In winter, that view often includes a beautiful sunset. (Koto-ku, Tokyo)

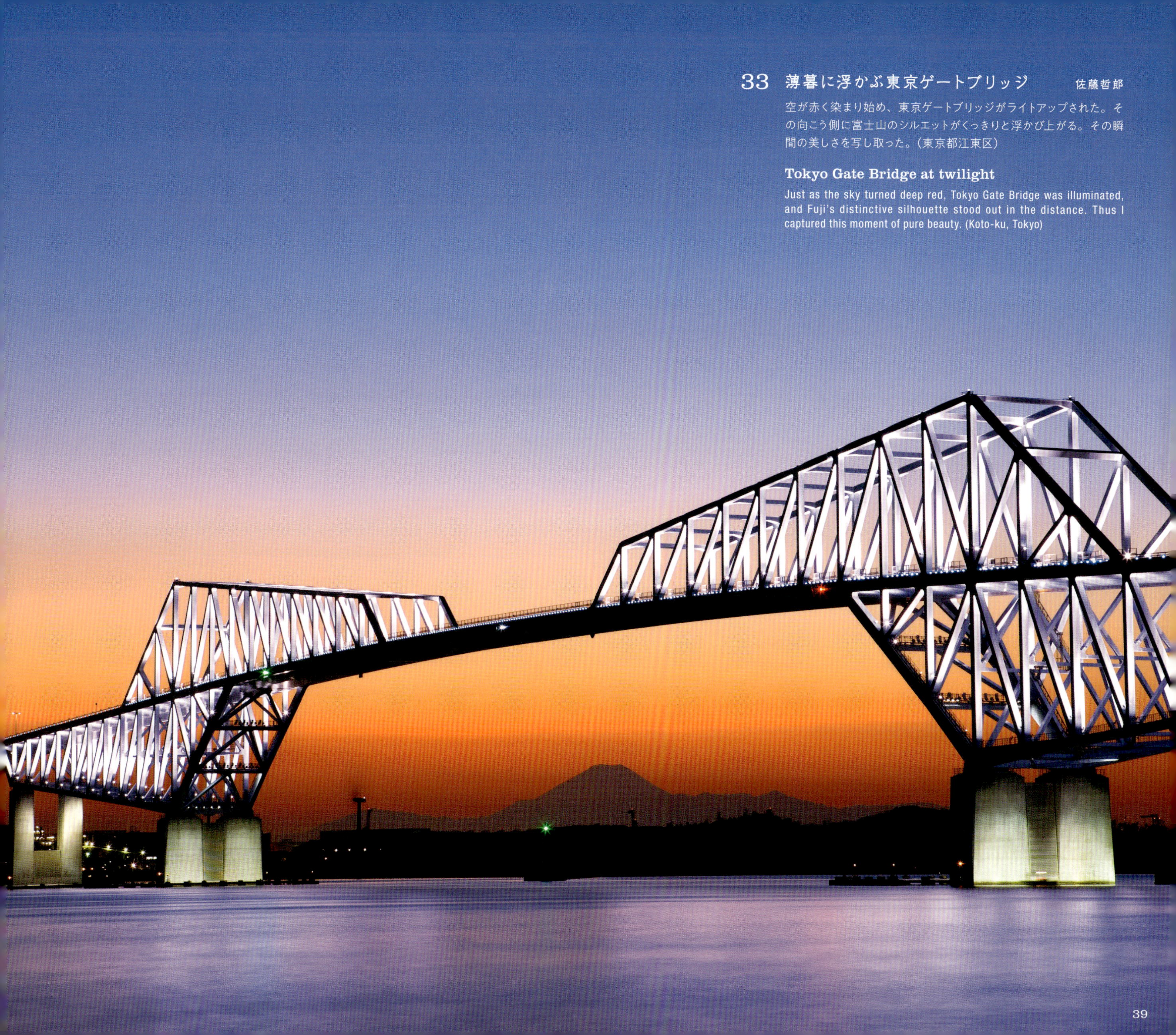

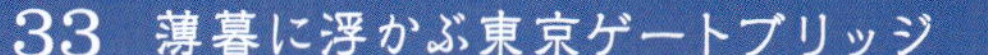

空が赤く染まり始め、東京ゲートブリッジがライトアップされた。その向こう側に富士山のシルエットがくっきりと浮かび上がる。その瞬間の美しさを写し取った。（東京都江東区）

Tokyo Gate Bridge at twilight

Just as the sky turned deep red, Tokyo Gate Bridge was illuminated, and Fuji's distinctive silhouette stood out in the distance. Thus I captured this moment of pure beauty. (Koto-ku, Tokyo)

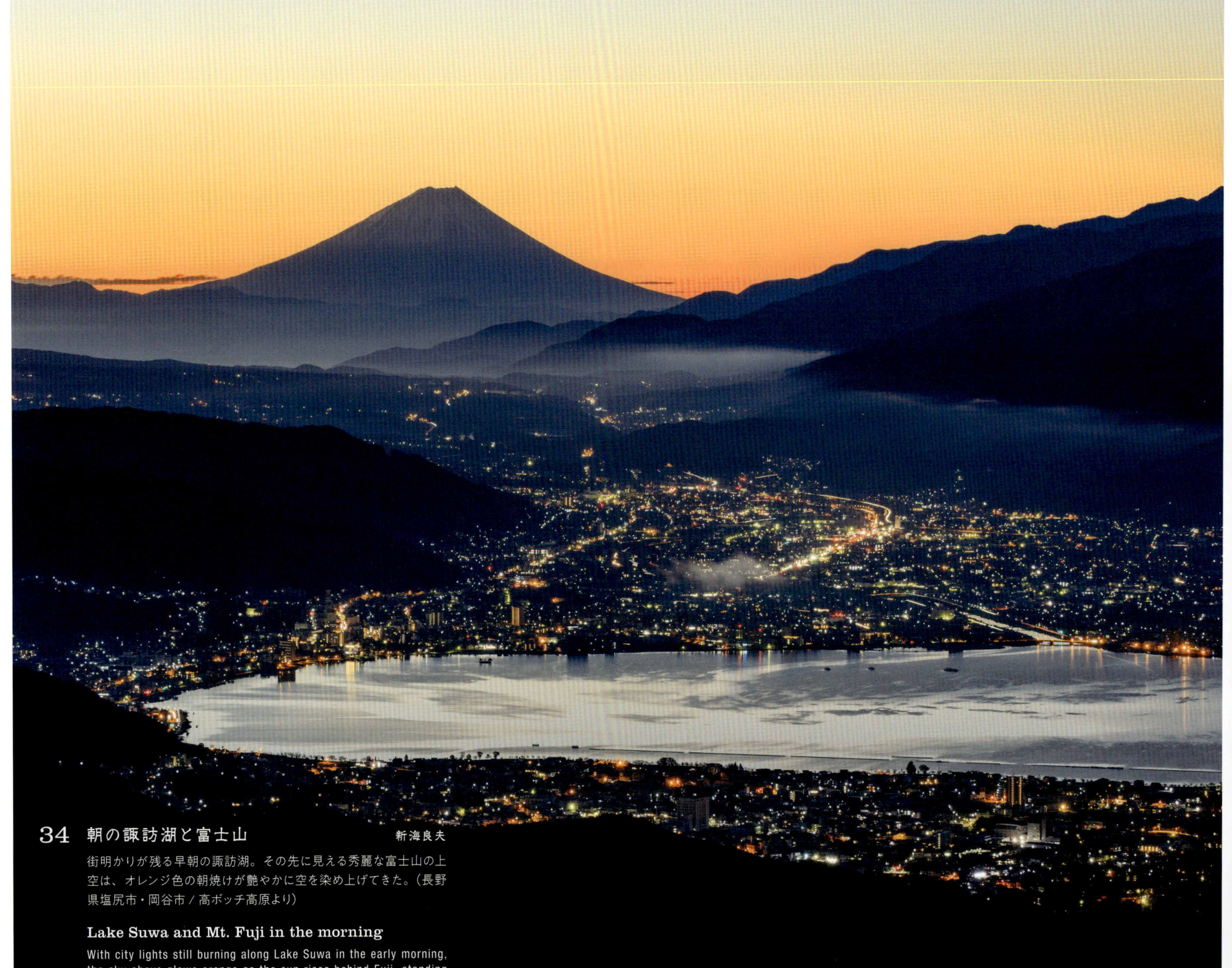

34　朝の諏訪湖と富士山

新海良夫

街明かりが残る早朝の諏訪湖。その先に見える秀麗な富士山の上空は、オレンジ色の朝焼けが艶やかに空を染め上げてきた。（長野県塩尻市・岡谷市 / 高ボッチ高原より）

Lake Suwa and Mt. Fuji in the morning

With city lights still burning along Lake Suwa in the early morning, the sky above glows orange as the sun rises behind Fuji, standing gracefully in the distance. (Shiojiri and Okaya, Nagano / From the Takabocchi Highlands)

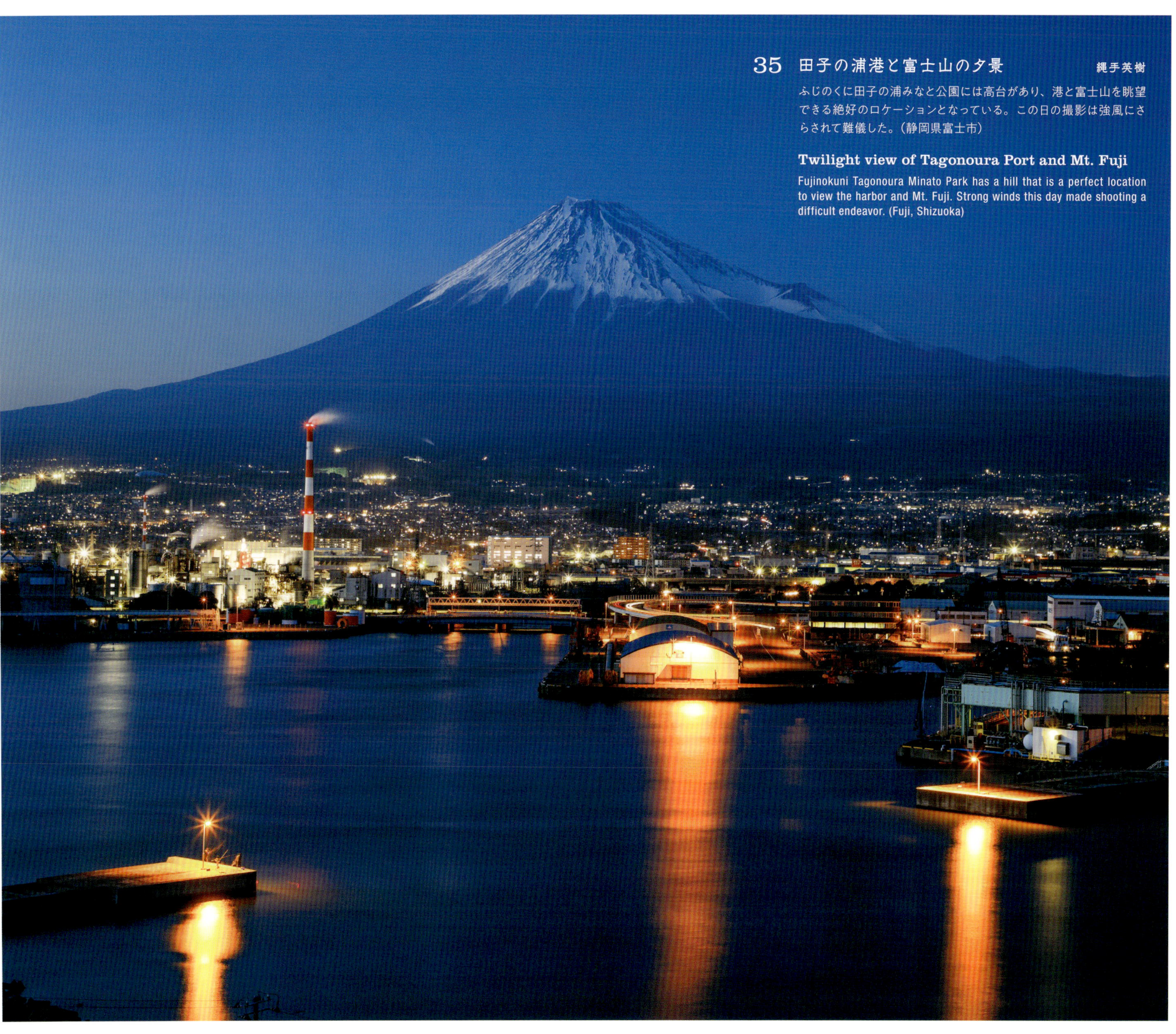

35　田子の浦港と富士山の夕景　　　縄手英樹

ふじのくに田子の浦みなと公園には高台があり、港と富士山を眺望
できる絶好のロケーションとなっている。この日の撮影は強風にさ
らされて難儀した。（静岡県富士市）

Twilight view of Tagonoura Port and Mt. Fuji
Fujinokuni Tagonoura Minato Park has a hill that is a perfect location
to view the harbor and Mt. Fuji. Strong winds this day made shooting a
difficult endeavor. (Fuji, Shizuoka)

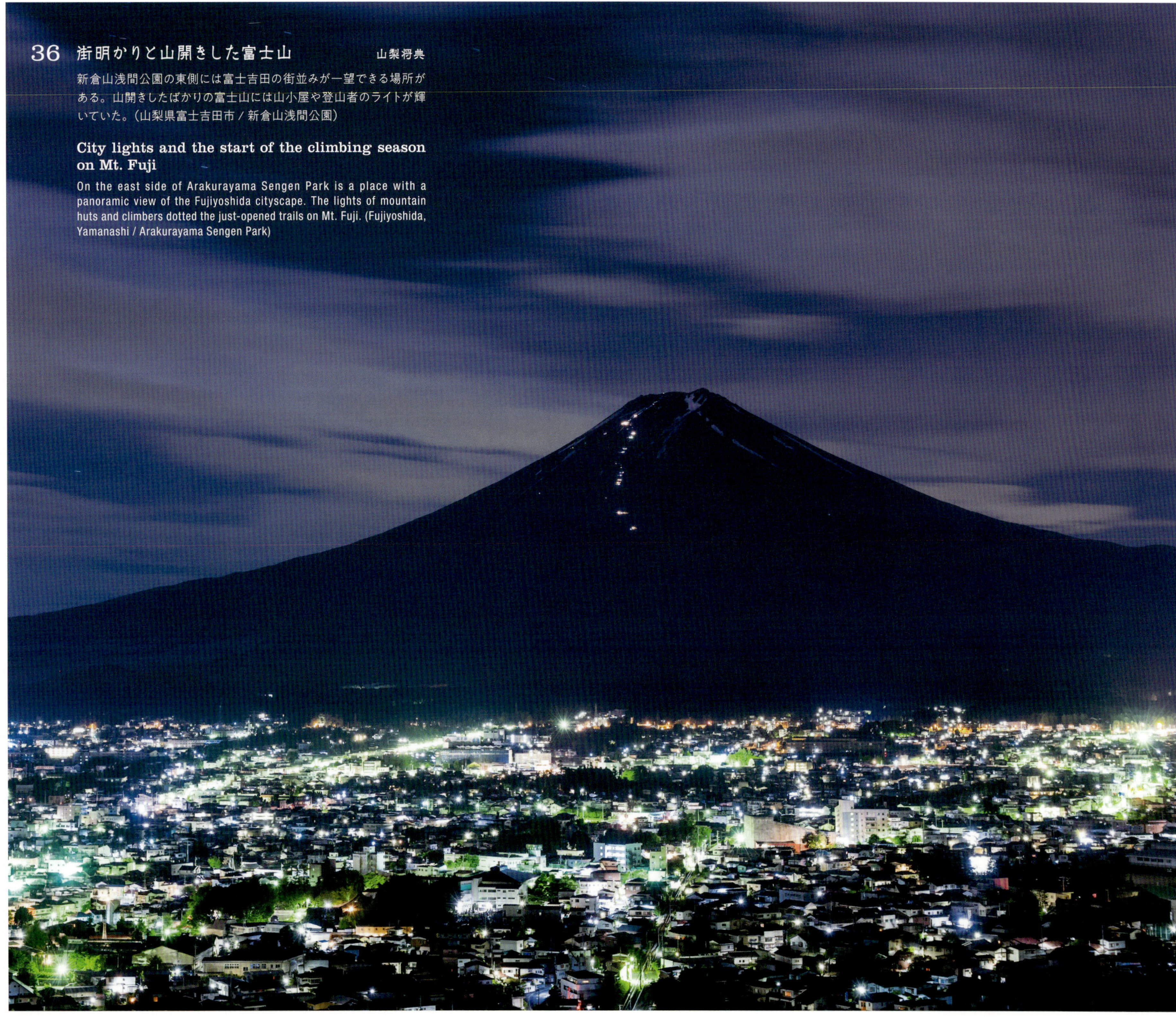

新倉山浅間公園の東側には富士吉田の街並みが一望できる場所がある。山開きしたばかりの富士山には山小屋や登山者のライトが輝いていた。(山梨県富士吉田市／新倉山浅間公園)

City lights and the start of the climbing season on Mt. Fuji

On the east side of Arakurayama Sengen Park is a place with a panoramic view of the Fujiyoshida cityscape. The lights of mountain huts and climbers dotted the just-opened trails on Mt. Fuji. (Fujiyoshida, Yamanashi / Arakurayama Sengen Park)

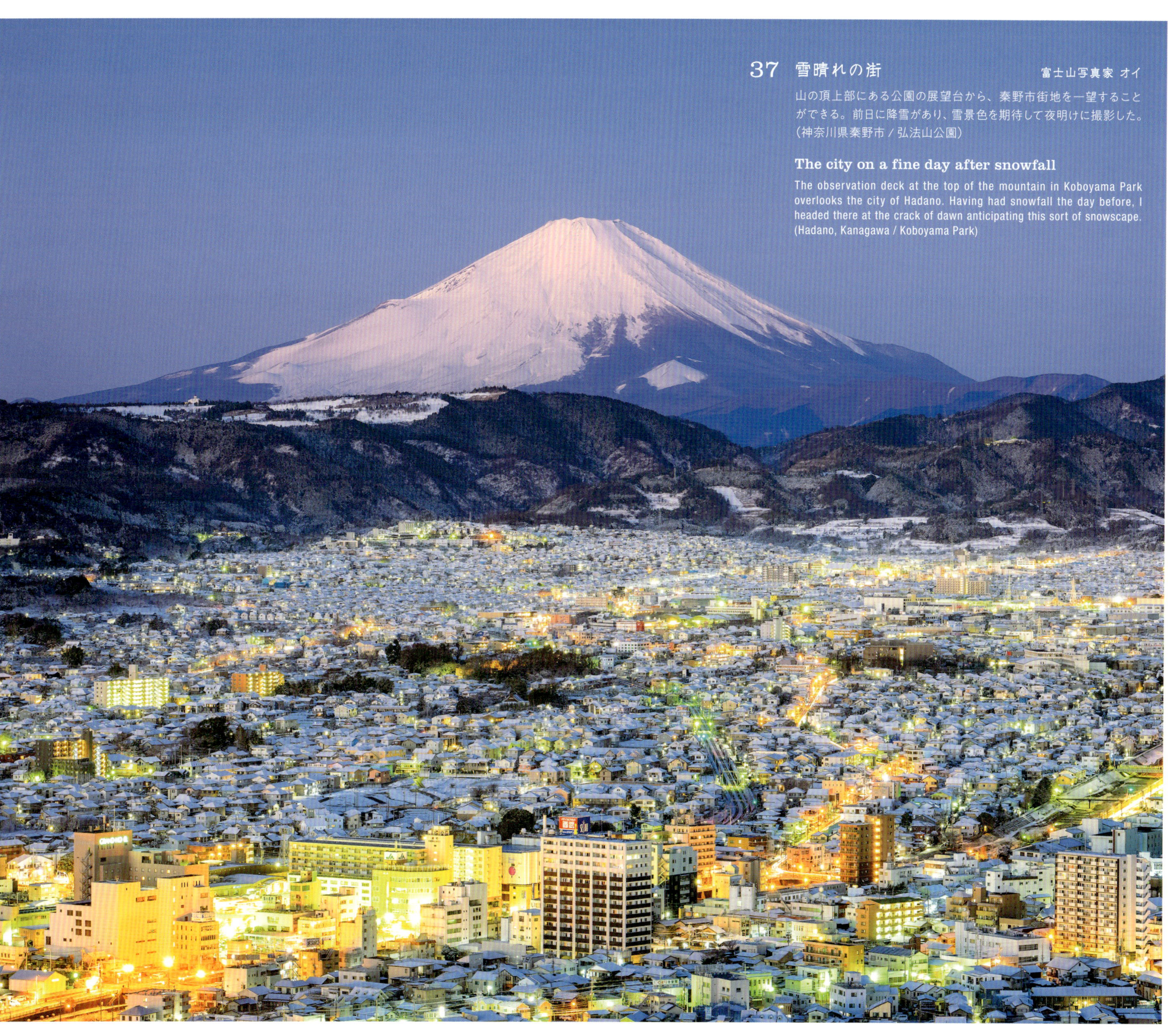

37 雪晴れの街
富士山写真家 オイ
山の頂上部にある公園の展望台から、秦野市街地を一望することができる。前日に降雪があり、雪景色を期待して夜明けに撮影した。
（神奈川県秦野市 / 弘法山公園）
The city on a fine day after snowfall
The observation deck at the top of the mountain in Koboyama Park overlooks the city of Hadano. Having had snowfall the day before, I headed there at the crack of dawn anticipating this sort of snowscape.
(Hadano, Kanagawa / Koboyama Park)

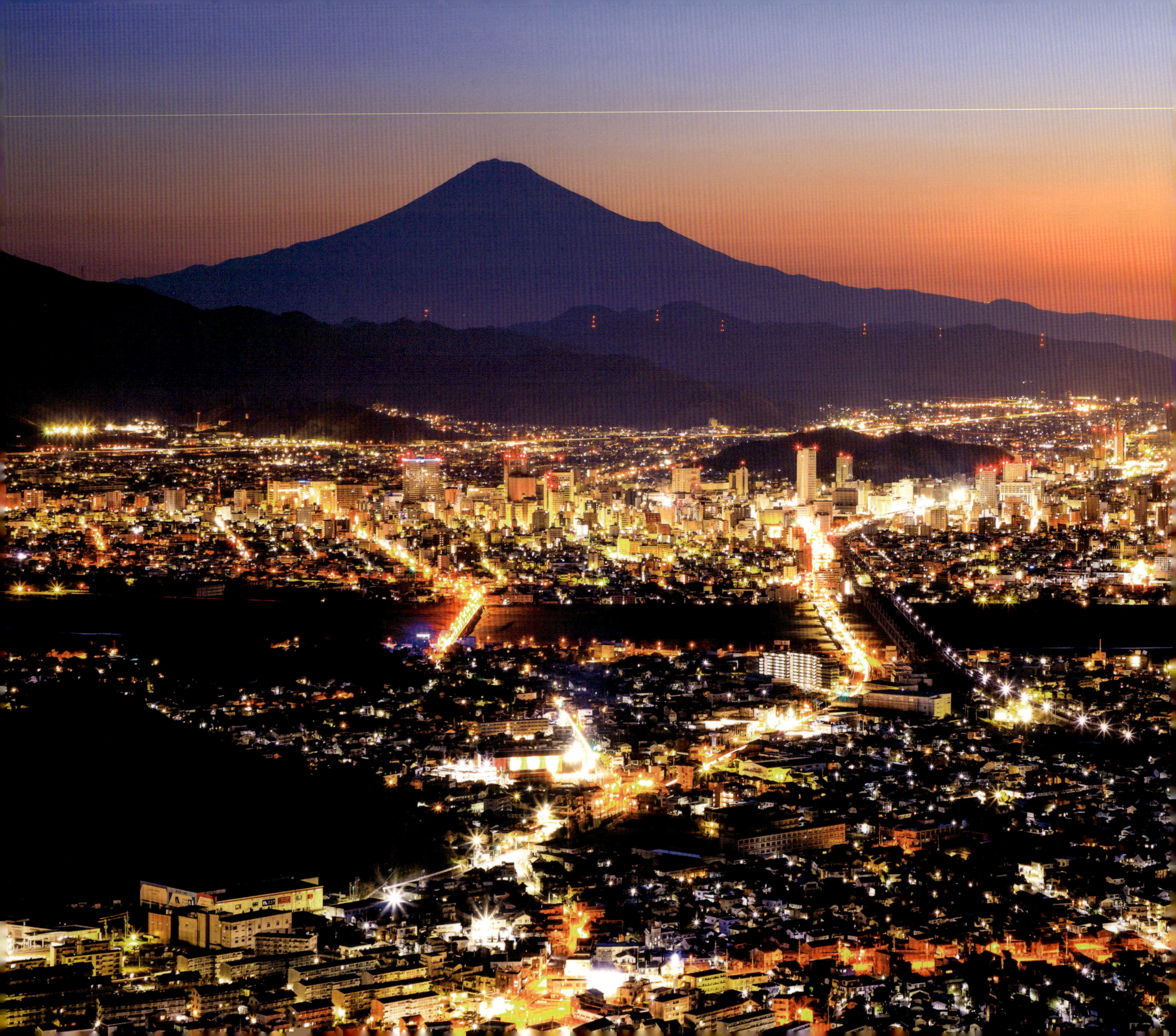

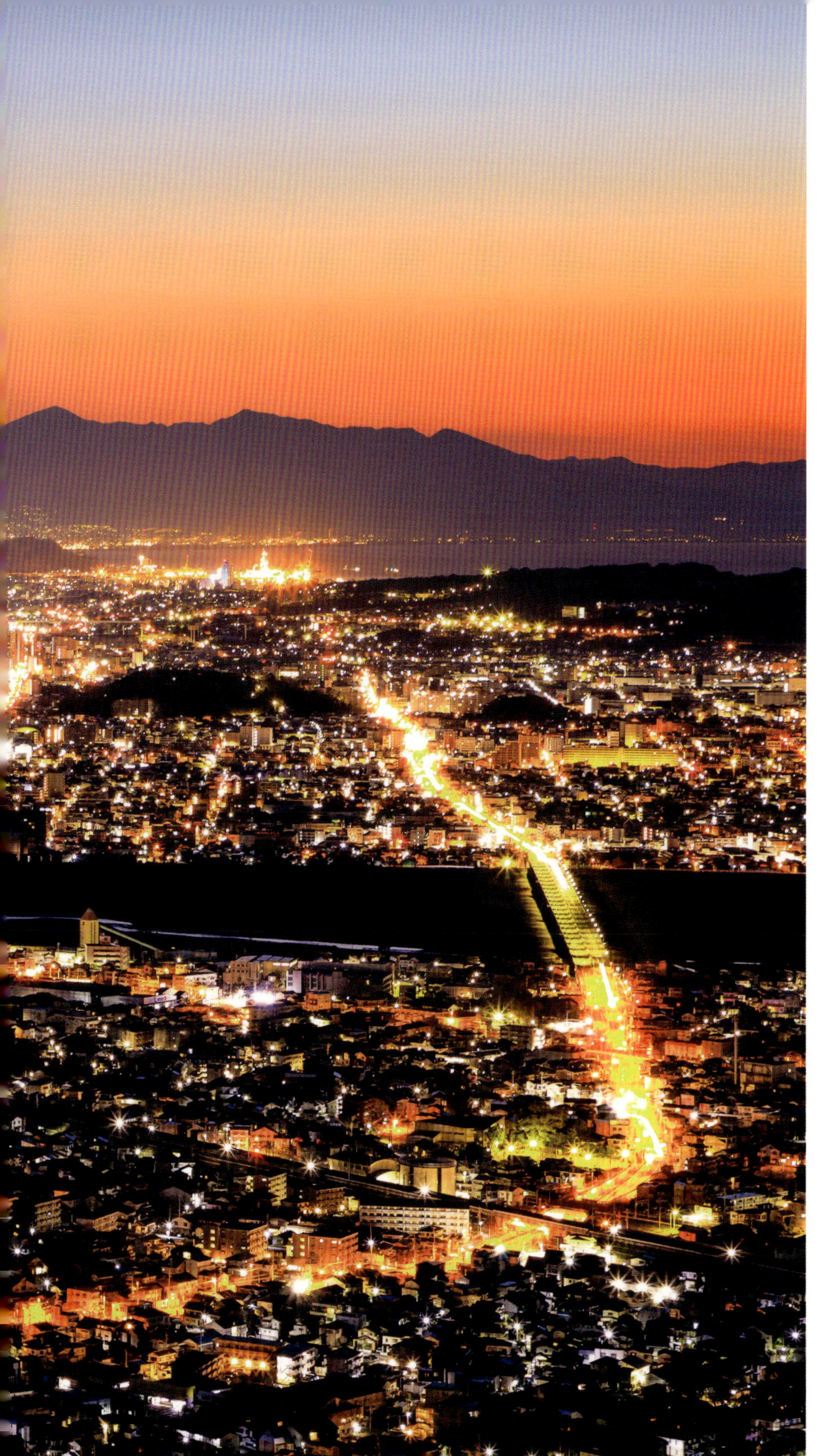

38 朝鮮岩から望む夜明けの富士山　　　縄手英樹

朝鮮岩へは４０分ほど登山しなければならないが、駿河湾や富士山、静岡市街の夜景を見られる好展望地である。（静岡県静岡市）

Mt. Fuji at dawn from Chosen Iwa

A 40-minute climb up to Chosen Iwa afforded this panoramic nighttime view of Suruga Bay, Mt. Fuji and the city of Shizuoka. (Shizuoka, Shizuoka)

毎年1月中旬から2月の土日の夜20分間打ち上げられる冬花火は河口
湖の夜を華やかに彩る。河口湖北岸の離れた場所から万全の防寒対策
で花火の打ち上げを待った。(山梨県南都留郡富士河口湖町／河口湖畔)

Winter fireworks at Lake Kawaguchi

Winter fireworks, launched for 20 minutes every Saturday and Sunday
night from mid-January to February, color the night sky of Lake
Kawaguchi. From a remote location on the northern shore of the
lake, I waited for the fireworks to start, fully protected from the cold.
(Fujikawaguchiko, Yamanashi / Lake Kawaguchi)

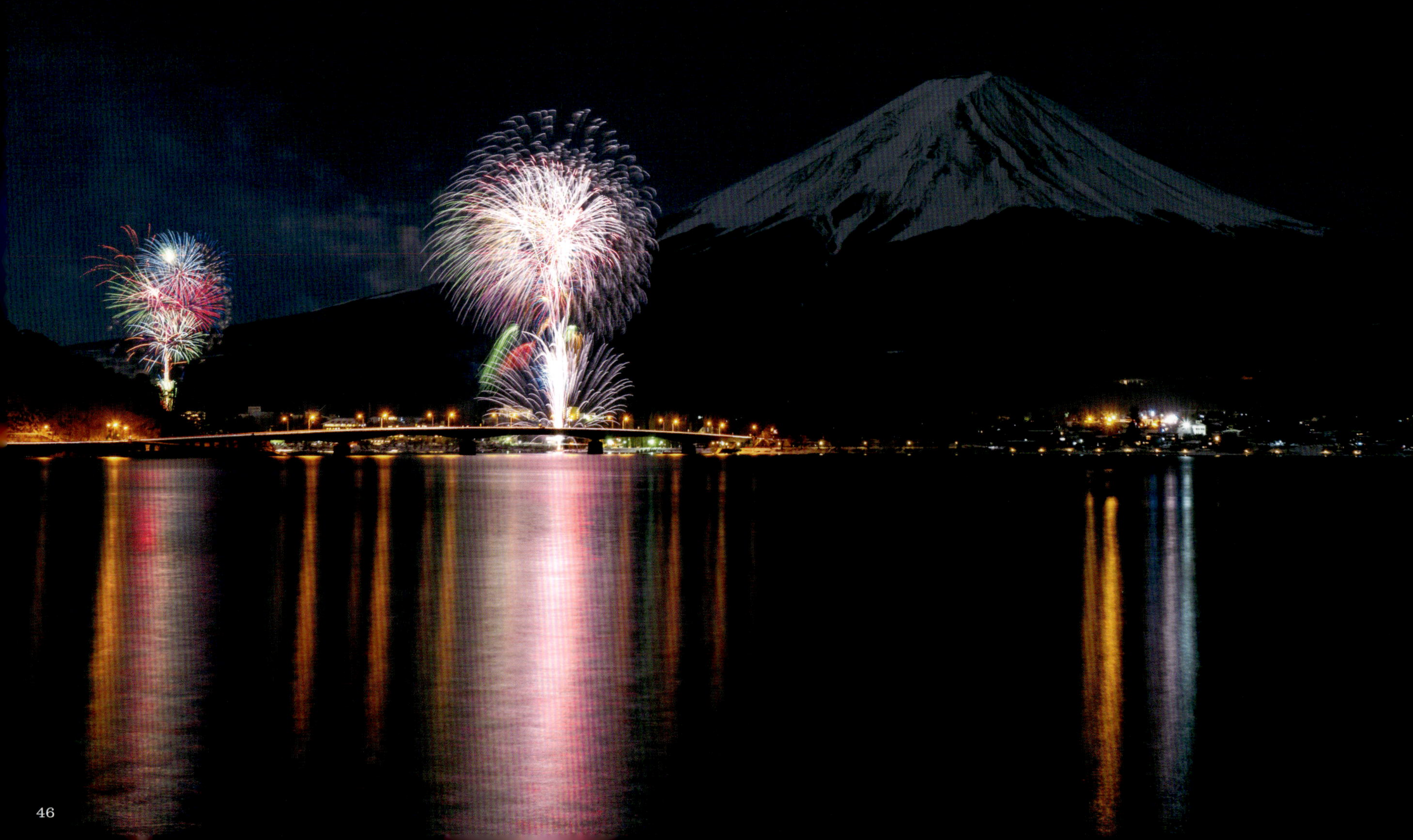

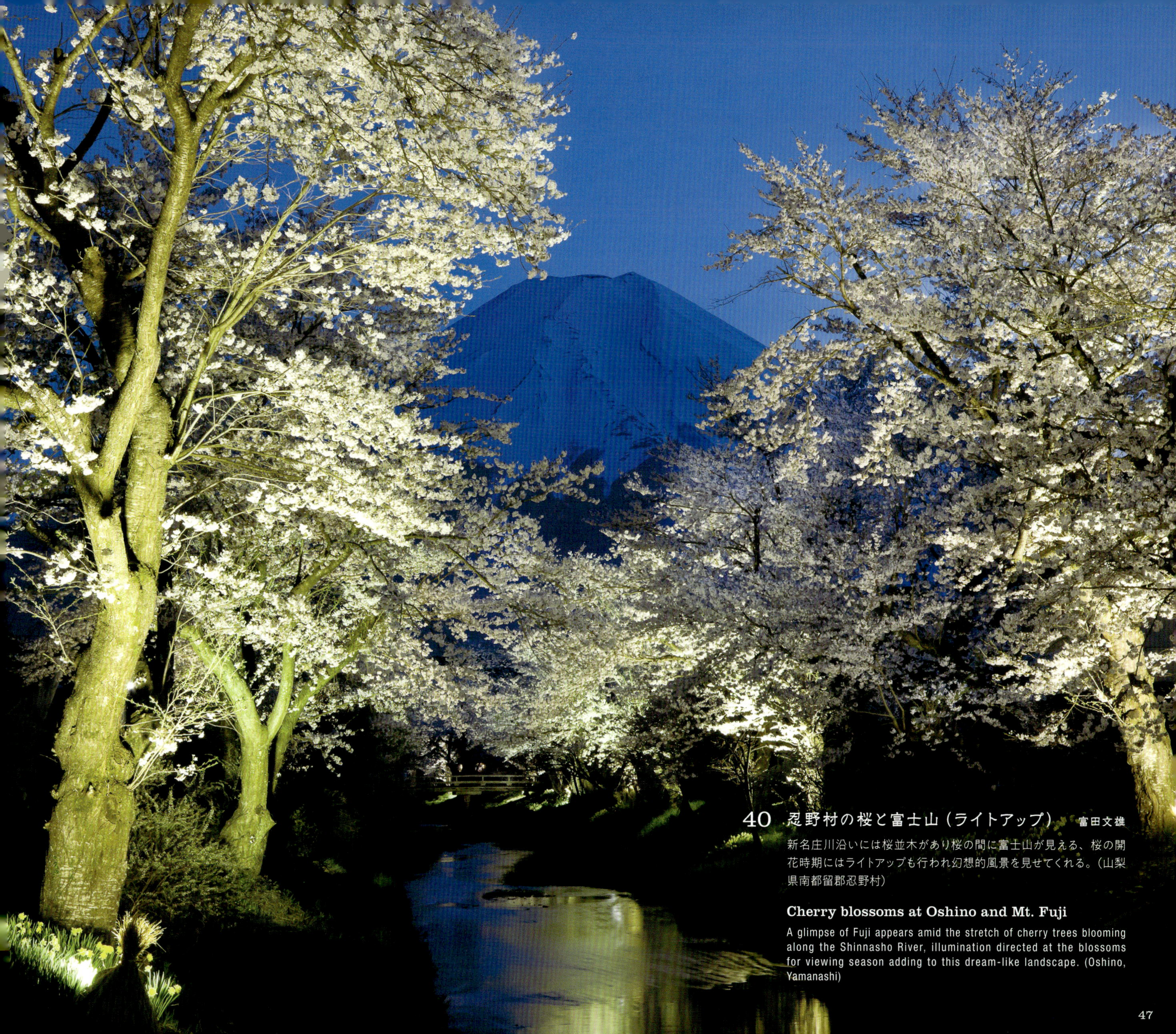

40 忍野村の桜と富士山（ライトアップ）　富田文雄

新名庄川沿いには桜並木があり桜の間に富士山が見える、桜の開花時期にはライトアップも行われ幻想的風景を見せてくれる。（山梨県南都留郡忍野村）

Cherry blossoms at Oshino and Mt. Fuji

A glimpse of Fuji appears amid the stretch of cherry trees blooming along the Shinnasho River, illumination directed at the blossoms for viewing season adding to this dream-like landscape. (Oshino, Yamanashi)

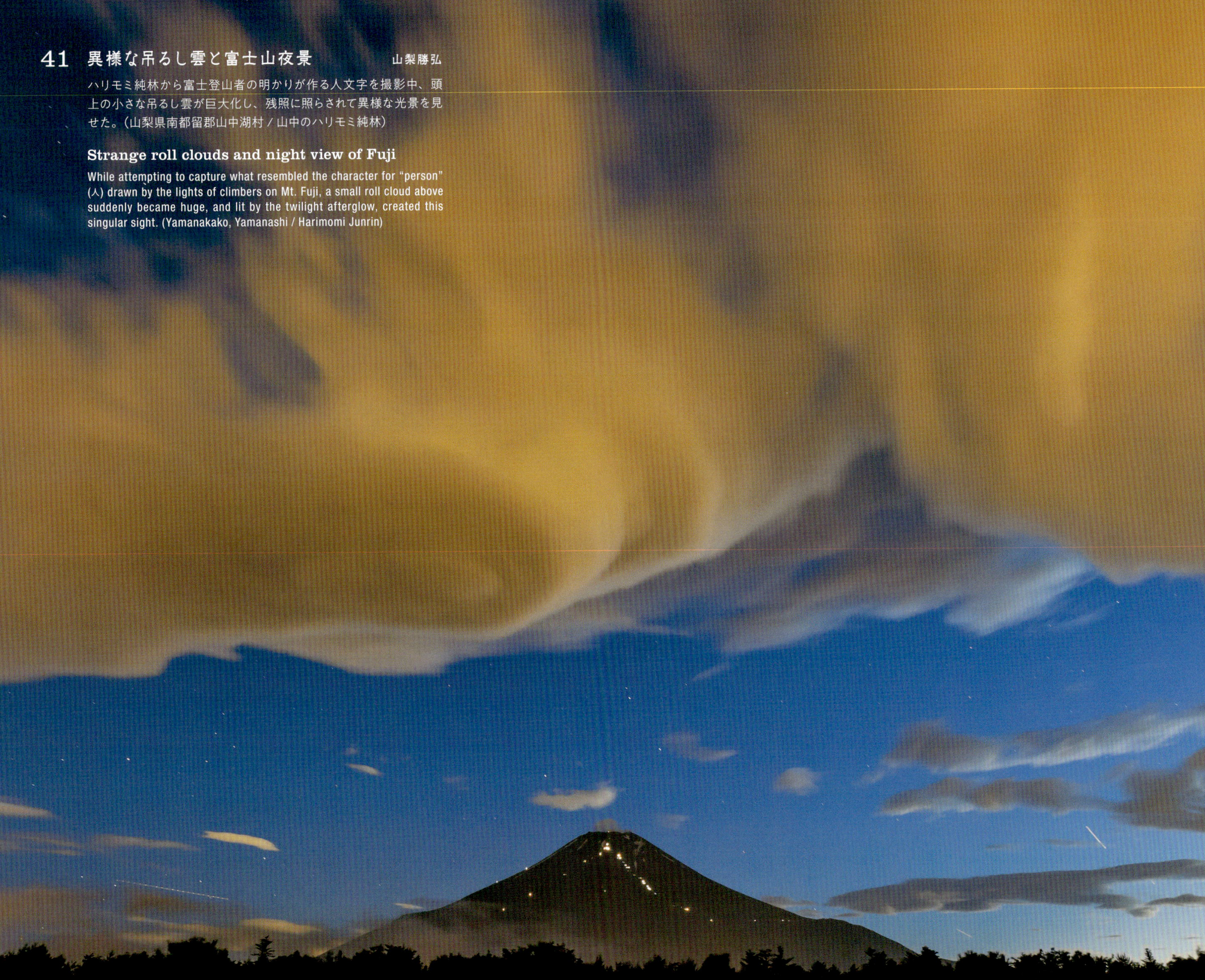

41　異様な吊るし雲と富士山夜景　　　　　山梨勝弘

ハリモミ純林から富士登山者の明かりが作る人文字を撮影中、頭
上の小さな吊るし雲が巨大化し、残照に照らされて異様な光景を見
せた。（山梨県南都留郡山中湖村／山中のハリモミ純林）

Strange roll clouds and night view of Fuji

While attempting to capture what resembled the character for "person"
(人) drawn by the lights of climbers on Mt. Fuji, a small roll cloud above
suddenly became huge, and lit by the twilight afterglow, created this
singular sight. (Yamanakako, Yamanashi / Harimomi Junrin)

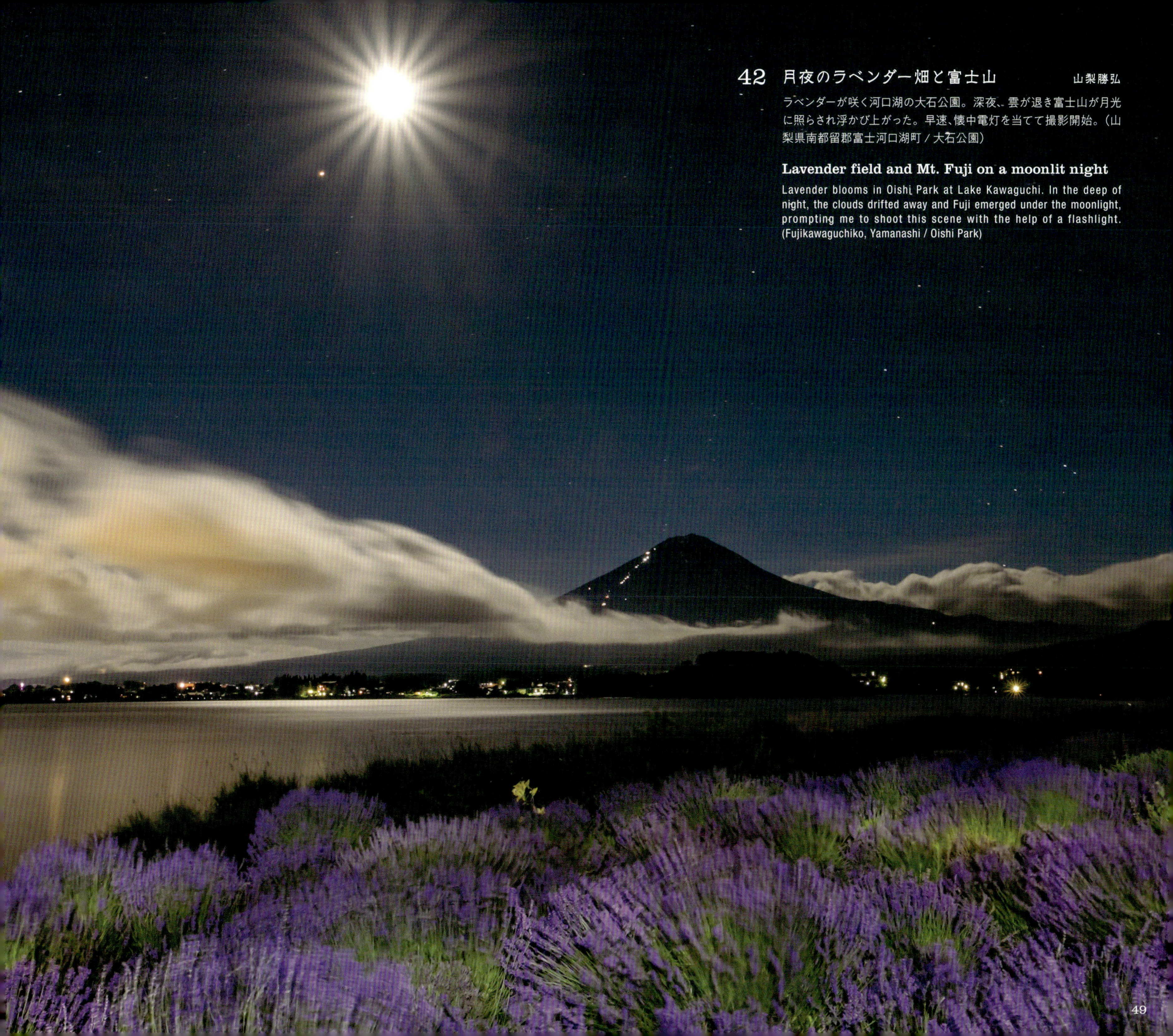

42　月夜のラベンダー畑と富士山　　　　山梨勝弘

ラベンダーが咲く河口湖の大石公園。深夜、雲が退き富士山が月光
に照らされ浮かび上がった。早速、懐中電灯を当てて撮影開始。（山
梨県南都留郡富士河口湖町／大石公園）

Lavender field and Mt. Fuji on a moonlit night

Lavender blooms in Oishi Park at Lake Kawaguchi. In the deep of
night, the clouds drifted away and Fuji emerged under the moonlight,
prompting me to shoot this scene with the help of a flashlight.
(Fujikawaguchiko, Yamanashi / Oishi Park)

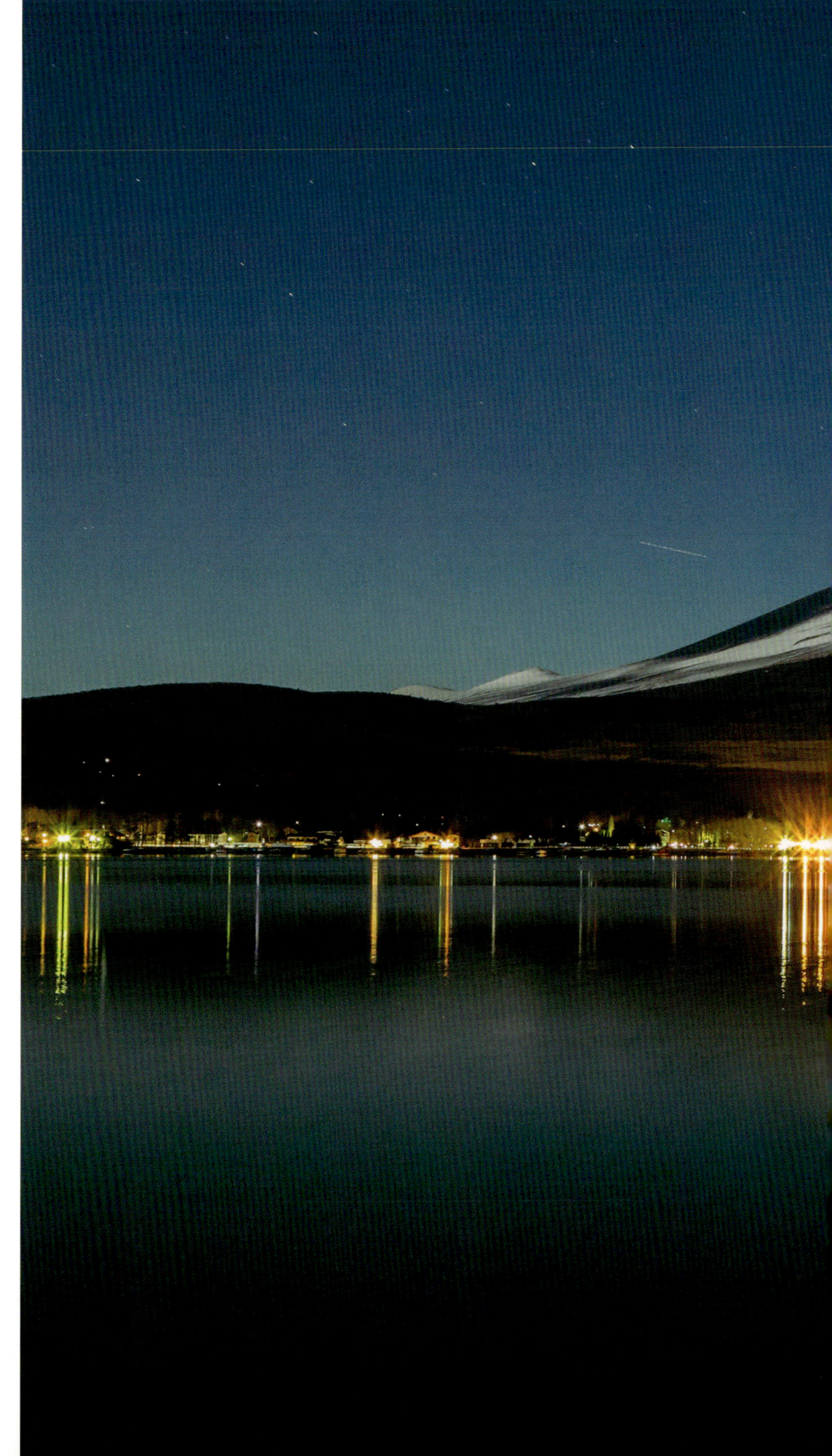

43　満月に浮かぶ富士山　　　山梨勝弘

山中湖畔で車中泊。放射冷却により底冷えのする夜だった。快晴
の空、煌煌と射す月明かりが富士山を明るく浮かび上がらせていた。
（山梨県南都留郡山中湖村 / 山中湖）

Mt. Fuji lit by the full moon

I spent the night in my car on the shore of Laka Yamanaka, a chilly night
due to radiative cooling. Clear skies and brightly shining moonlight lit
Fuji fully, brilliantly. (Yamanakako, Yamanashi / Lake Yamanaka)

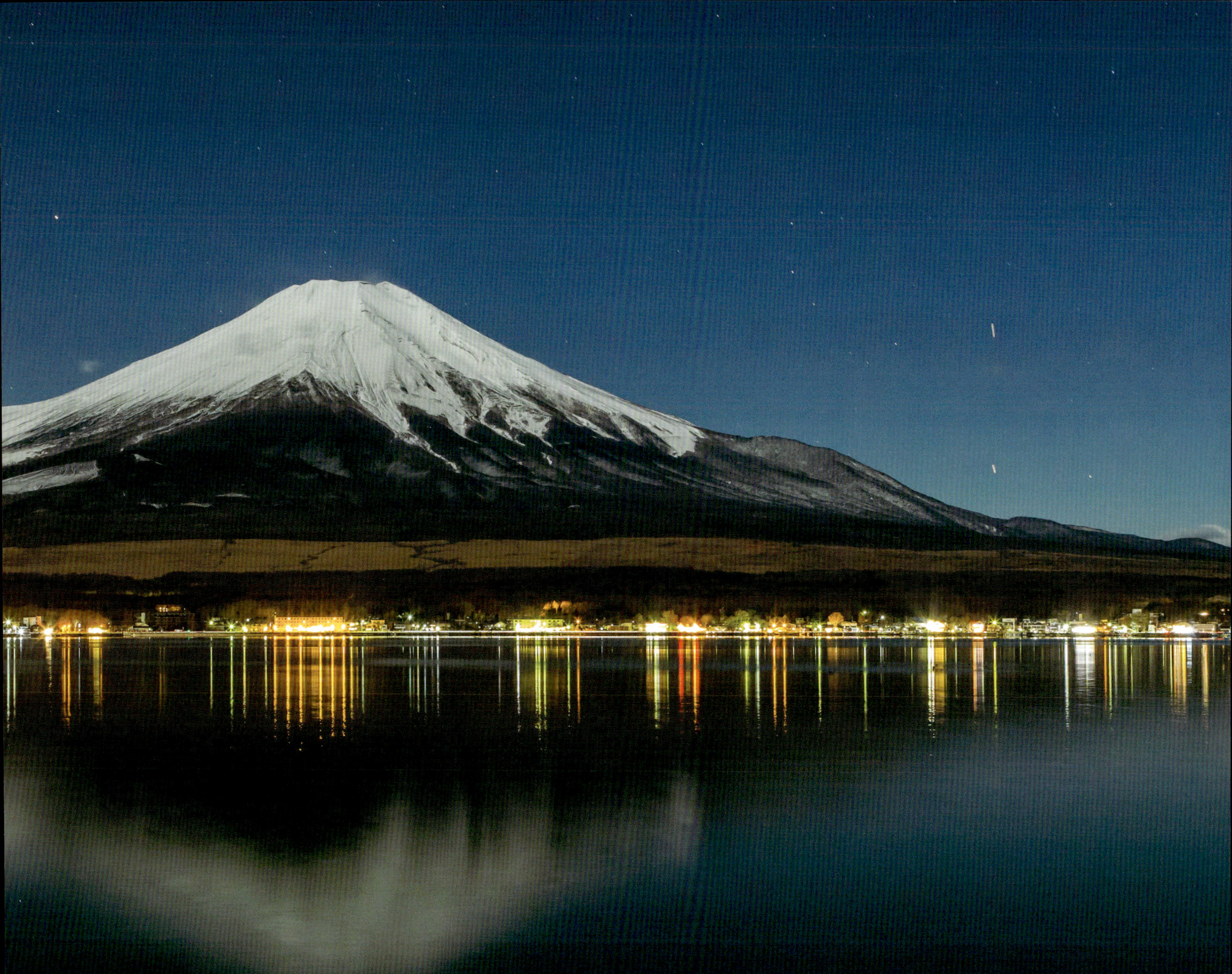

44 富士山暮色〈陣馬山（じんばさん）より〉　　富田文雄

東京都と神奈川県の境にある陣馬山から見る富士山は雄大だ。夕暮
れのあと赤く染まり夜を迎える富士山には特別な趣がある。（神奈
川県相模原市）

Mt. Fuji at dusk from Mt. Jinba

Mt. Fuji seen from Mt. Jinba on the border between Tokyo and
Kanagawa is magnificent, and took on a special aura against this
crimson-stained sky of twilight (Sagamihara, Kanagawa)

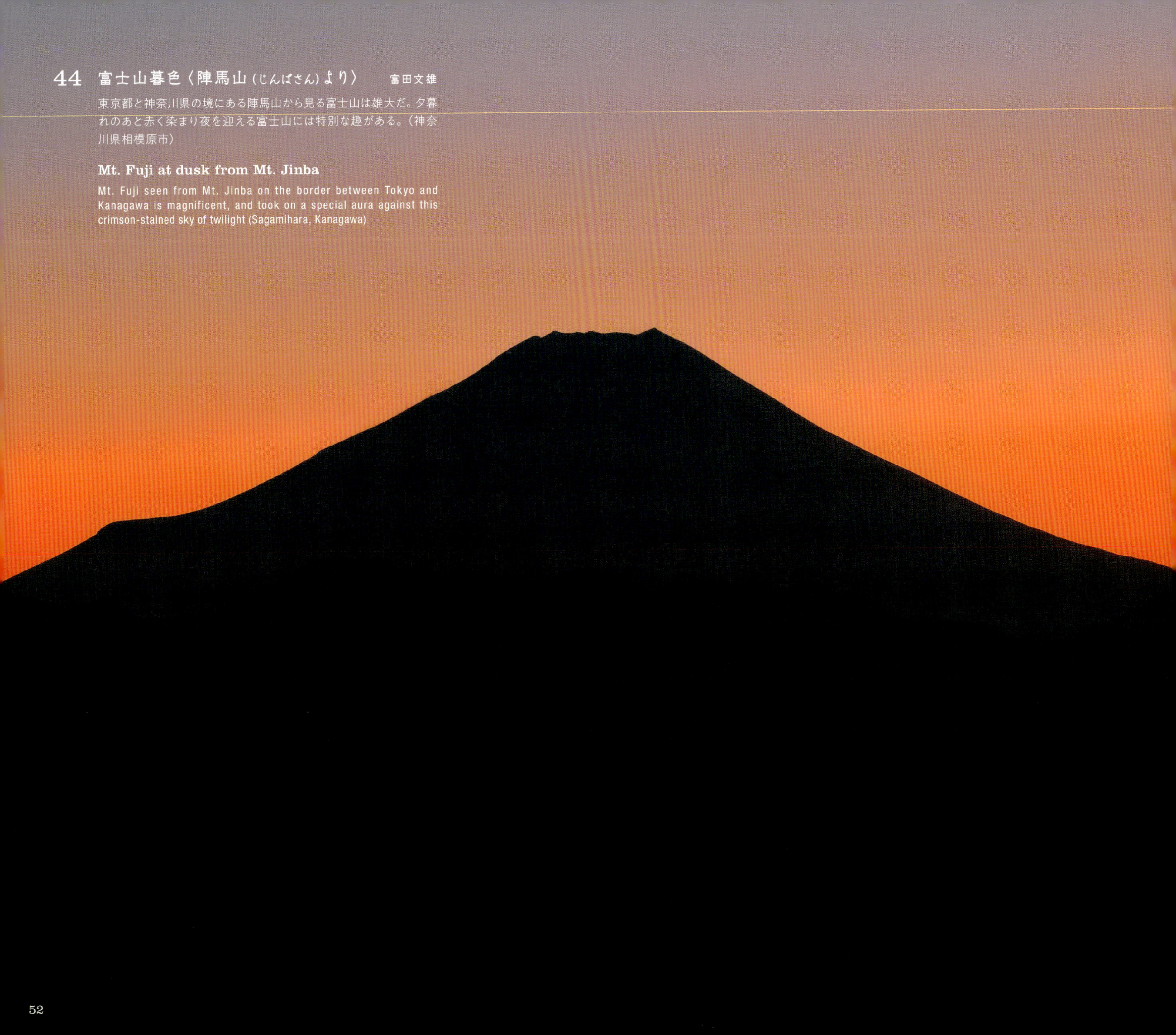

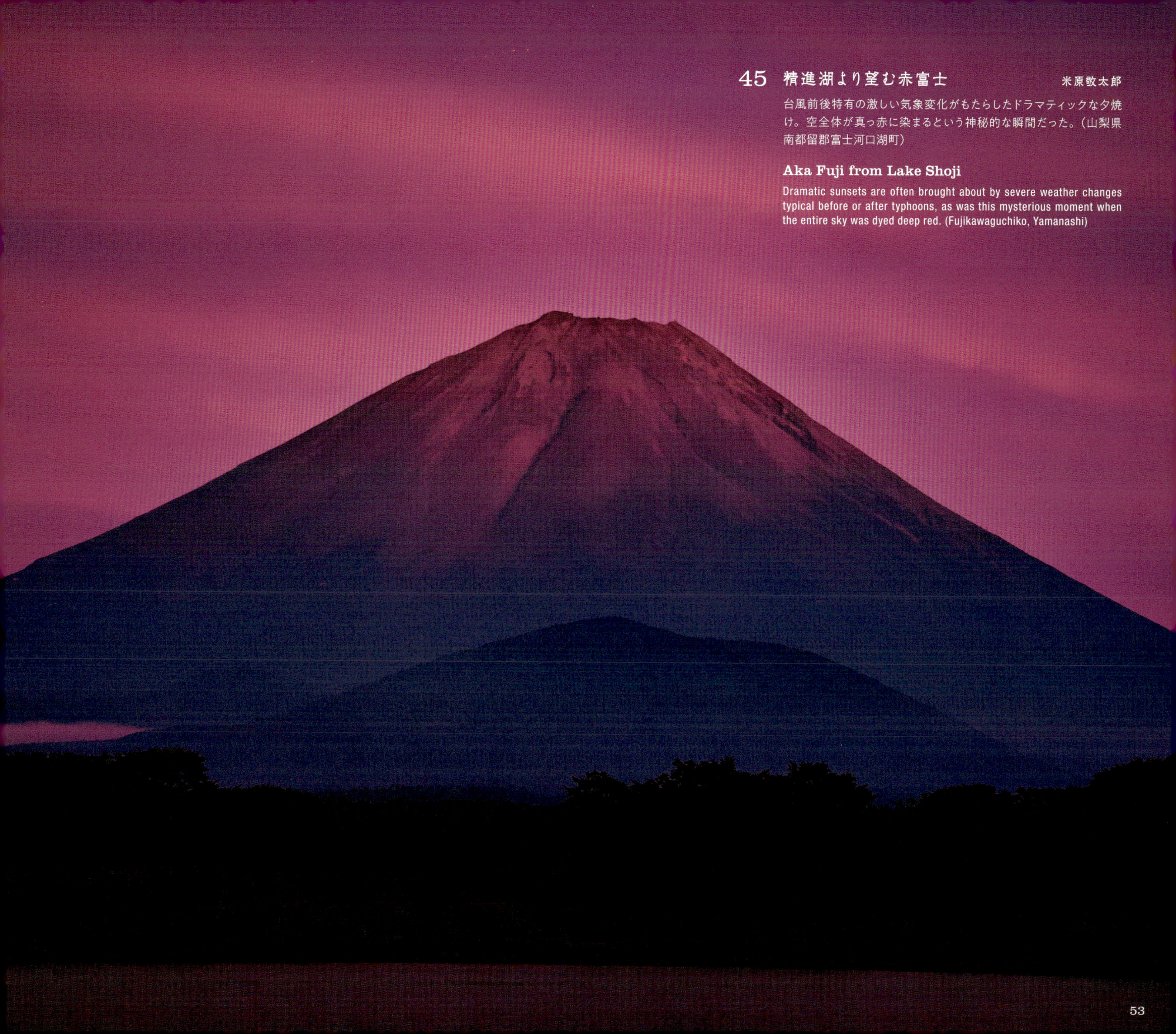

45　精進湖より望む赤富士　　　　　　　　米原敬太郎

台風前後特有の激しい気象変化がもたらしたドラマティックな夕焼
け。空全体が真っ赤に染まるという神秘的な瞬間だった。（山梨県
南都留郡富士河口湖町）

Aka Fuji from Lake Shoji
Dramatic sunsets are often brought about by severe weather changes
typical before or after typhoons, as was this mysterious moment when
the entire sky was dyed deep red. (Fujikawaguchiko, Yamanashi)

46 夜明け前の富士山 鎌形久

日の出前、富士山の麓に広がる朝霧高原から、星空と月とシルエットの富士をねらう。昼間とは違うドラマティックな表情を見せてくれた。（静岡県富士宮市）

Mt. Fuji before daybreak

Before sunrise, aiming to shoot the moon and Fuji's shadow-like silhouette against the starry sky from Asagiri Kogen at the foot of the mountain, I captured this dramatically different look from that of daytime. (Fujinomiya, Shizuoka)

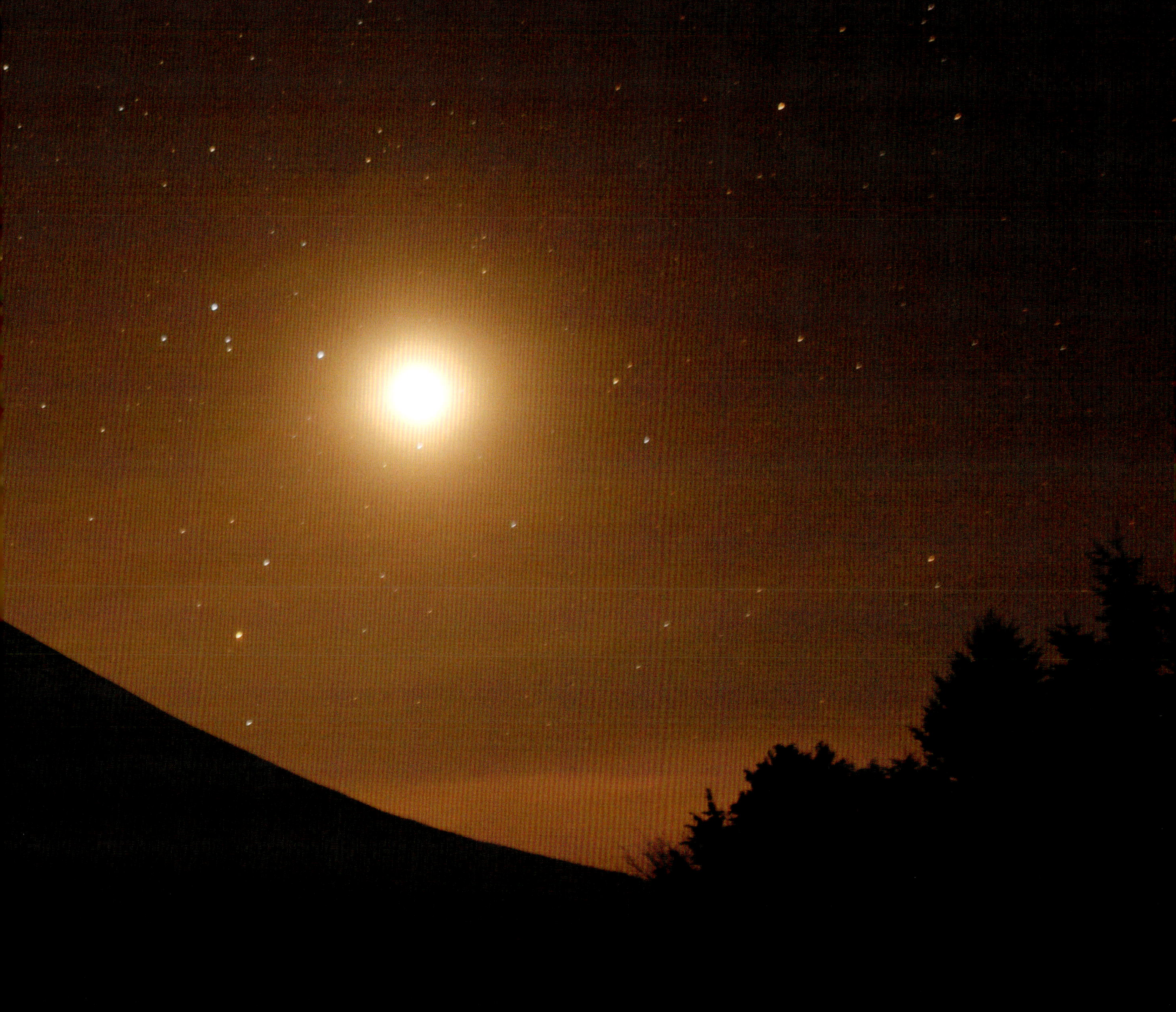

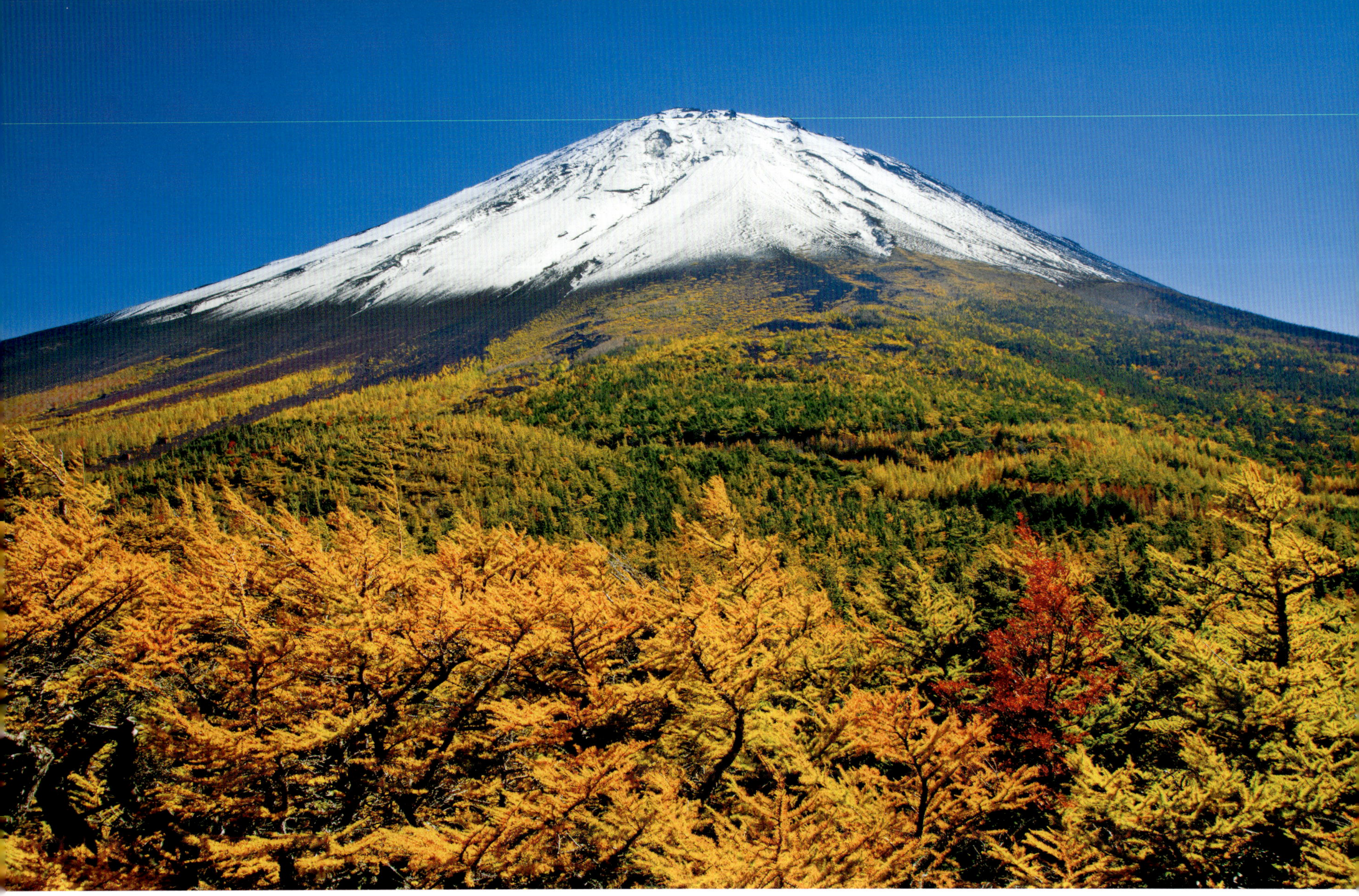

47　黄葉と新雪の富士山　　　　富田文雄

富士スバルライン奥庭駐車場から歩くこと約20分で奥庭展望台に
着く。ここからは秋のカラマツが一面黄金色に染まり新雪の富士山
とのコントラストが美しい。（山梨県南都留郡鳴沢村奥庭）

Mt. Fuji with autumn foliage and fresh snow

It takes about 20 minutes to walk from the Fuji Subaru Line parking
lot to the Okuniwa lookout, where Fuji's fresh white cap contrasted
beautifully with the broad expanse of golden larches covering the lower
reaches of the mountain. (Okuniwa, Narusawa, Yamanashi)

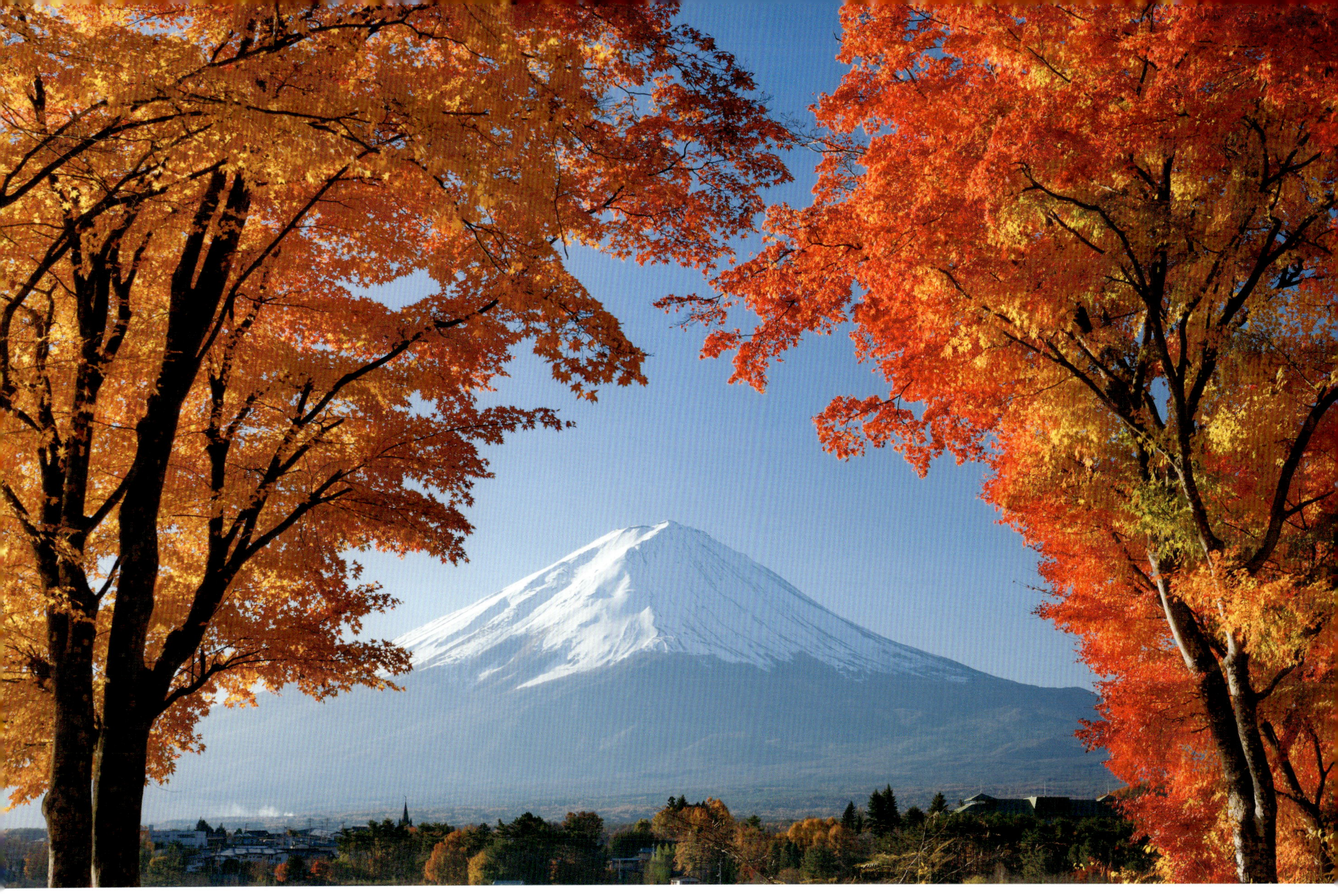

48　錦秋の富士　　　　　　　　　　　　館野二朗

河口湖畔沿いに紅葉した 2 本の木があり、その間から冠雪した富士
山を望んだ。朝の斜光が紅葉の葉を透過して輝いていた。（山梨県
南都留郡富士河口湖町）

Mt. Fuji framed in autumn brocade

Two trees showing off their autumn tints on the shore of Lake Kawaguchi
framed this view of a snow-capped Fuji. Morning light filtering through
the leaves set them ablaze in color. (Fujikawaguchiko, Yamanashi)

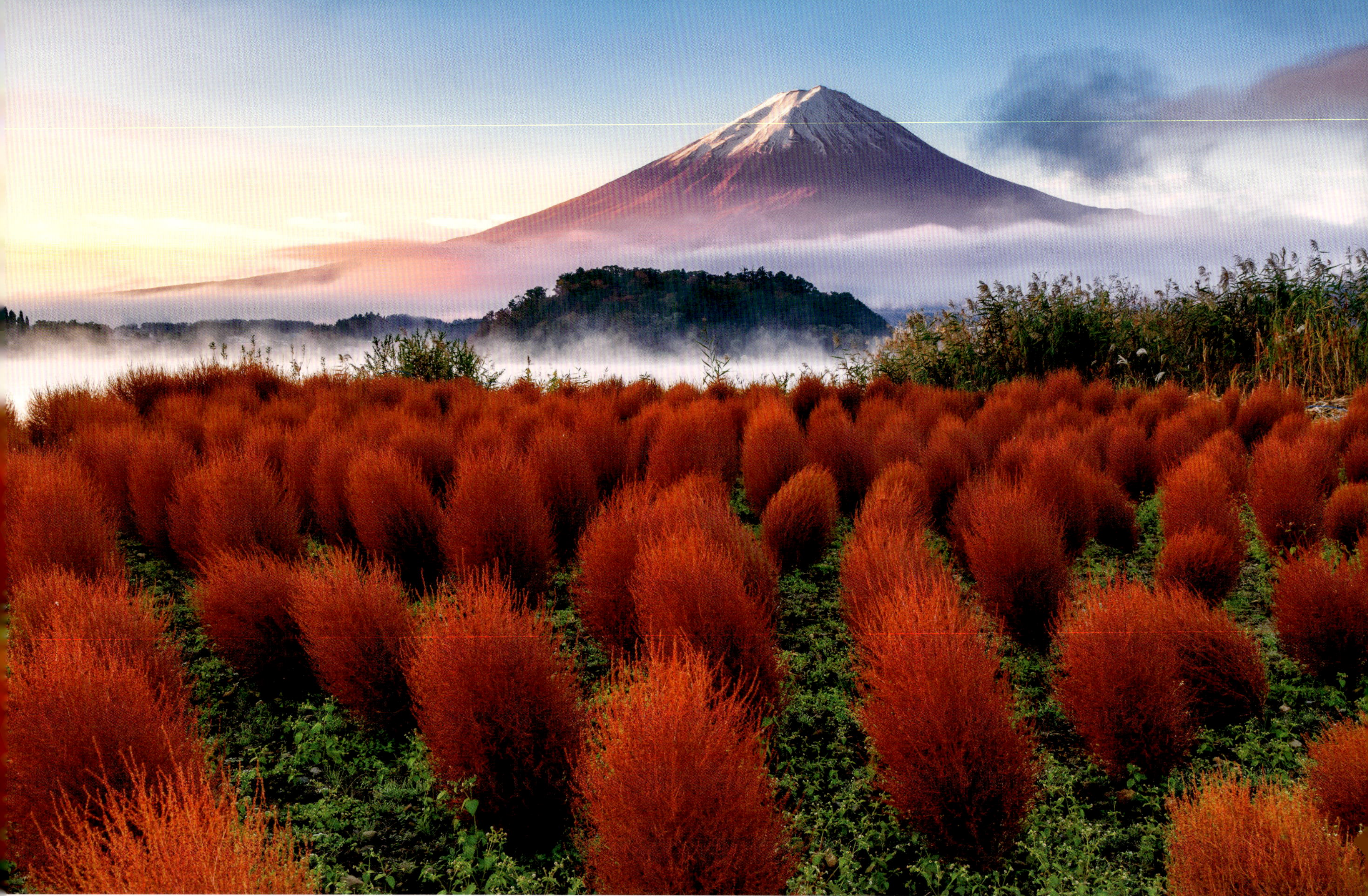

49　真紅のコキアと赤富士

高椋俊樹

朝日に照らされた富士山と、河口湖畔の大石公園のコキアの紅葉が
色彩を競う。誰でも早朝から散策できる。（山梨県南都留郡富士河
口湖町）

Crimson summer cypresses and Aka Fuji

The coloration of Fuji tinged by the morning sun and the crimson leaves
of the summer cypress in Oishi Park at Lake Kawaguchi are evenly
matched in beauty. The park is open to all for early morning strolling.
(Fujikawaguchiko, Yamanashi)

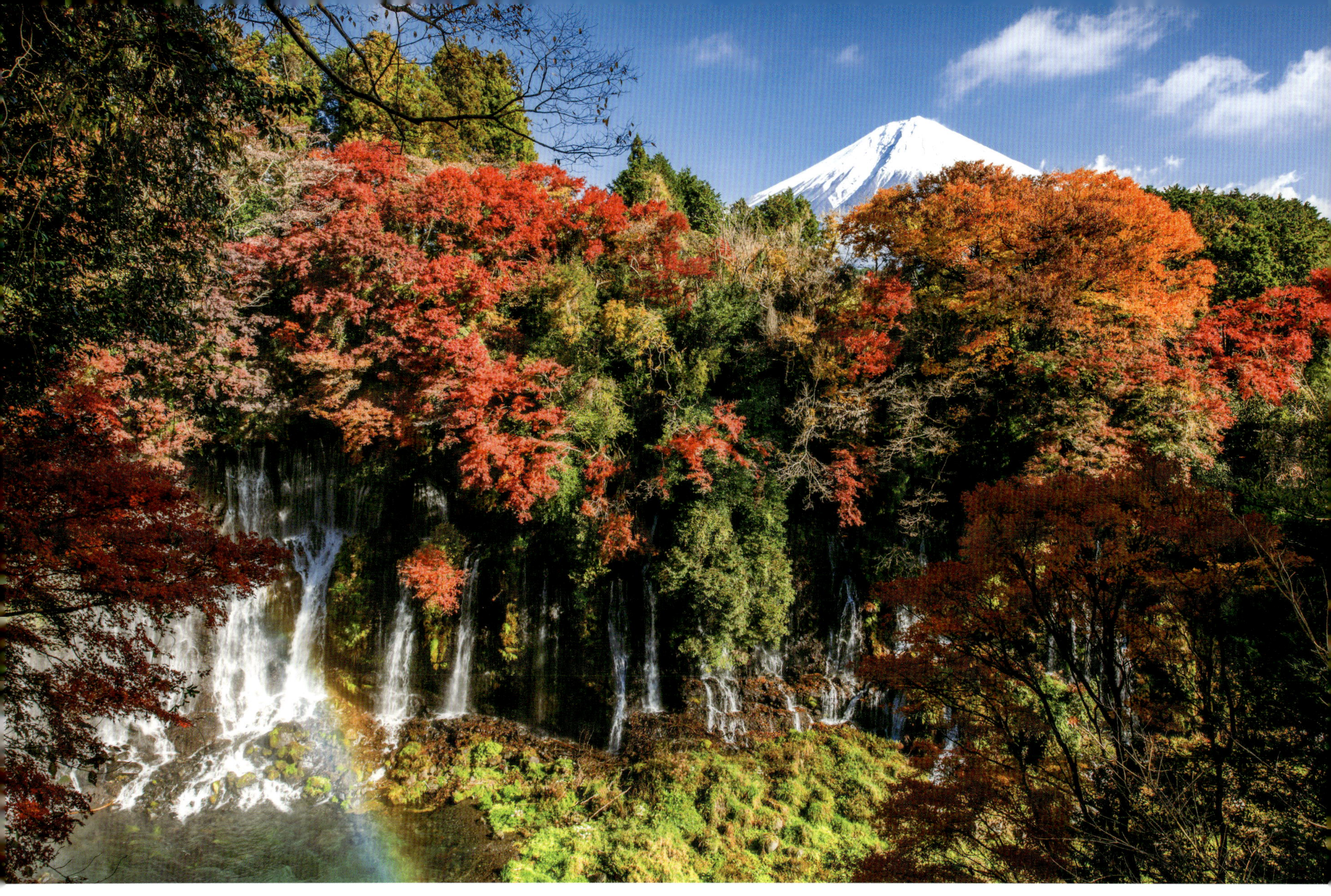

50　白糸ノ滝からの富士山

片岡巖

白糸ノ滝は富士山の雪解け水が絶壁から流れる名瀑で、国の名勝、天然記念物に指定されている。時間帯によっては豊かな水の流れに虹がかかることもあり、さらに美しさを増す。（静岡県富士宮市）

Mt. Fuji from Shiraito Falls

Ranked among the most beautiful waterfalls in Japan and bestowed natural monument status, Shiraito Falls is fed by snowmelt from Mt. Fuji that flows in thin white streams off the edge of a high cliff. When the sun strikes it right at certain times of day, the cascade's spray hosts a rainbow, making it all the more beautiful. (Fujinomiya, Shizuoka)

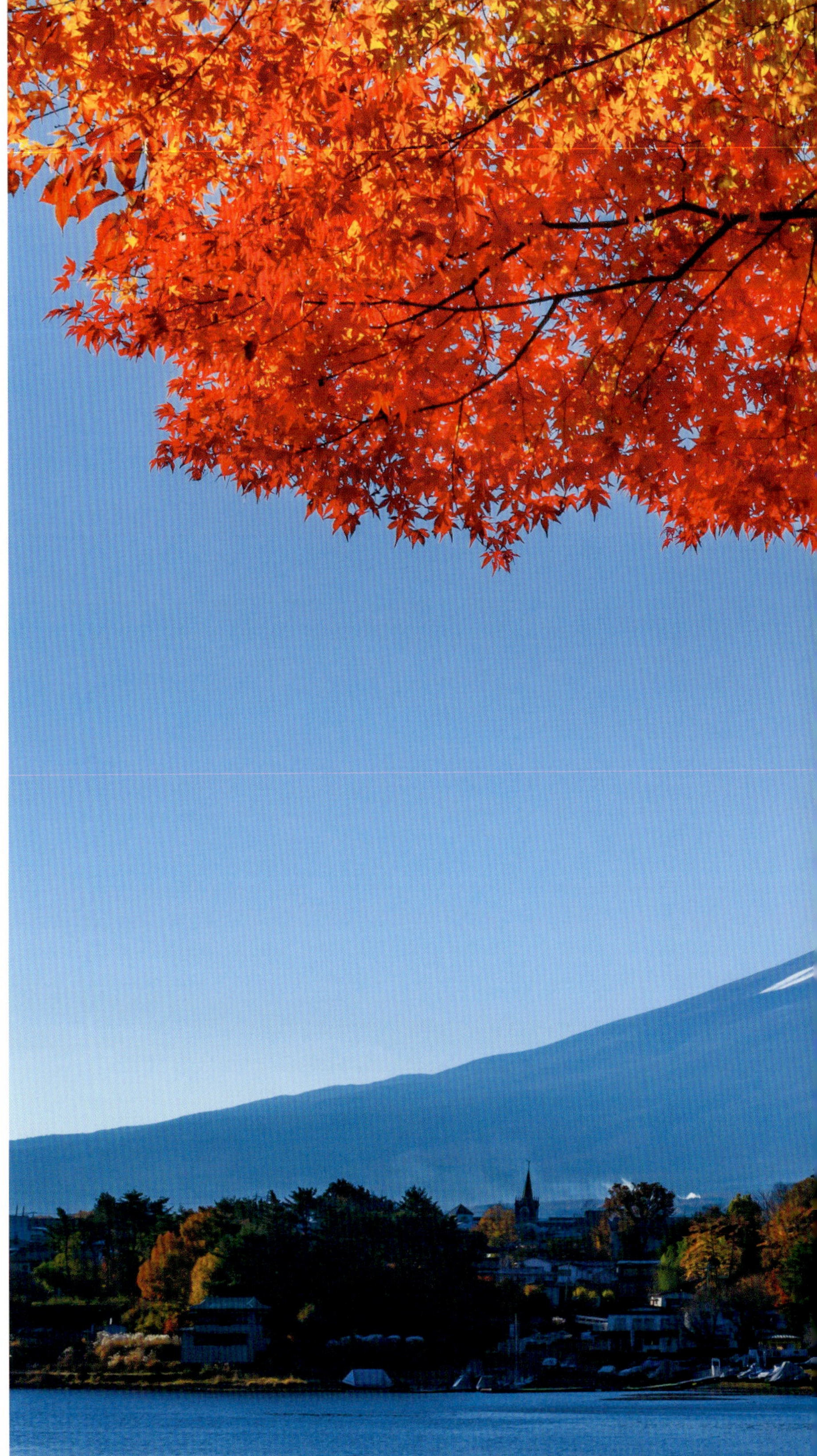

51 河口湖からの紅葉と富士山　　　山梨勝弘

河口湖の北岸には紅葉のポイントが何箇所かあり、11 月中旬から下旬が見頃だ。爽やかな朝の陽光に透かして見る紅葉は実に鮮やかだ。（山梨県南都留郡富士河口湖町／河口湖畔）

Autumn tints and Mt. Fuji from Lake Kawaguchi

The north shore of Lake Kawaguchi features a number of spots for viewing autumn tints, which are at their peak from mid to late November. In clear morning light, the colors are blazingly vivid. (Fujikawaguchiko, Yamanashi / Lake Kawaguchi)

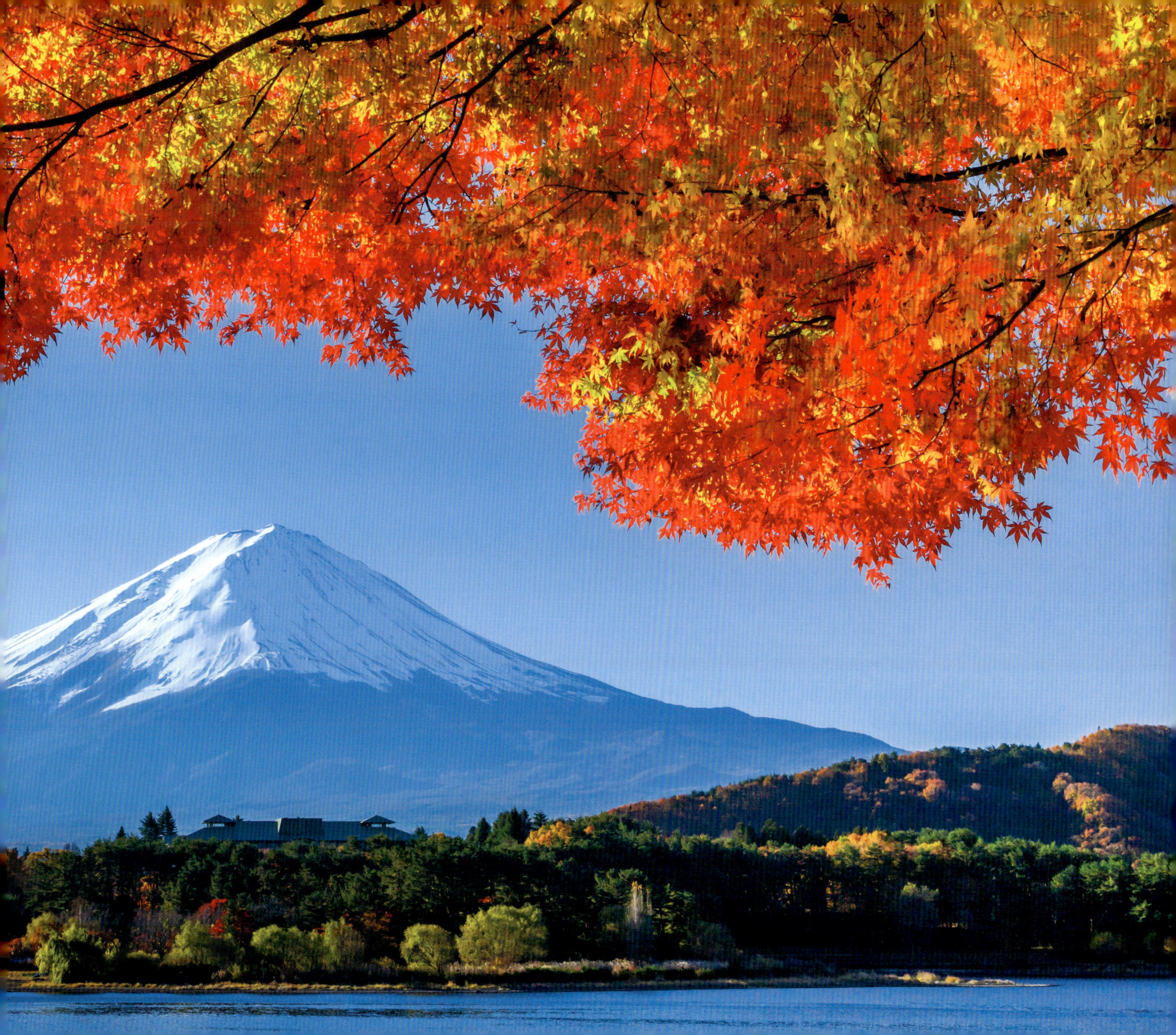

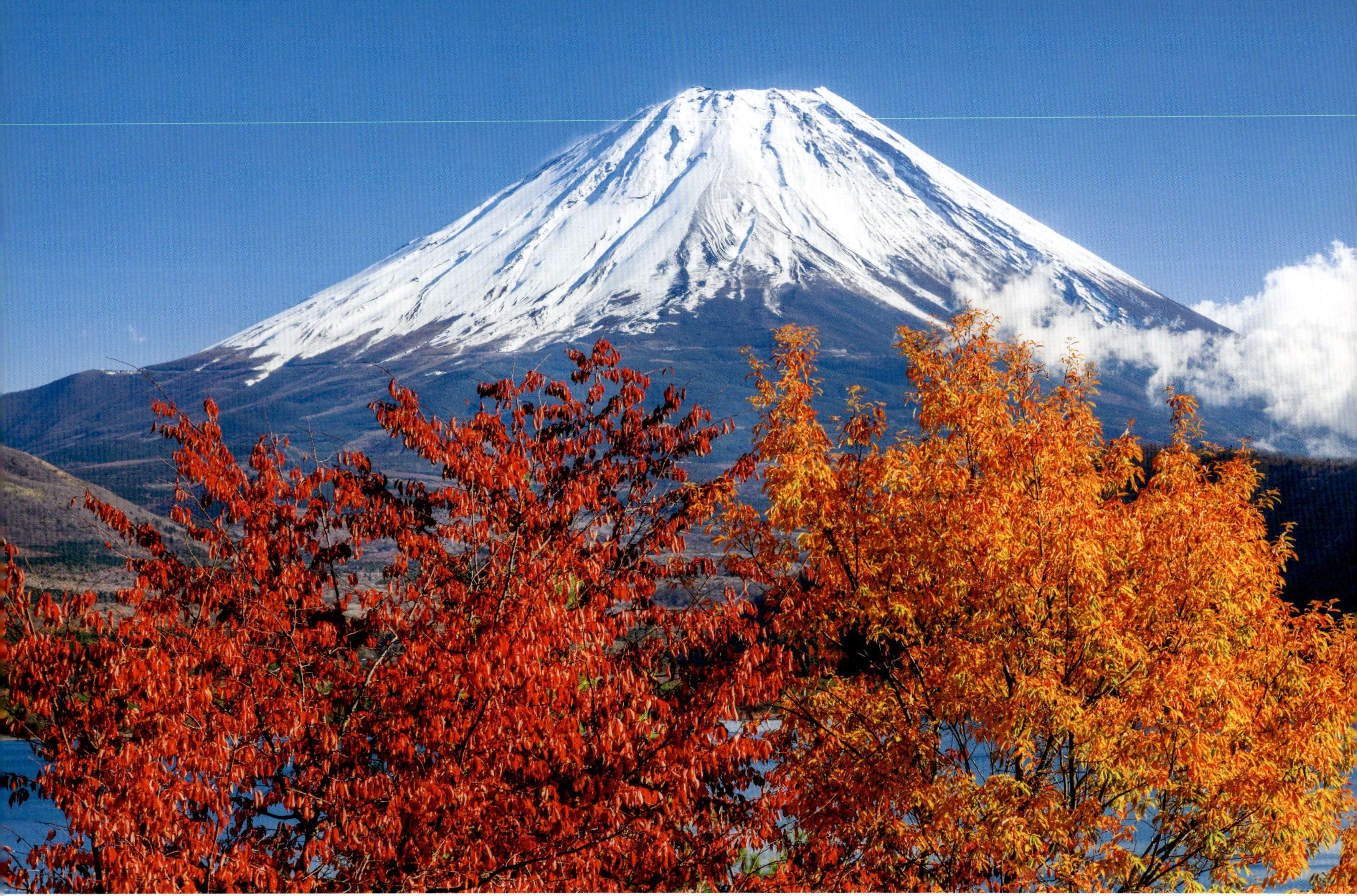

52　紅葉と富士山

山梨勝弘

身延町と富士河口湖町にまたがる本栖湖。身延町からの富士山は
千円札の裏に使われているビューポイントで、特に秋の彩りが美し
い。（山梨県南巨摩郡身延町／本栖湖）

Autumn tints and Mt. Fuij

Lake Motosu straddles the towns of Fujikawaguchiko and Minobu. The
view of Mt. Fuji and Lake Motosu featured on the back of the Japanese
1000-yen note is that seen from Minobu, where the colors of autumn
are also particularly beautiful. (Minobu, Yamanashi / Lake Motosu)

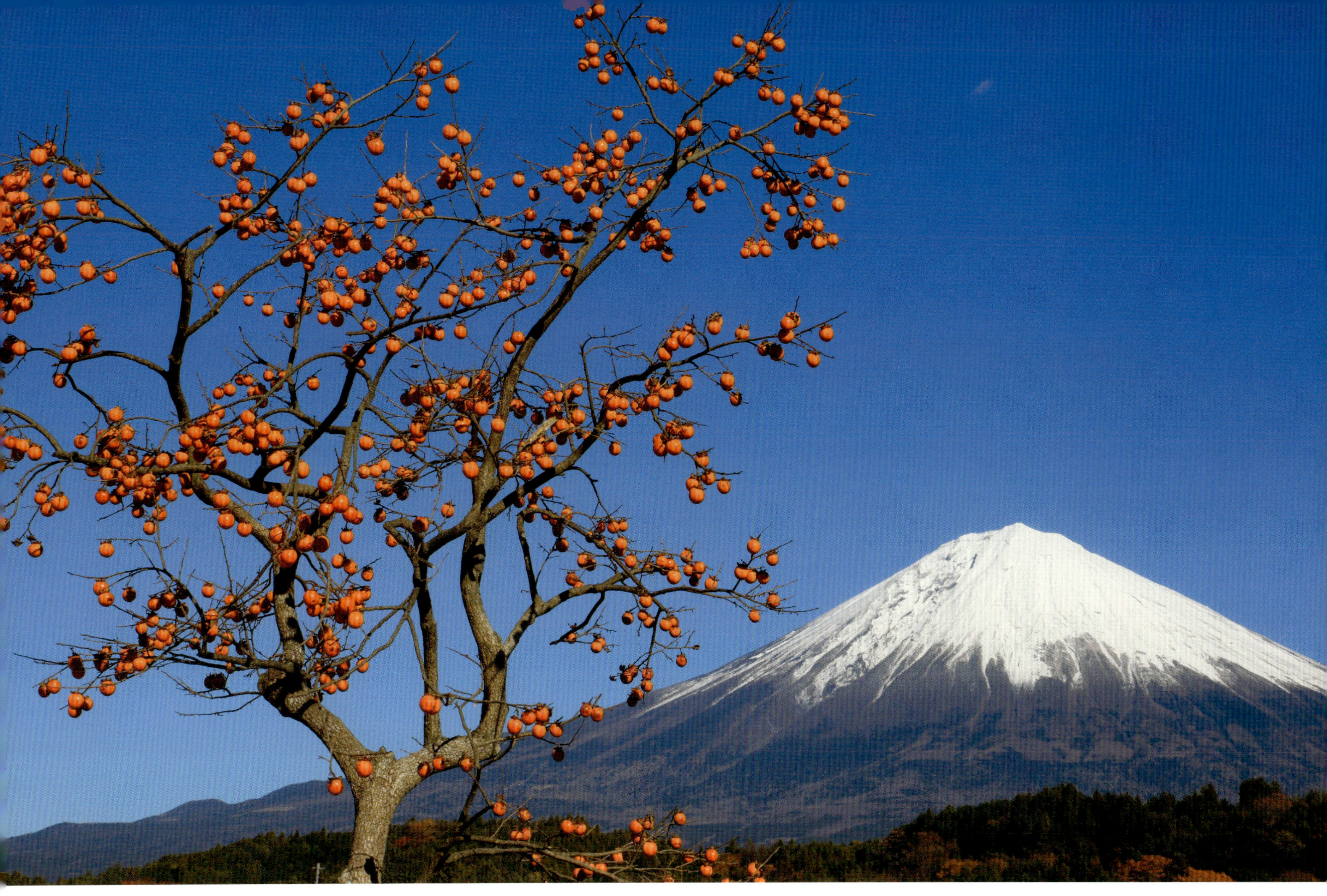

53　柿の実と白い富士

竹内トキ子

のどかな田園地帯に柿の木が一本。白雪の富士と落葉し実だけに
なった柿が、午後の光の中で晩秋の碧空に溶け込んでいた。（静岡
県富士宮市）

Persimmons and White Fuji

A single persimmon tree standing in the tranquil countryside. Snow-
capped Fuji and the leafless fruit-laden tree melted into the clear blue
sky in the afternoon light of late autumn. (Fujinomiya, Shizuoka)

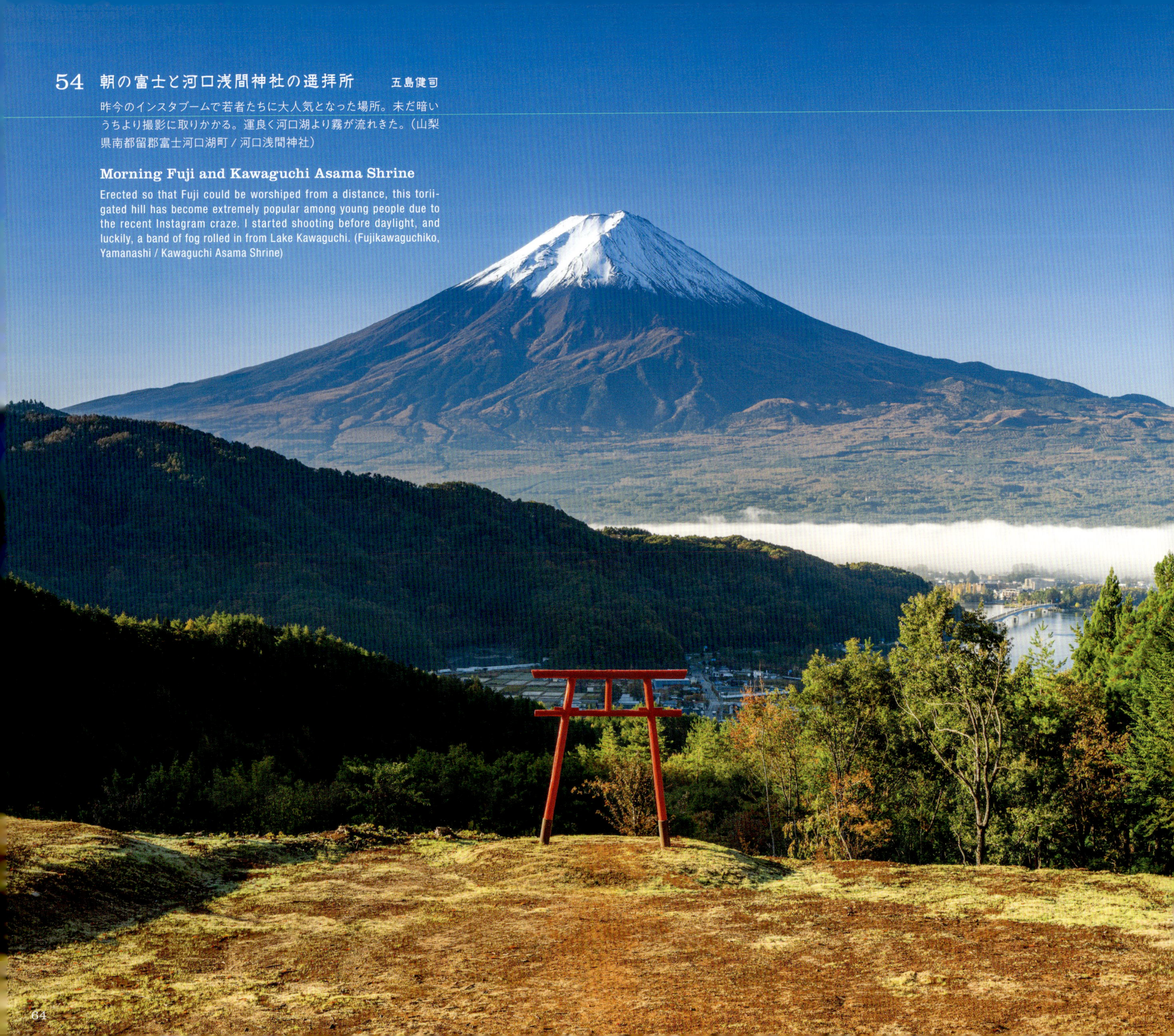

54　朝の富士と河口浅間神社の遥拝所　　　五島健司

昨今のインスタブームで若者たちに大人気となった場所。未だ暗い
うちより撮影に取りかかる。運良く河口湖より霧が流れきた。（山梨
県南都留郡富士河口湖町 / 河口浅間神社）

Morning Fuji and Kawaguchi Asama Shrine

Erected so that Fuji could be worshiped from a distance, this torii-
gated hill has become extremely popular among young people due to
the recent Instagram craze. I started shooting before daylight, and
luckily, a band of fog rolled in from Lake Kawaguchi. (Fujikawaguchiko,
Yamanashi / Kawaguchi Asama Shrine)

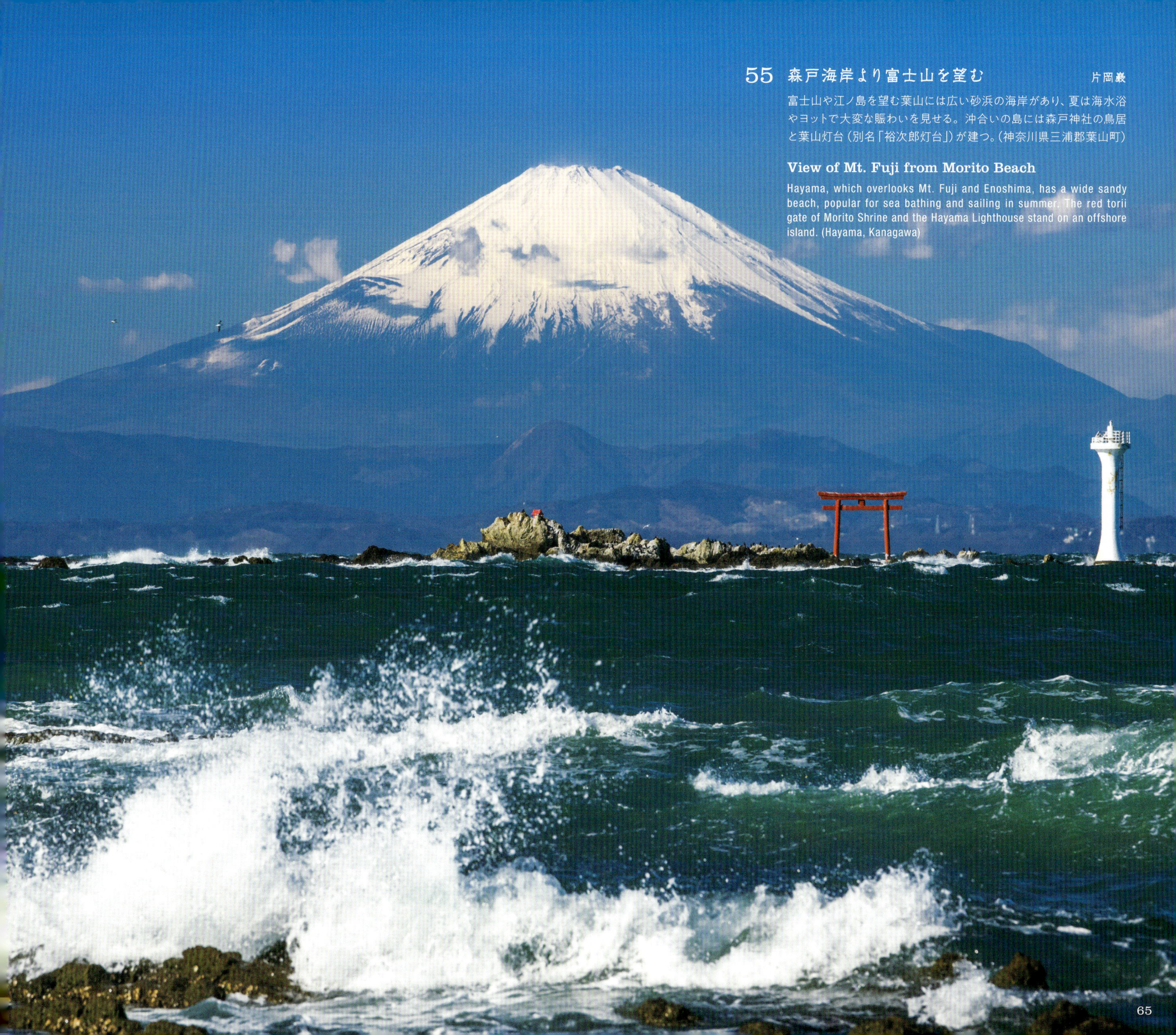

55　森戸海岸より富士山を望む　　　　片岡巖

富士山や江ノ島を望む葉山には広い砂浜の海岸があり、夏は海水浴
やヨットで大変な賑わいを見せる。沖合いの島には森戸神社の鳥居
と葉山灯台（別名「裕次郎灯台」）が建つ。（神奈川県三浦郡葉山町）

View of Mt. Fuji from Morito Beach
Hayama, which overlooks Mt. Fuji and Enoshima, has a wide sandy
beach, popular for sea bathing and sailing in summer. The red torii
gate of Morito Shrine and the Hayama Lighthouse stand on an offshore
island. (Hayama, Kanagawa)

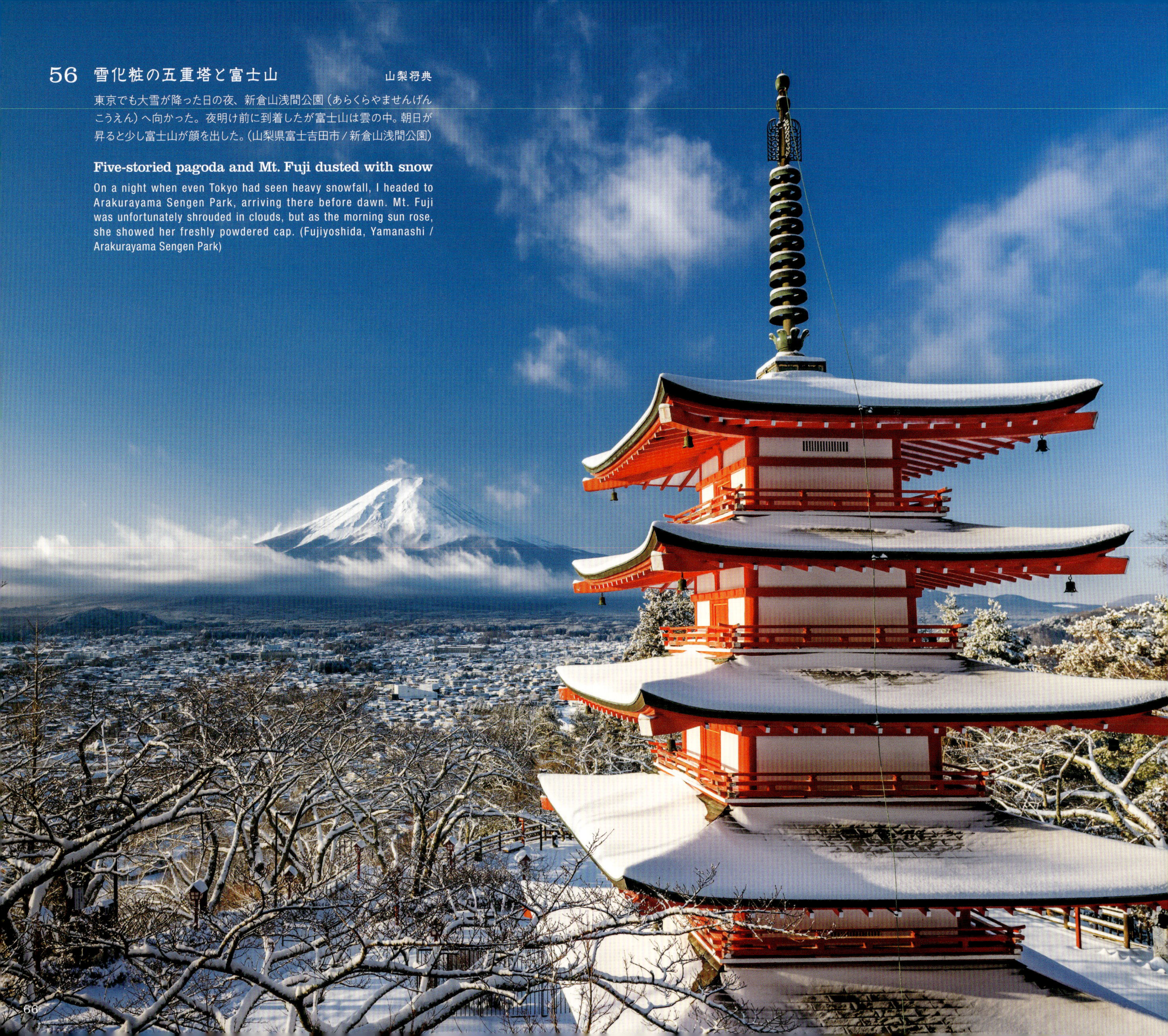

雪化粧の五重塔と富士山　　　　山梨将典

東京でも大雪が降った日の夜、新倉山浅間公園（あらくらやませんげん
こうえん）へ向かった。夜明け前に到着したが富士山は雲の中。朝日が
昇ると少し富士山が顔を出した。（山梨県富士吉田市／新倉山浅間公園）

Five-storied pagoda and Mt. Fuji dusted with snow

On a night when even Tokyo had seen heavy snowfall, I headed to
Arakurayama Sengen Park, arriving there before dawn. Mt. Fuji
was unfortunately shrouded in clouds, but as the morning sun rose,
she showed her freshly powdered cap. (Fujiyoshida, Yamanashi /
Arakurayama Sengen Park)

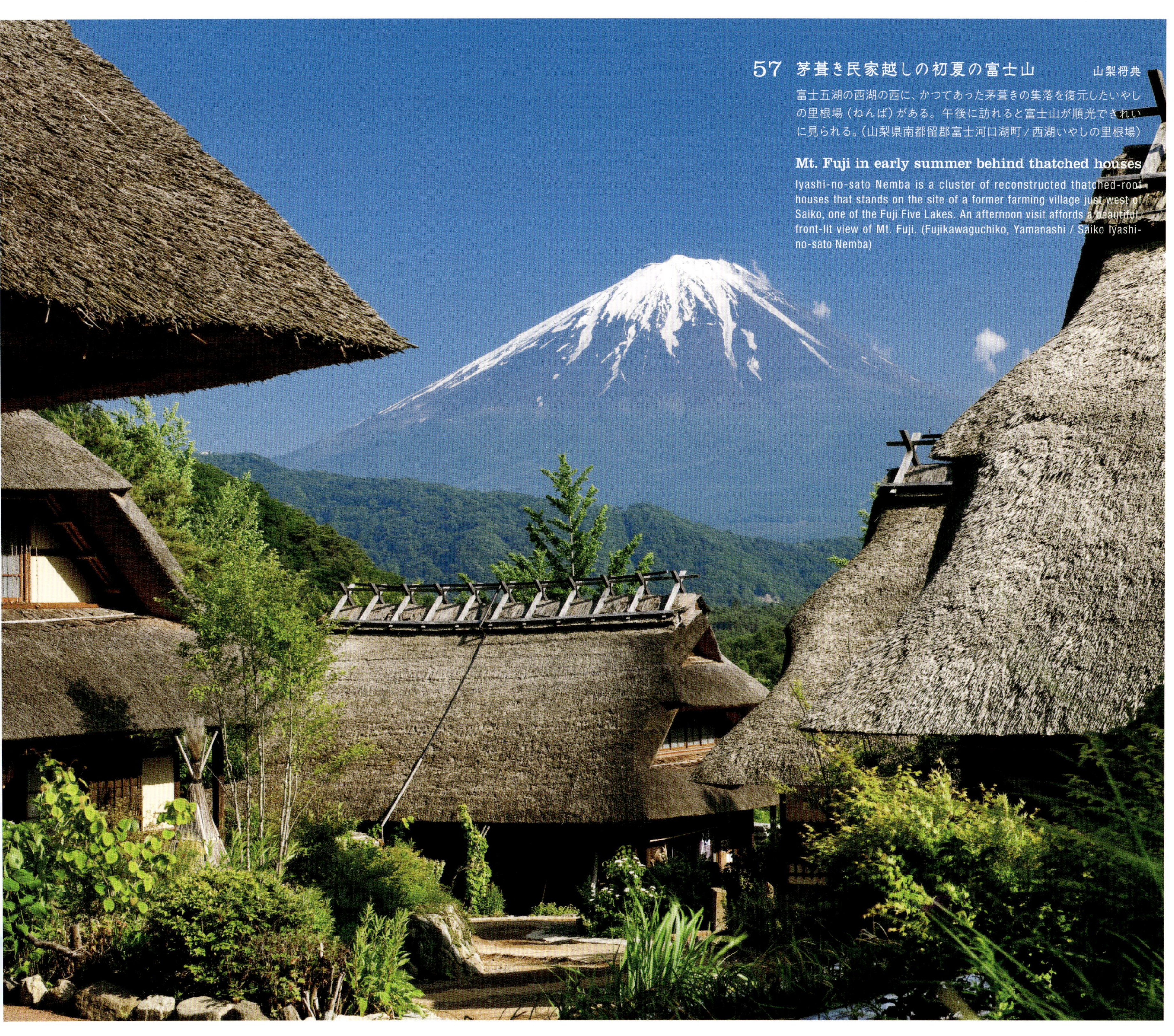

57　茅葺き民家越しの初夏の富士山　　　山梨将典

富士五湖の西湖の西に、かつてあった茅葺きの集落を復元したいやしの里根場（ねんば）がある。午後に訪れると富士山が順光できれいに見られる。(山梨県南都留郡富士河口湖町／西湖いやしの里根場)

Mt. Fuji in early summer behind thatched houses

Iyashi-no-sato Nemba is a cluster of reconstructed thatched-roof houses that stands on the site of a former farming village just west of Saiko, one of the Fuji Five Lakes. An afternoon visit affords a beautiful front-lit view of Mt. Fuji. (Fujikawaguchiko, Yamanashi / Saiko Iyashi-no-sato Nemba)

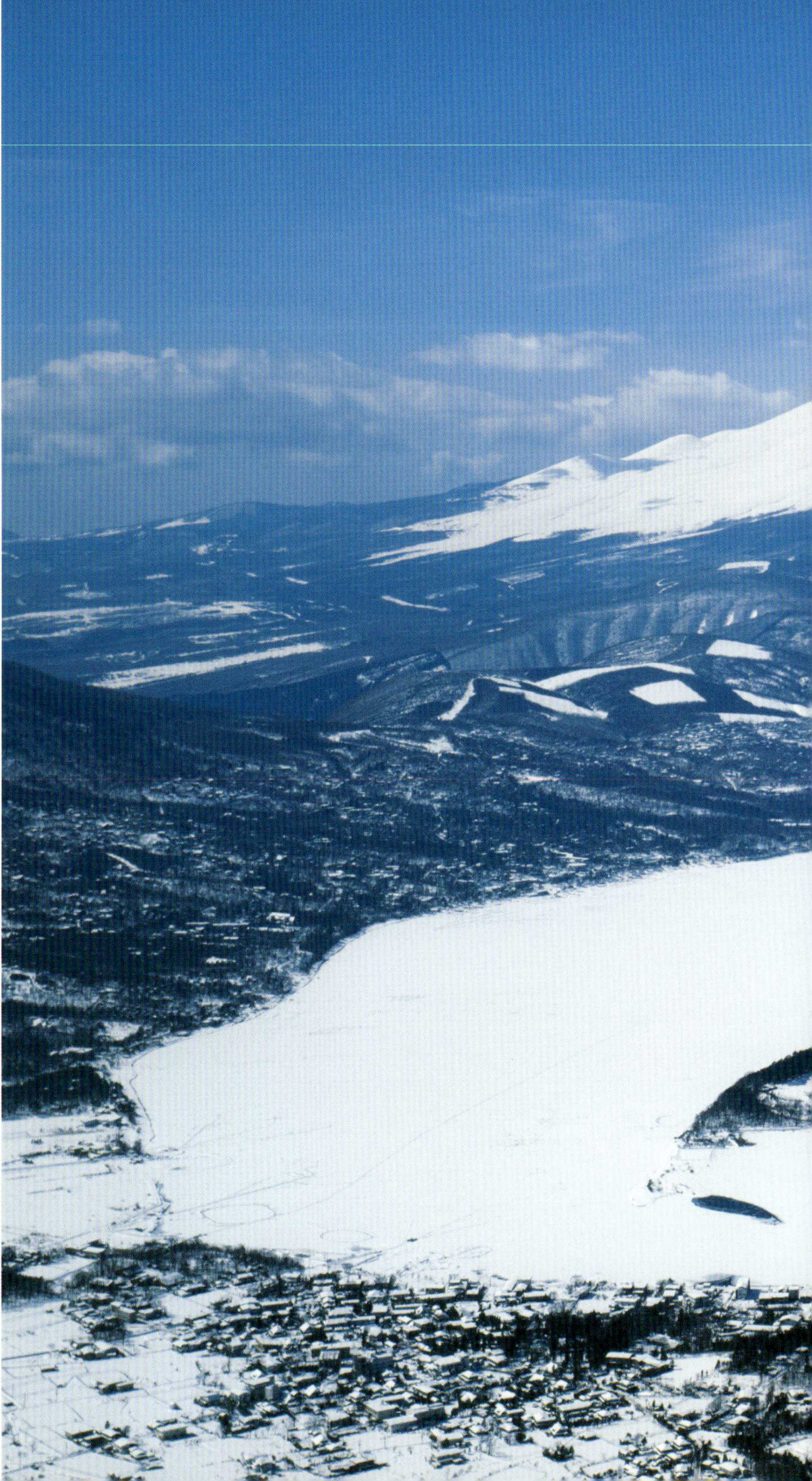

58 冬晴れの富士山 豊高隆三

昨晩の大雪から一転した快晴の朝、今日は良い写真が撮れると確信し
フライトを始めた。山中湖の湖面もすっぽりと雪化粧をし、勾玉のよ
うな形が際立って見えた。（山梨県南都留郡山中湖村上空より）

Mt. Fuji on a clear winter's day

Clear skies the morning after a night of heavy snowfall promised to
yield some good pictures, so I took to the sky. The surface of Lake
Yamanaka was completely covered with snow, looking much like an
ancient Japanese comma-shaped magatama bead. (From the sky above
Yamanakako, Yamanashi)

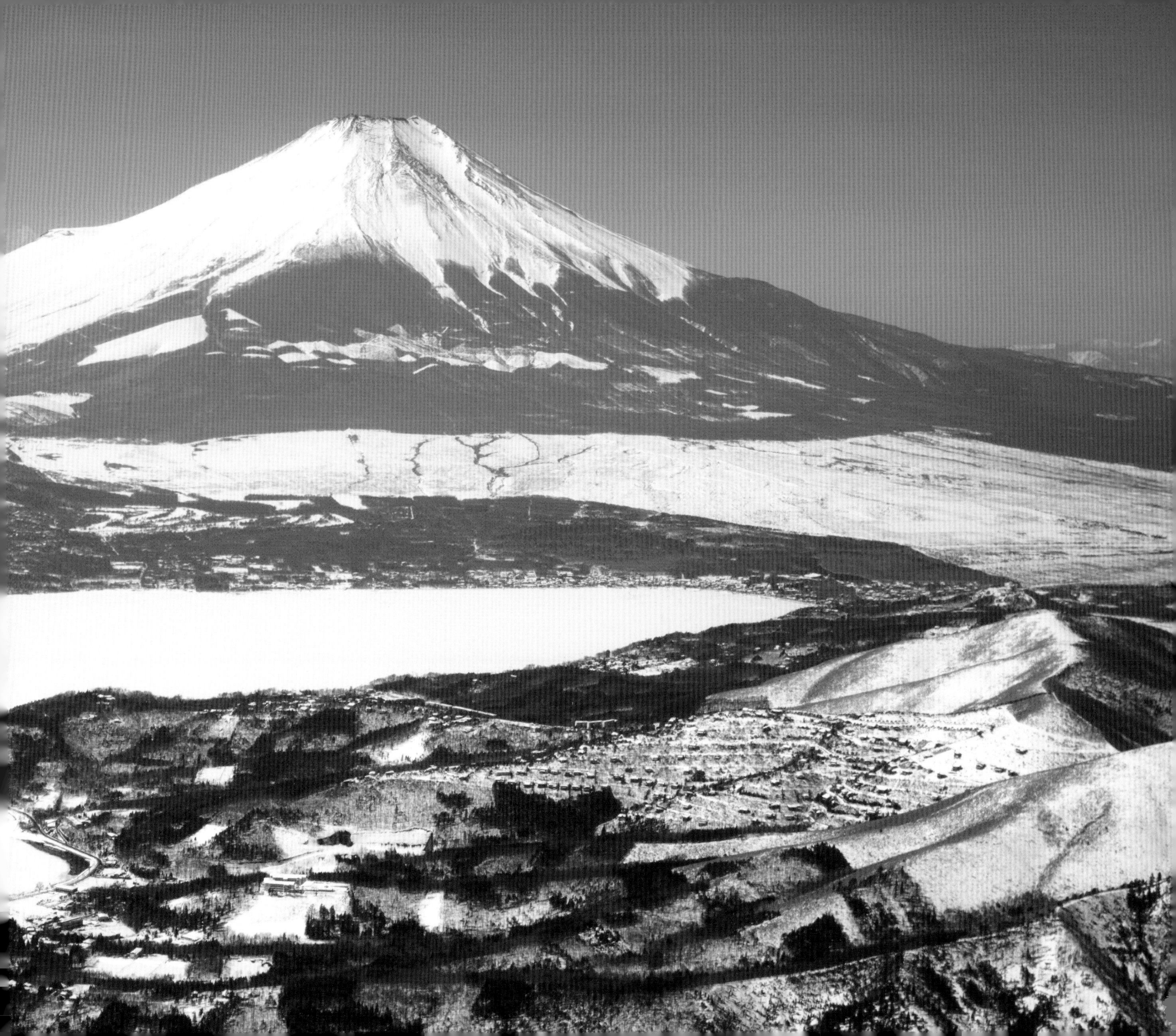

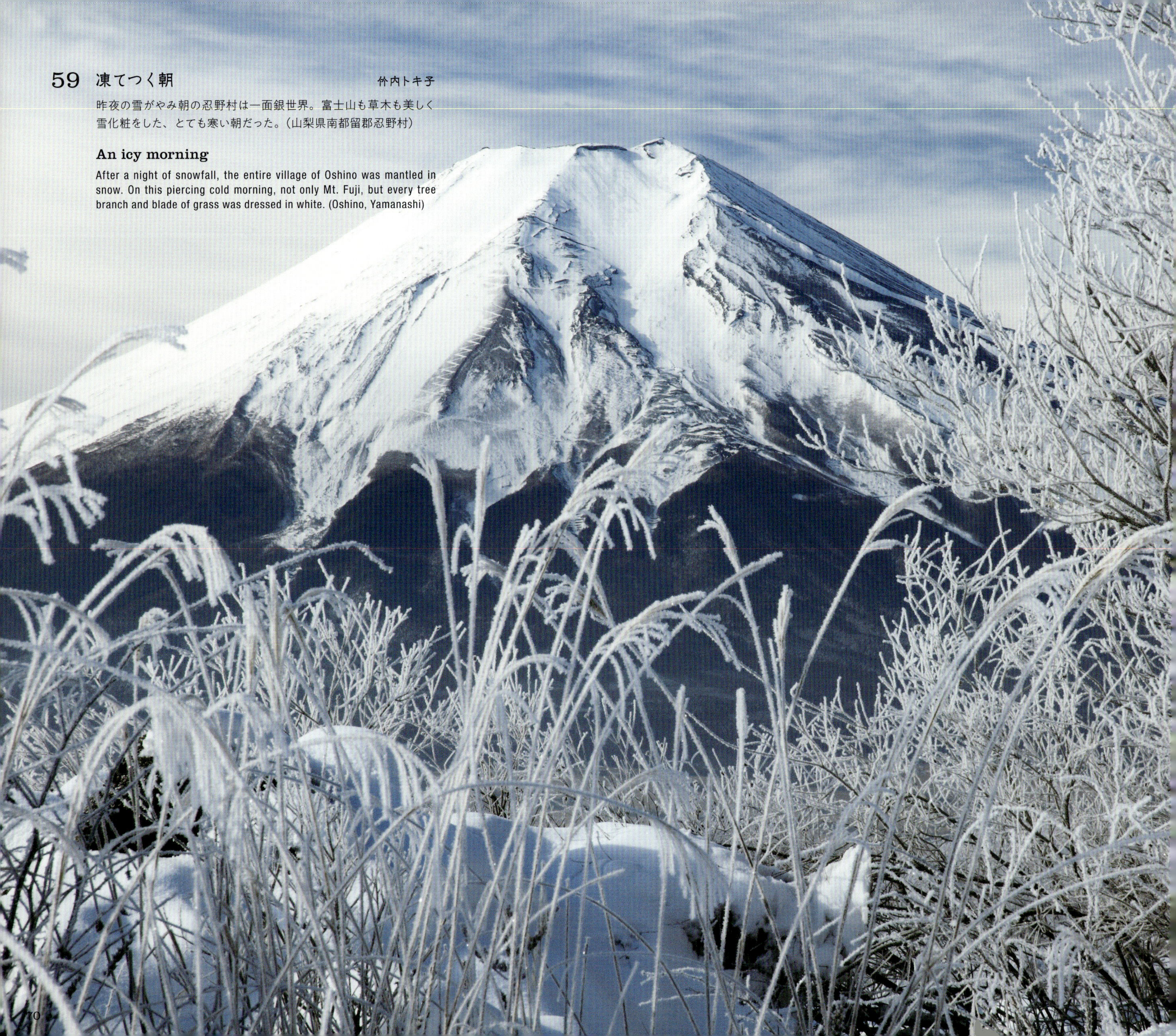
59　凍てつく朝　　　　　竹内トキ子
昨夜の雪がやみ朝の忍野村は一面銀世界。富士山も草木も美しく
雪化粧をした、とても寒い朝だった。（山梨県南都留郡忍野村）

An icy morning

After a night of snowfall, the entire village of Oshino was mantled in
snow. On this piercing cold morning, not only Mt. Fuji, but every tree
branch and blade of grass was dressed in white. (Oshino, Yamanashi)

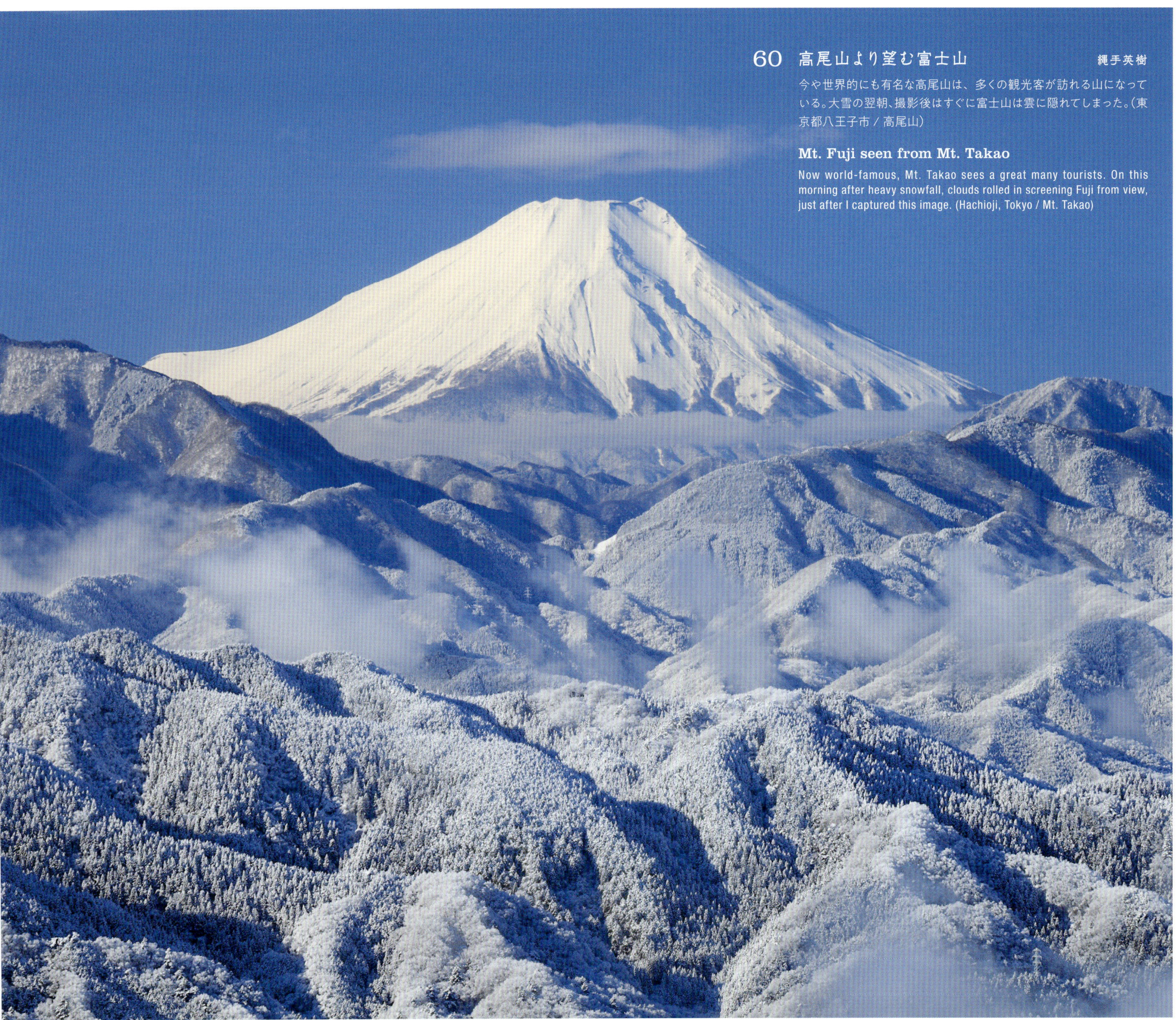

60　高尾山より望む富士山
縄手英樹
今や世界的にも有名な高尾山は、多くの観光客が訪れる山になっている。大雪の翌朝、撮影後はすぐに富士山は雲に隠れてしまった。(東京都八王子市 / 高尾山)

Mt. Fuji seen from Mt. Takao
Now world-famous, Mt. Takao sees a great many tourists. On this morning after heavy snowfall, clouds rolled in screening Fuji from view, just after I captured this image. (Hachioji, Tokyo / Mt. Takao)

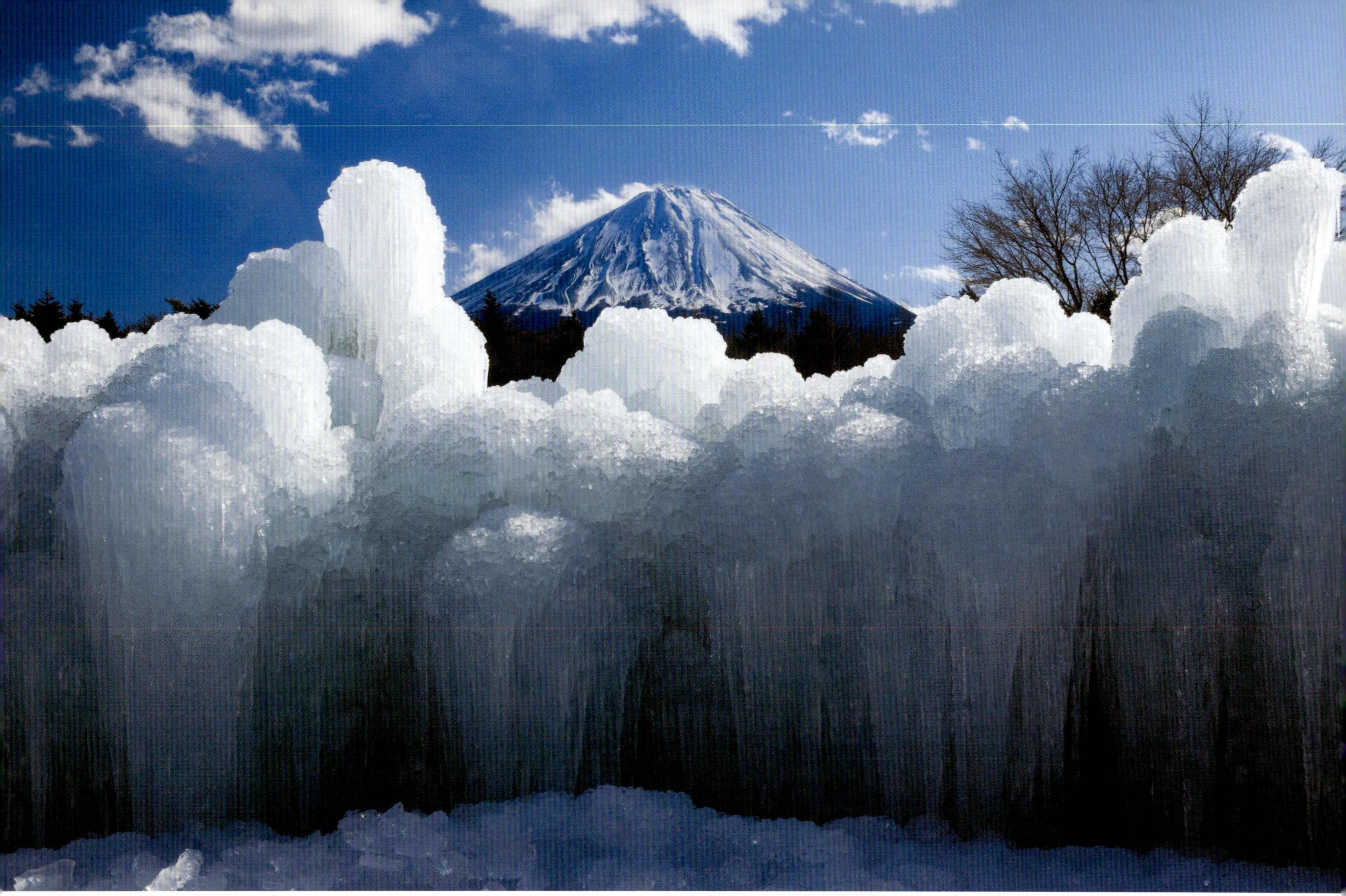

61 樹氷と富士山　　　　　　　　　　鎌形久

西湖野鳥の森公園で例年行われる「西湖樹氷まつり」の人工的に
作られた樹氷。造形的な樹氷と富士山の組み合わせが青空に映え
ていた。(山梨県南都留郡富士河口湖町)

Ice-covered trees and Mt. Fuji

Artificially created rime covers trees at the Saiko Ice Festival, held
annually at Saiko Yachonomori Park. Blue sky set off this combination
of sculptural ice formations and Mt. Fuji to perfection. (Fujikawaguchiko,
Yamanashi)

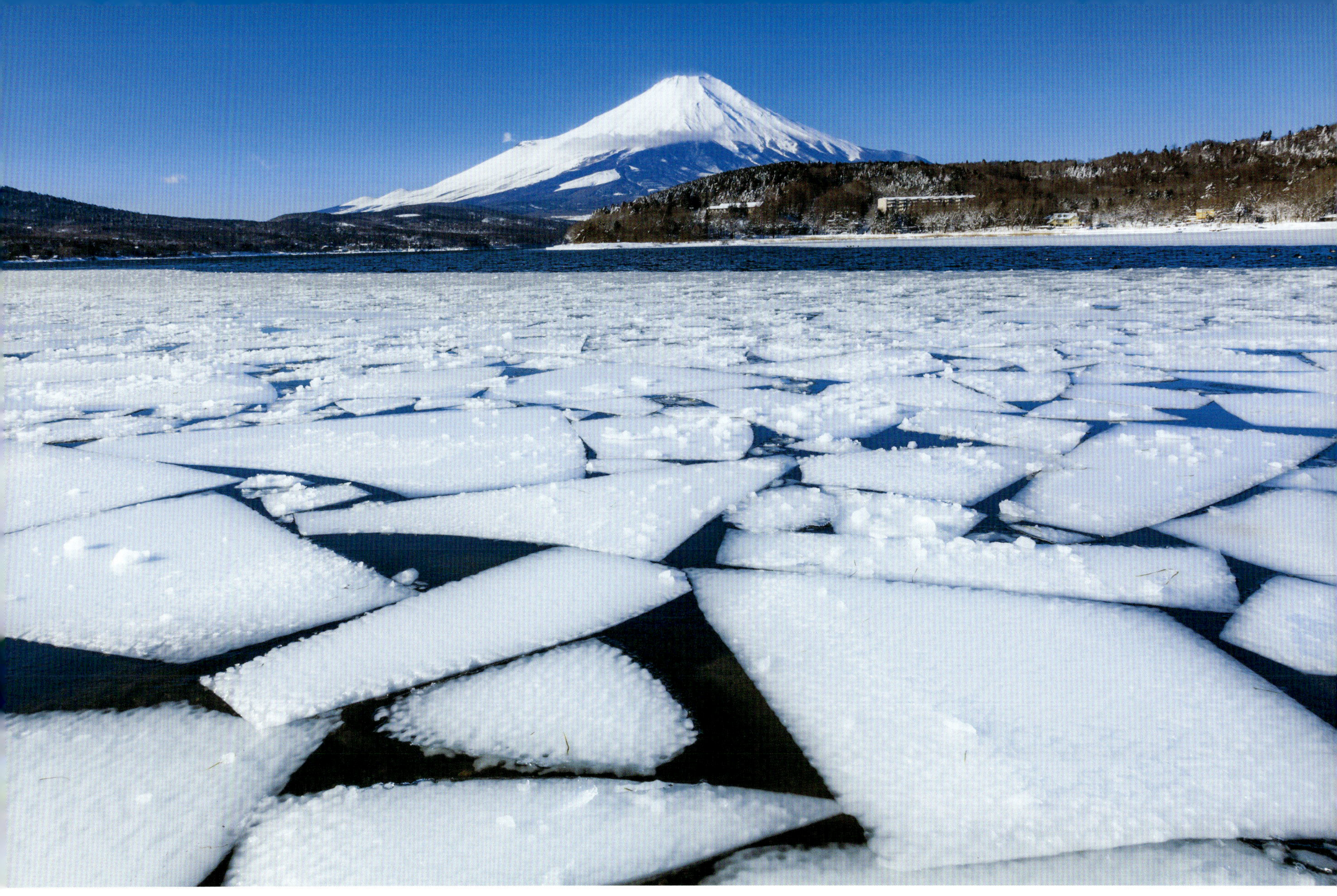

62　氷漂う山中湖と富士山　　　　　　　　　　山梨勝弘

平野地区に位置する山中湖の東岸は穏やかな入り江になっている。
寒波によって湖岸に張り詰めた薄氷が割れ、湖上に幾何学模様を
作り上げた。（山梨県南都留郡山中湖村／山中湖）

Floating ice on Lake Yamanaka and Mt. Fuji

The Hirano-district east shore of Lake Yamanaka is a gentle inlet. The
thin ice that had formed on the lake as a result of a cold spell fractured,
creating a geometric pattern on the water's surface. (Yamanakako,
Yamanashi / Lake Yamanaka)

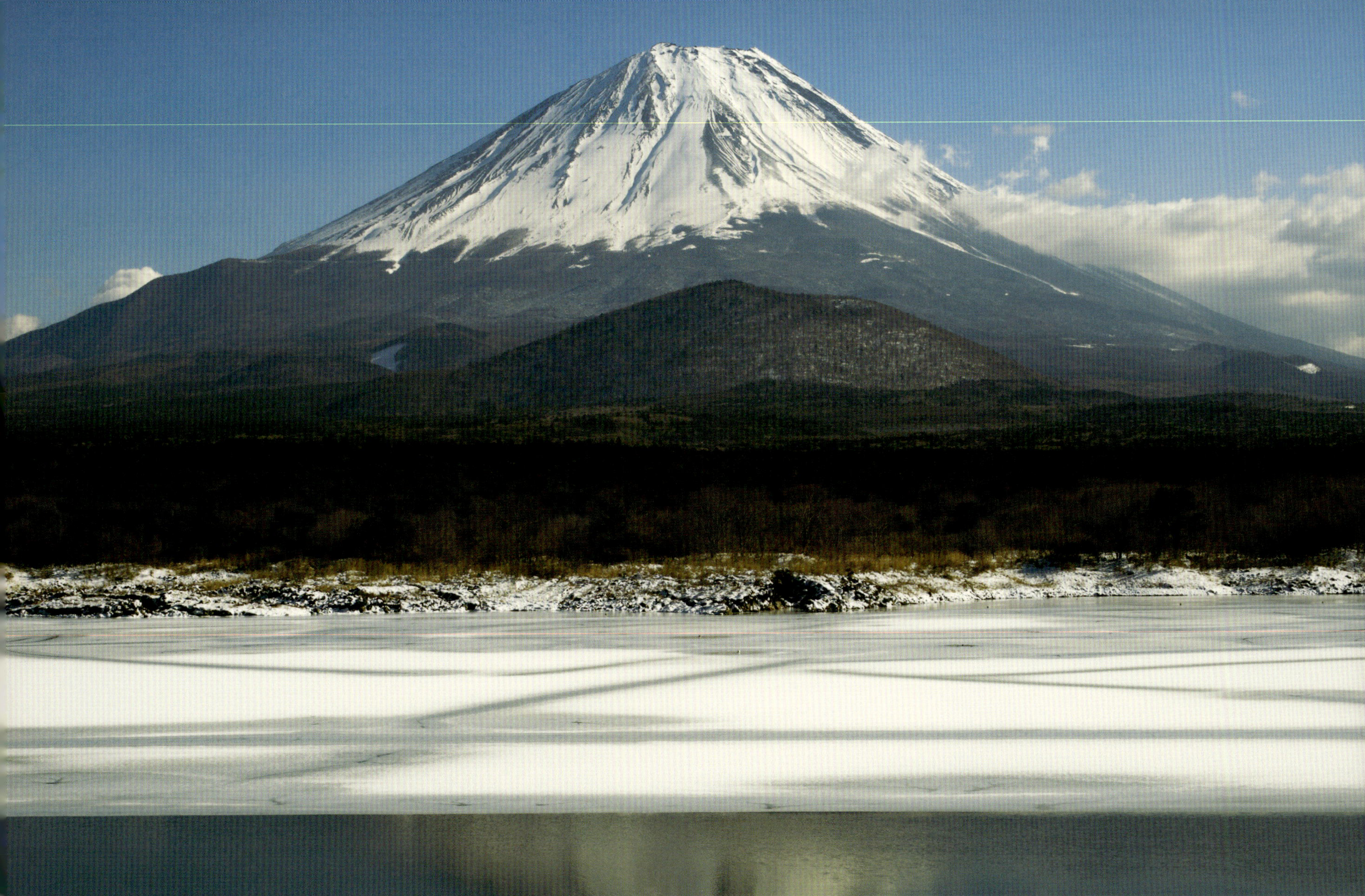

精進湖から見る富士は手前の大室山（おおむろやま）を抱いているように見えることから「子抱き富士」と呼ばれる。（山梨県南都留郡富士河口湖町）

Frost on Lake Shoji and Kodaki Fuji

Mt. Fuji, as seen from Lake Shoji, appears to be cradling Mt. Omuro in the foreground, and is thus called "Kodaki Fuji" ("Fuji holding a child"). The section of the lake not frozen over also mirrored an "inverted Fuji." (Fujikawaguchiko, Yamanashi)

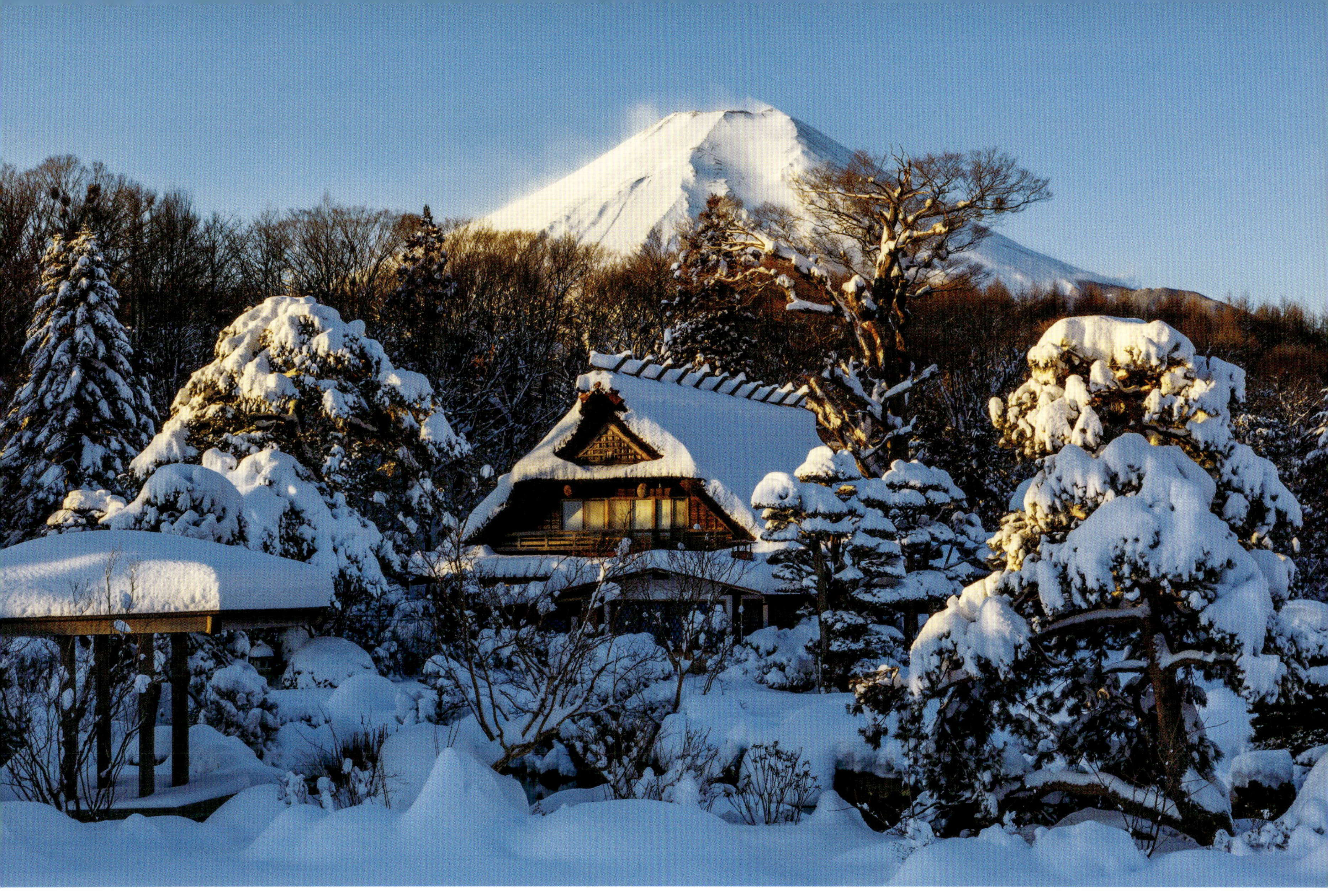

64　朝日を浴びる新雪の富士山　　　　山梨勝弘

大雪情報を聞いて忍野（おしの）に向かう。翌早朝、周辺の木々は
新雪を重たげに纏っていた。朝の光が差し込むと小枝の雪がサラサ
ラと宙を舞った。（山梨県南都留郡忍野村 / 鱒の家）

Mt. Fuji with virgin snow bathed in morning sunlight

With heavy snow in the forecast, I headed to Oshino. Early the next
day, the trees were laden with fresh snow. The powdery snow on their
branches danced in the air, spot-lit by rays of the morning sun. (Oshino,
Yamanashi / Masu-no-ie)

65　雲海と富士山　　　　　　　　　　　　豊高隆三

空一面の雲海の中にぽっかりと頭を出す富士山。長年富士山上空を
飛んでいるがこの姿にはめったに出会えない。童謡「ふじの山」の一
節さながらの光景であった。(山梨県南都留郡富士河口湖町上空より)

Mt. Fuji in a sea of clouds

Mt. Fuji pops its head out of a sea of cloud cover. Having flown over
Fuji countless times over the years, I can attest to how rare this sight
is; embodying as it were the first verse of the Japanese children's song
"Fuji no yama": "Holding its head high above the clouds." (From the sky
above Fujikawaguchiko, Yamanashi)

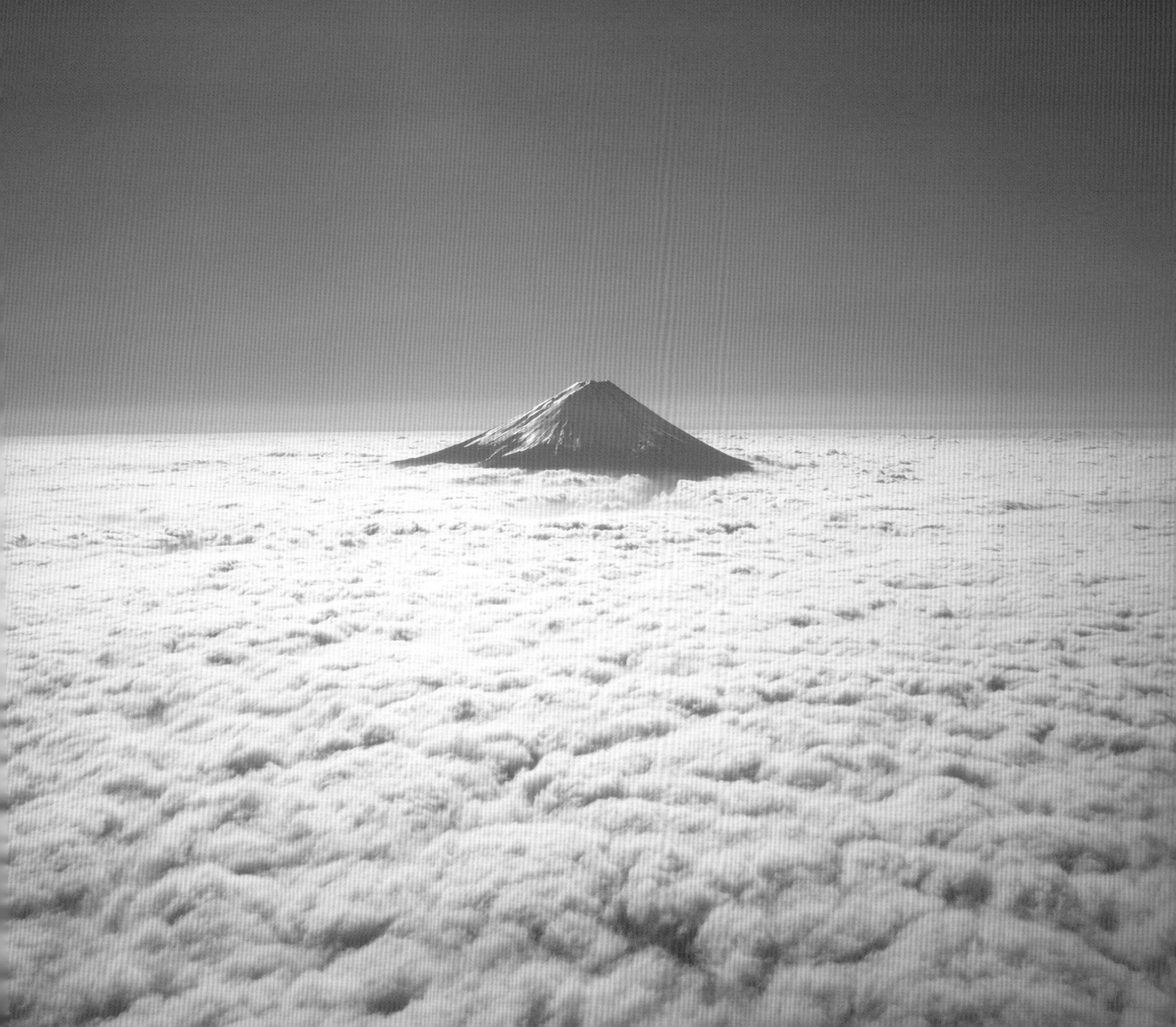

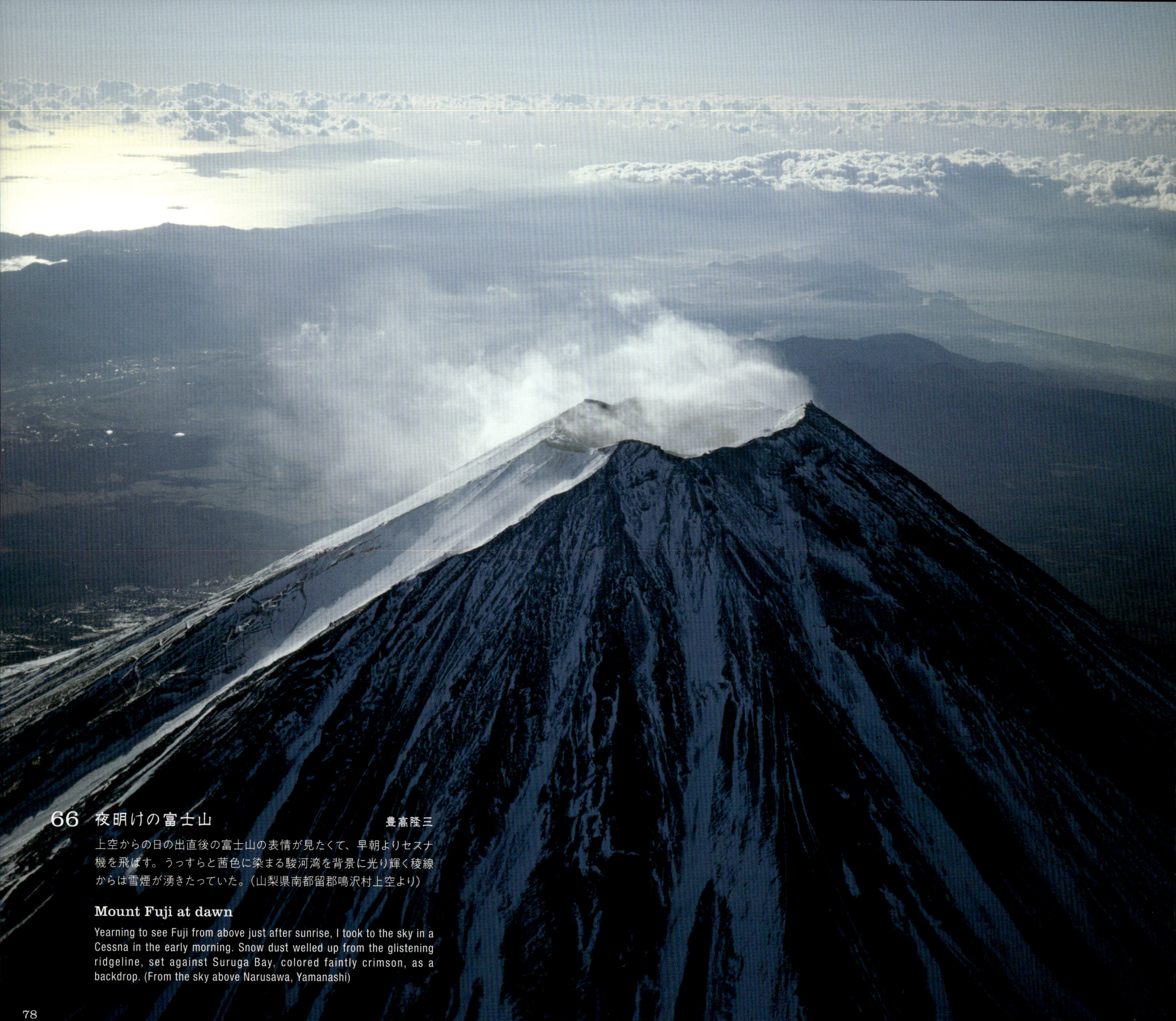

66　夜明けの富士山　　　　　　　豊高隆三

上空からの日の出直後の富士山の表情が見たくて、早朝よりセスナ機を飛ばす。うっすらと茜色に染まる駿河湾を背景に光り輝く稜線からは雪煙が湧きたっていた。（山梨県南都留郡鳴沢村上空より）

Mount Fuji at dawn

Yearning to see Fuji from above just after sunrise, I took to the sky in a Cessna in the early morning. Snow dust welled up from the glistening ridgeline, set against Suruga Bay, colored faintly crimson, as a backdrop. (From the sky above Narusawa, Yamanashi)

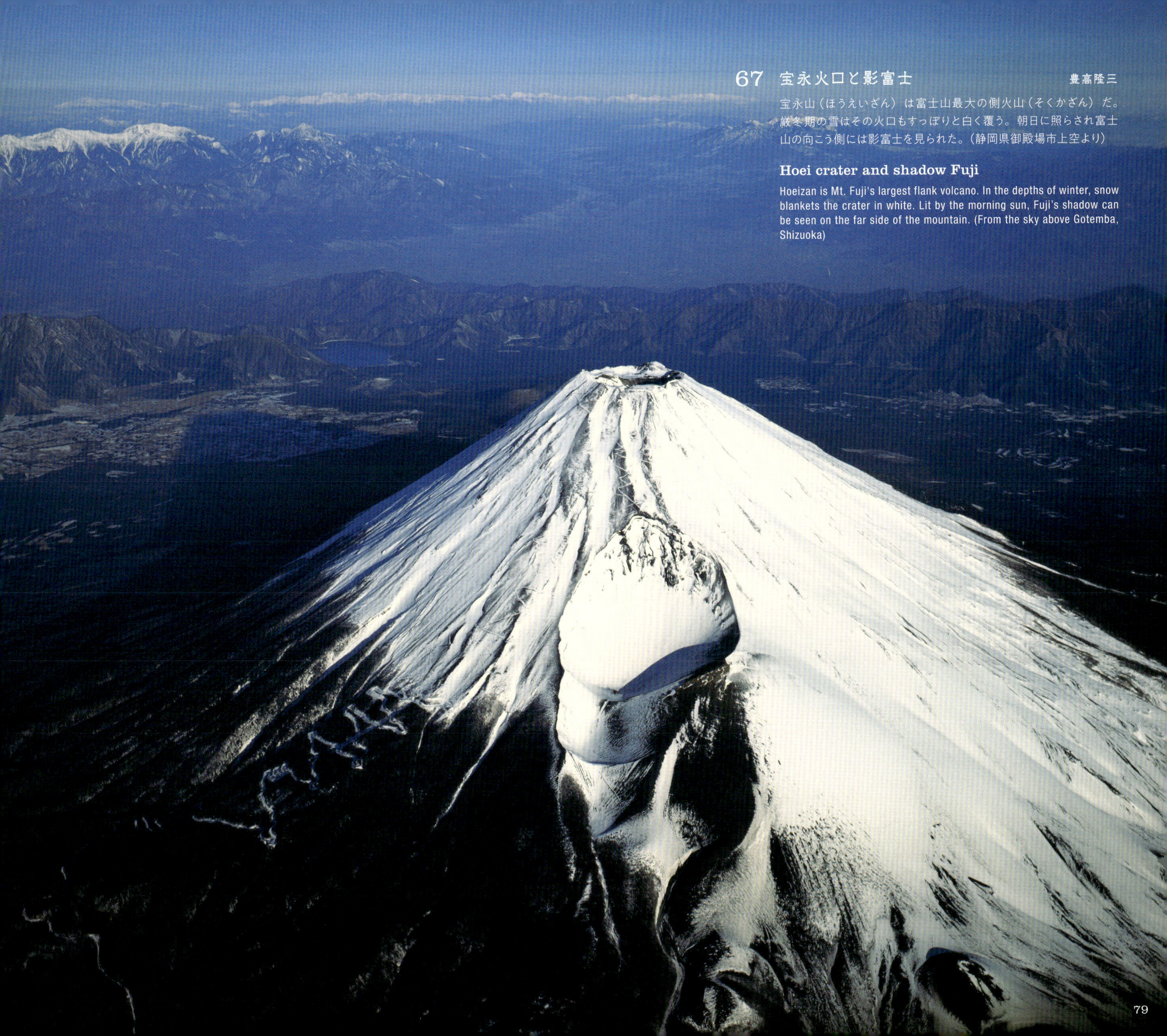

67　宝永火口と影富士　　　　　　　　　豊高隆三

宝永山（ほうえいざん）は富士山最大の側火山（そくかざん）だ。
厳冬期の雪はその火口もすっぽりと白く覆う。朝日に照らされ富士
山の向こう側には影富士を見られた。（静岡県御殿場市上空より）

Hoei crater and shadow Fuji

Hoeizan is Mt. Fuji's largest flank volcano. In the depths of winter, snow
blankets the crater in white. Lit by the morning sun, Fuji's shadow can
be seen on the far side of the mountain. (From the sky above Gotemba,
Shizuoka)

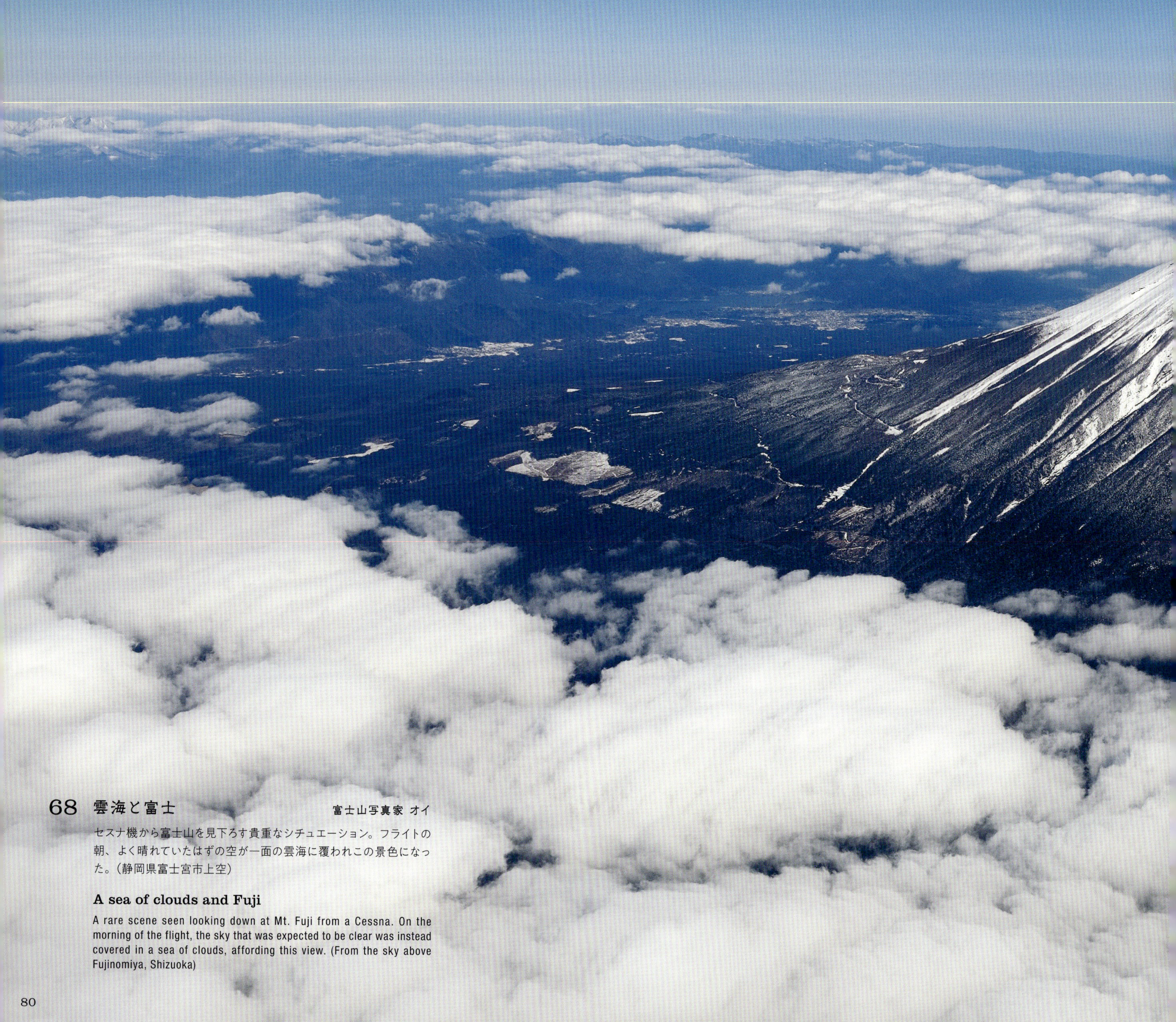

68 雲海と富士

富士山写真家 オイ

セスナ機から富士山を見下ろす貴重なシチュエーション。フライトの朝、よく晴れていたはずの空が一面の雲海に覆われこの景色になった。（静岡県富士宮市上空）

A sea of clouds and Fuji

A rare scene seen looking down at Mt. Fuji from a Cessna. On the morning of the flight, the sky that was expected to be clear was instead covered in a sea of clouds, affording this view. (From the sky above Fujinomiya, Shizuoka)

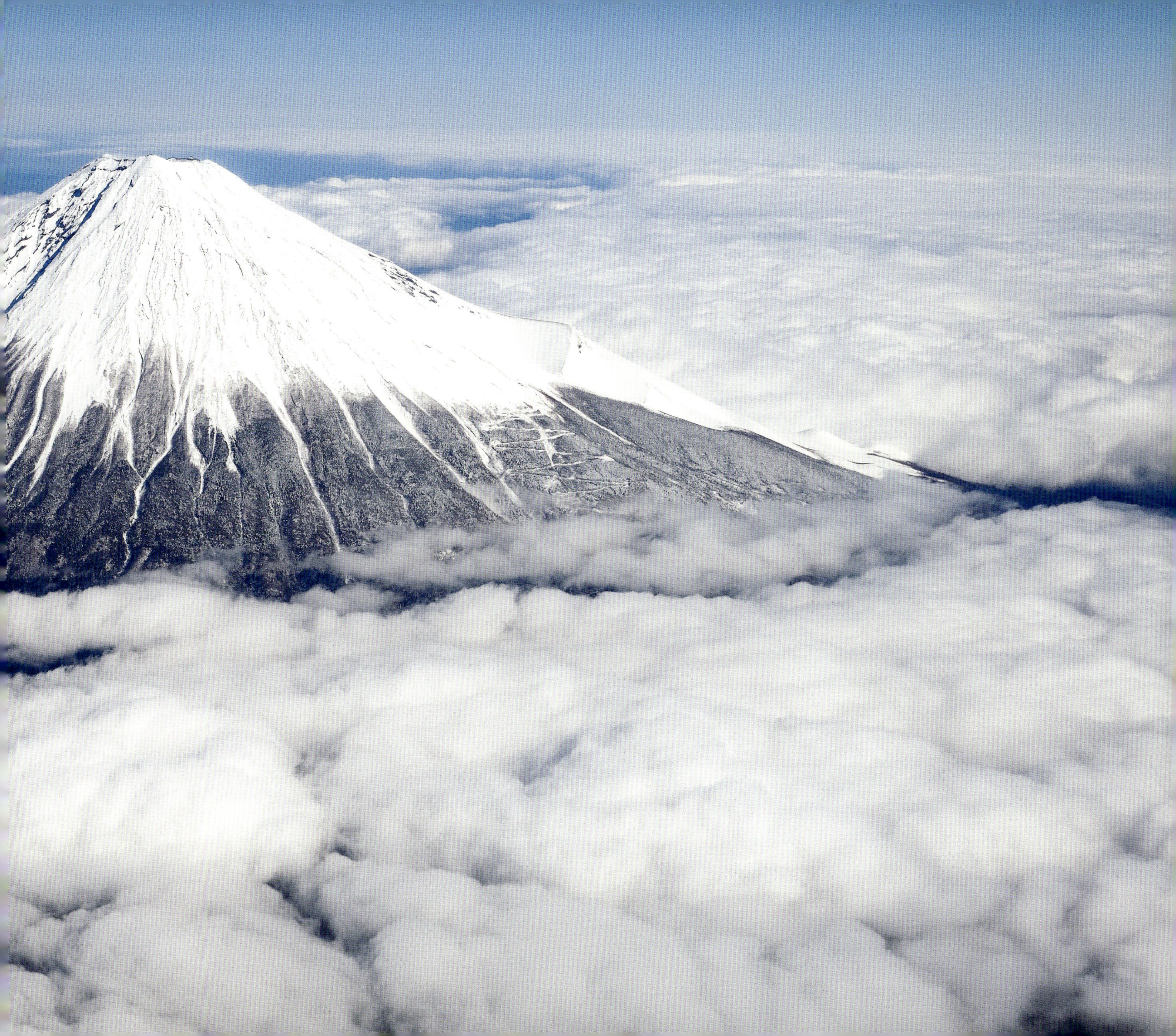

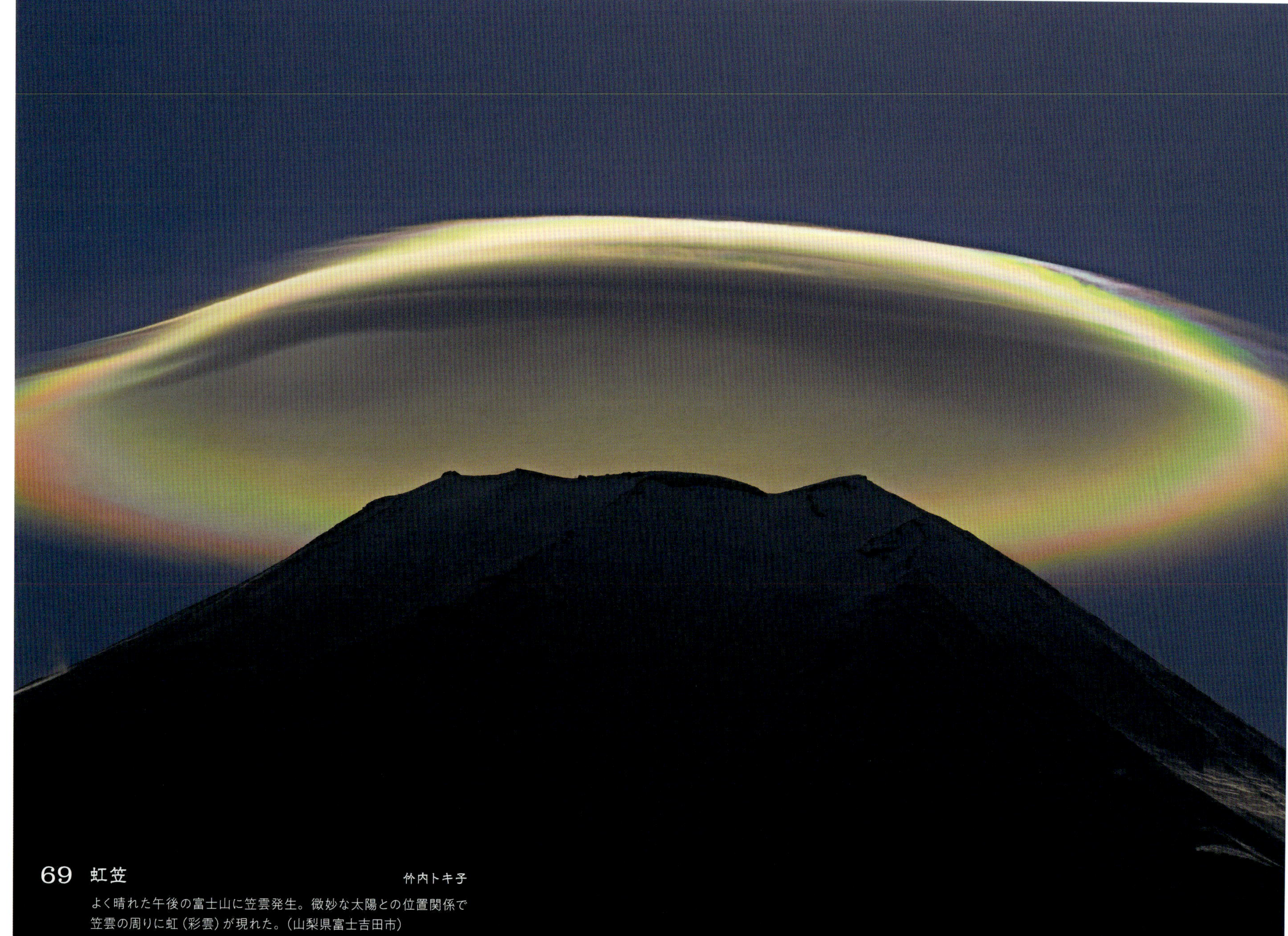

69　虹笠　　　　　　　　　　竹内トキ子

よく晴れた午後の富士山に笠雲発生。微妙な太陽との位置関係で
笠雲の周りに虹（彩雲）が現れた。（山梨県富士吉田市）

Rainbow lens

A lens-shaped cloud typically forms over Mt. Fuji on a sunny afternoon.
Striking the perfect relationship in its position with the sun, rainbow
colors appeared around the periphery of the cloud. (Fujiyoshida,
Yamanashi)

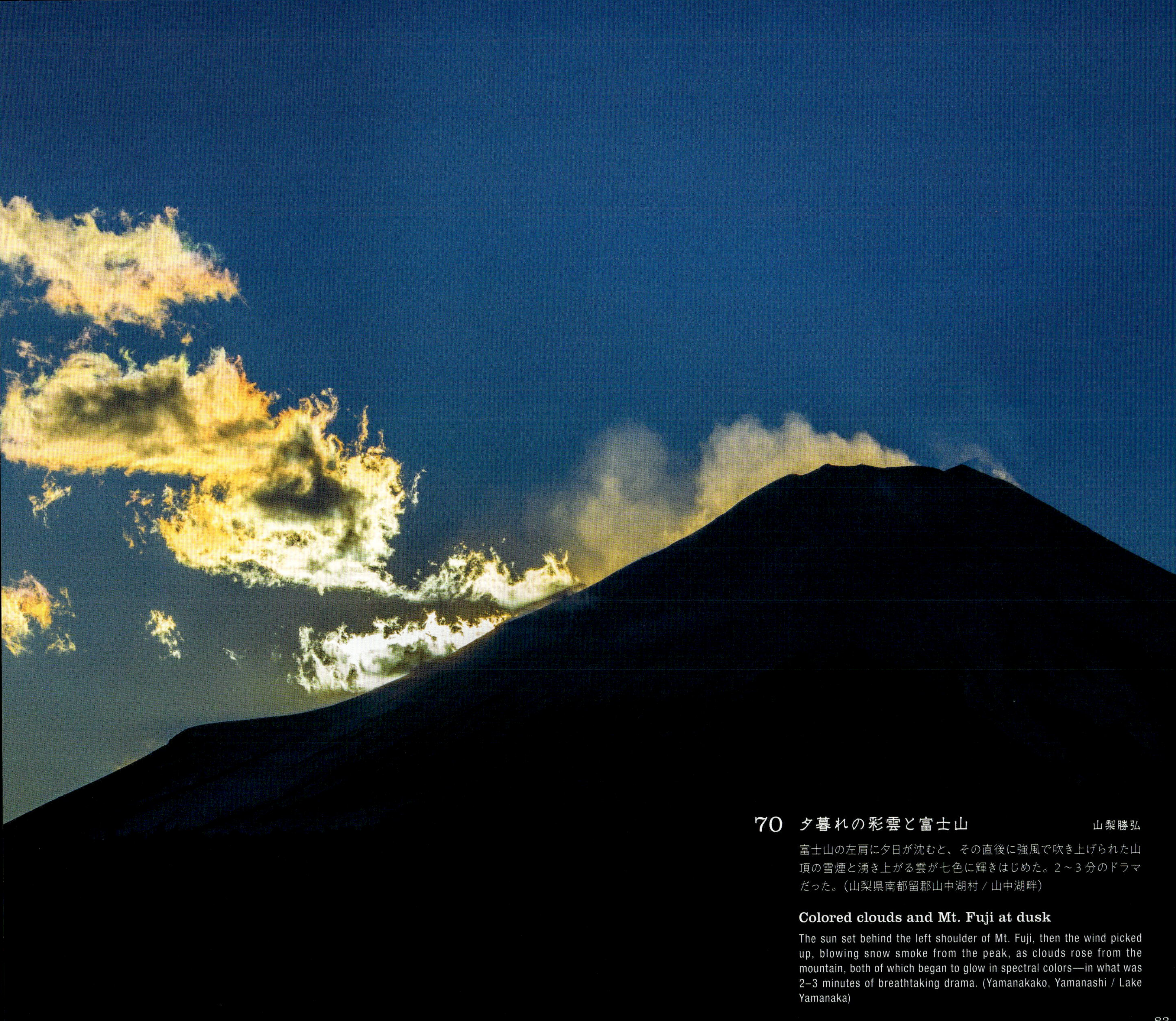

70 夕暮れの彩雲と富士山　　　　　　　　山梨勝弘

富士山の左肩に夕日が沈むと、その直後に強風で吹き上げられた山頂の雪煙と湧き上がる雲が七色に輝きはじめた。2〜3分のドラマだった。(山梨県南都留郡山中湖村 / 山中湖畔)

Colored clouds and Mt. Fuji at dusk

The sun set behind the left shoulder of Mt. Fuji, then the wind picked up, blowing snow smoke from the peak, as clouds rose from the mountain, both of which began to glow in spectral colors—in what was 2–3 minutes of breathtaking drama. (Yamanakako, Yamanashi / Lake Yamanaka)

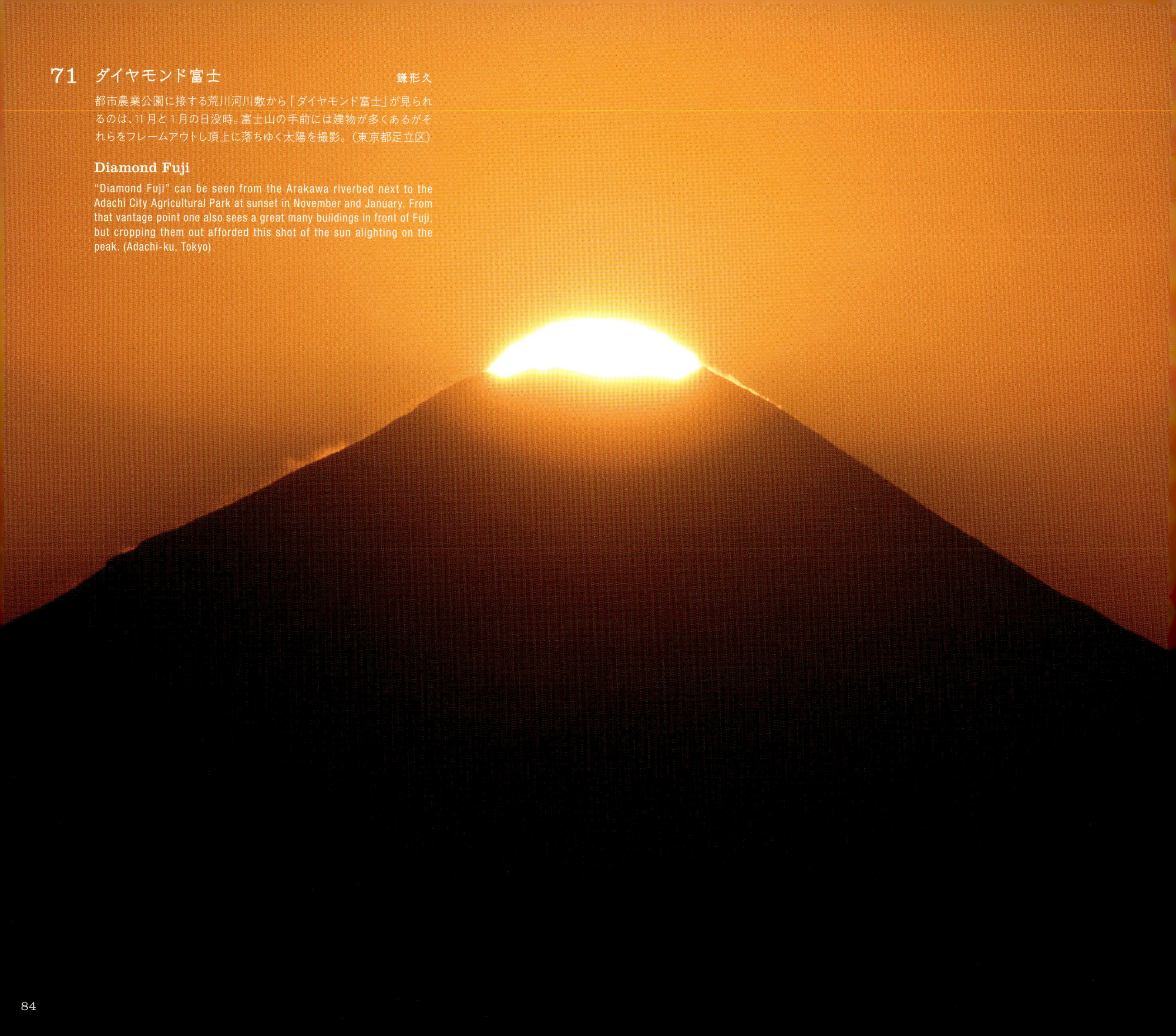

鎌形久

都市農業公園に接する荒川河川敷から「ダイヤモンド富士」が見られるのは、11月と1月の日没時。富士山の手前には建物が多くあるがそれらをフレームアウトし頂上に落ちゆく太陽を撮影。（東京都足立区）

Diamond Fuji

"Diamond Fuji" can be seen from the Arakawa riverbed next to the Adachi City Agricultural Park at sunset in November and January. From that vantage point one also sees a great many buildings in front of Fuji, but cropping them out afforded this shot of the sun alighting on the peak. (Adachi-ku, Tokyo)

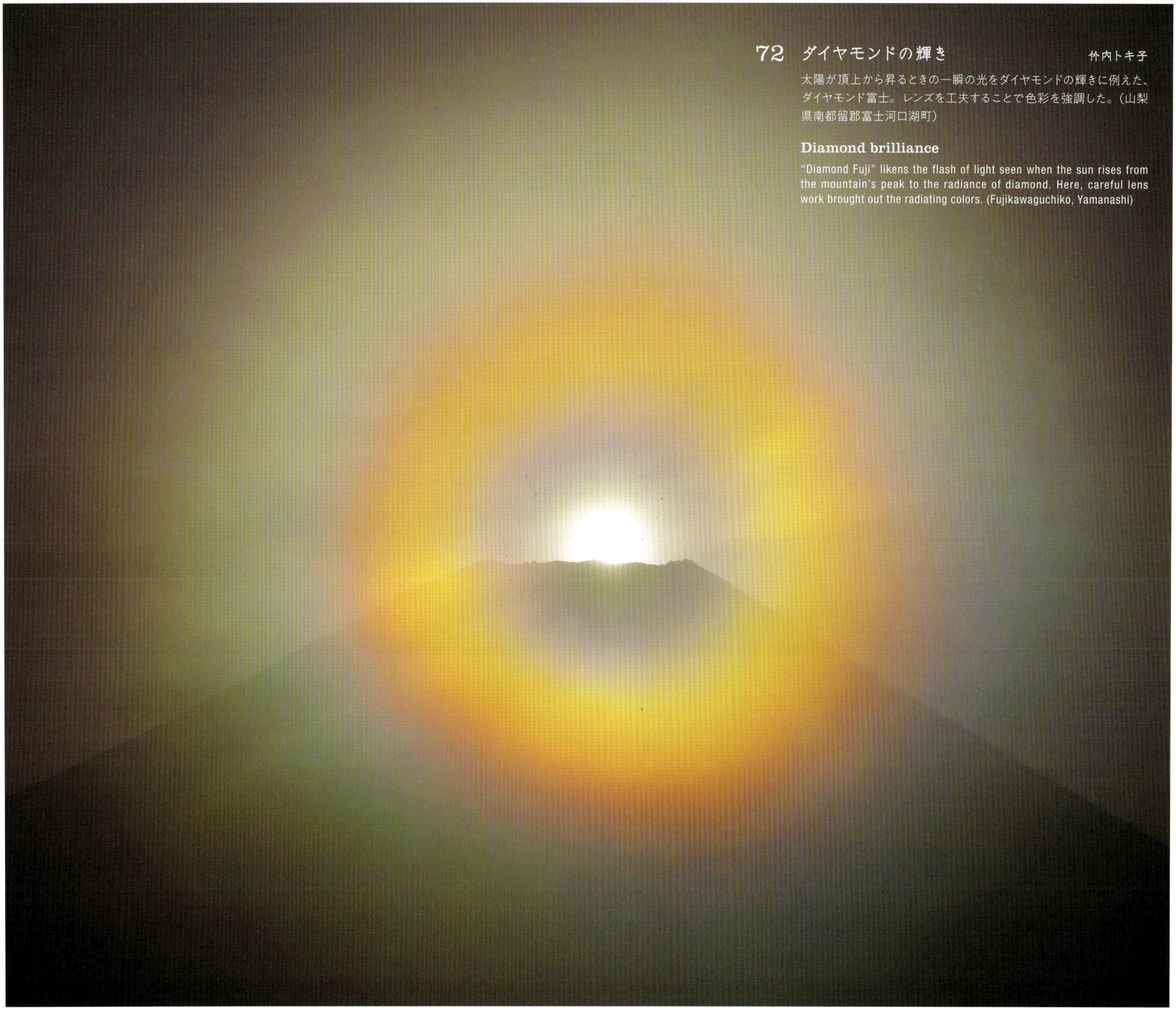

72　ダイヤモンドの輝き　　　竹内トキ子

太陽が頂上から昇るときの一瞬の光をダイヤモンドの輝きに例えた、
ダイヤモンド富士。レンズを工夫することで色彩を強調した。（山梨
県南都留郡富士河口湖町）

Diamond brilliance

"Diamond Fuji" likens the flash of light seen when the sun rises from
the mountain's peak to the radiance of diamond. Here, careful lens
work brought out the radiating colors. (Fujikawaguchiko, Yamanashi)

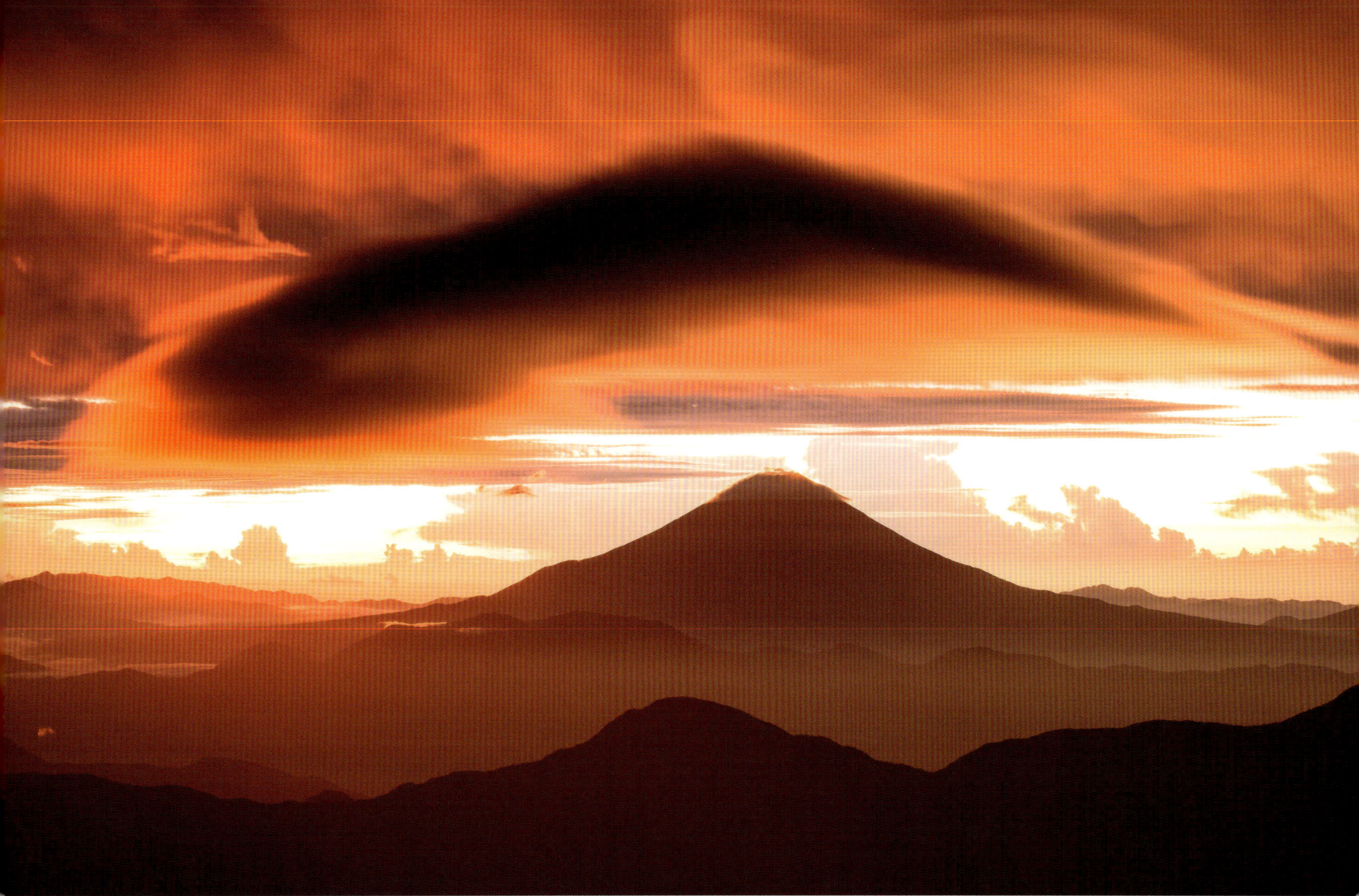

73　焼雲の襲来　　　　　　富士山写真家 オイ

南アルプス南部にある赤石岳は山深く厳しい場所だが、素晴らしい眺めが待っている。雲がざわつく日の出前、目の前を奇妙な形の雲が通り過ぎて行く。（長野県下伊那郡大鹿村・静岡県静岡市／赤石岳）

Clouds ablaze

Mt. Akaishi in the southern part of the Southern Alps is difficult to reach and tough to climb, but there awaits a wonderful view. Here, a strangely shaped cloud came and went with the stirrings in in the sky before sunrise. (Oshika, Nagano / Shizuoka City, Shizuoka / Mount Akaishi)

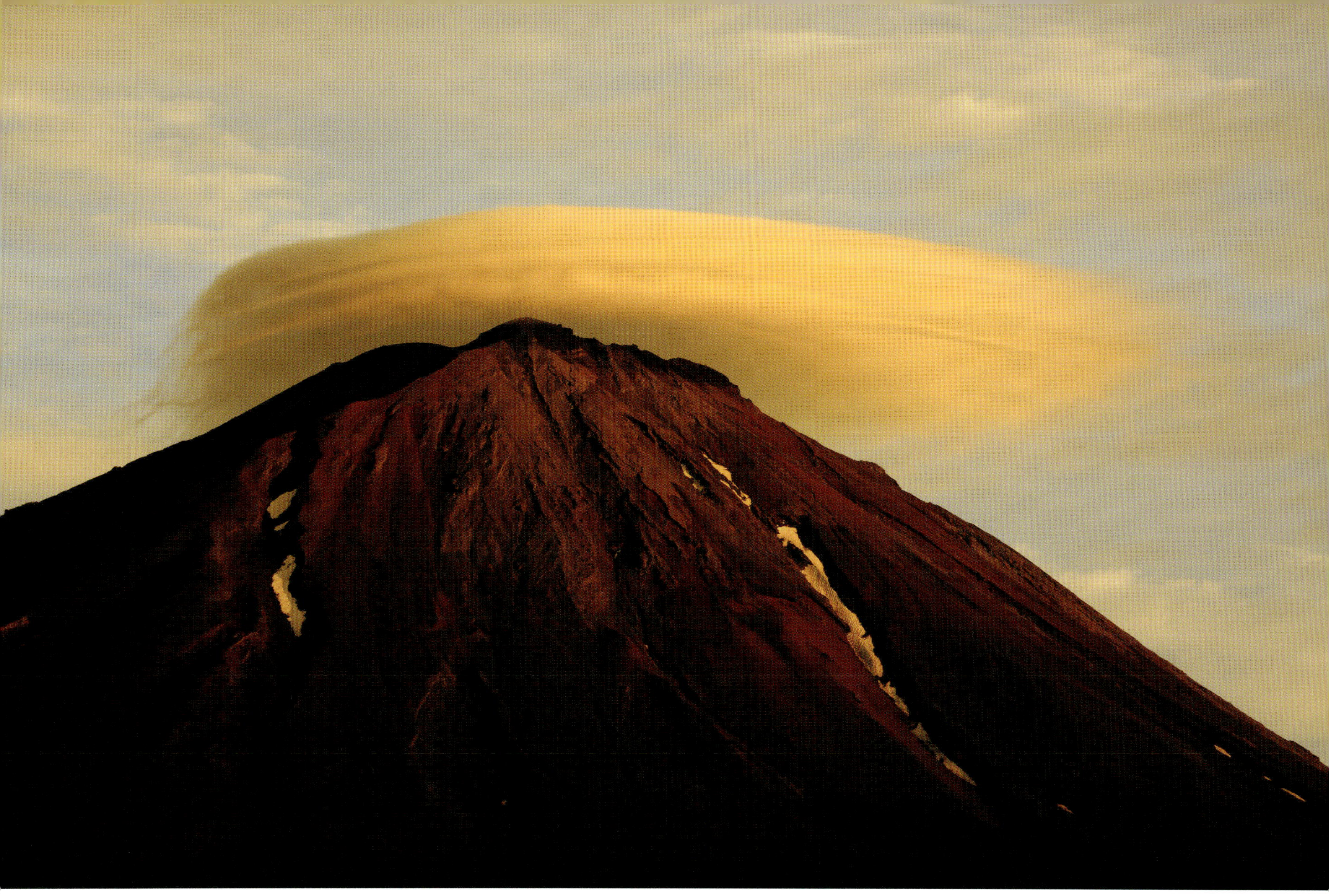

74 夕照の笠雲

竹内トキ子

真夏の富士山の地肌が夕日に染まるころ、近付いている低気圧の影響で発生した笠雲も色づいてきた。西の空は雲が多くなり、雨空に変わりつつある。（山梨県南都留郡鳴沢村）

UFO cloud at sunset

As the surface of Mt. Fuji in midsummer was tinted crimson by the setting sun, the UFO cloud above, formed by approaching low pressure, also took on color. Clouds gathering in the west would bring rainy skies. (Narusawa, Yamanashi)

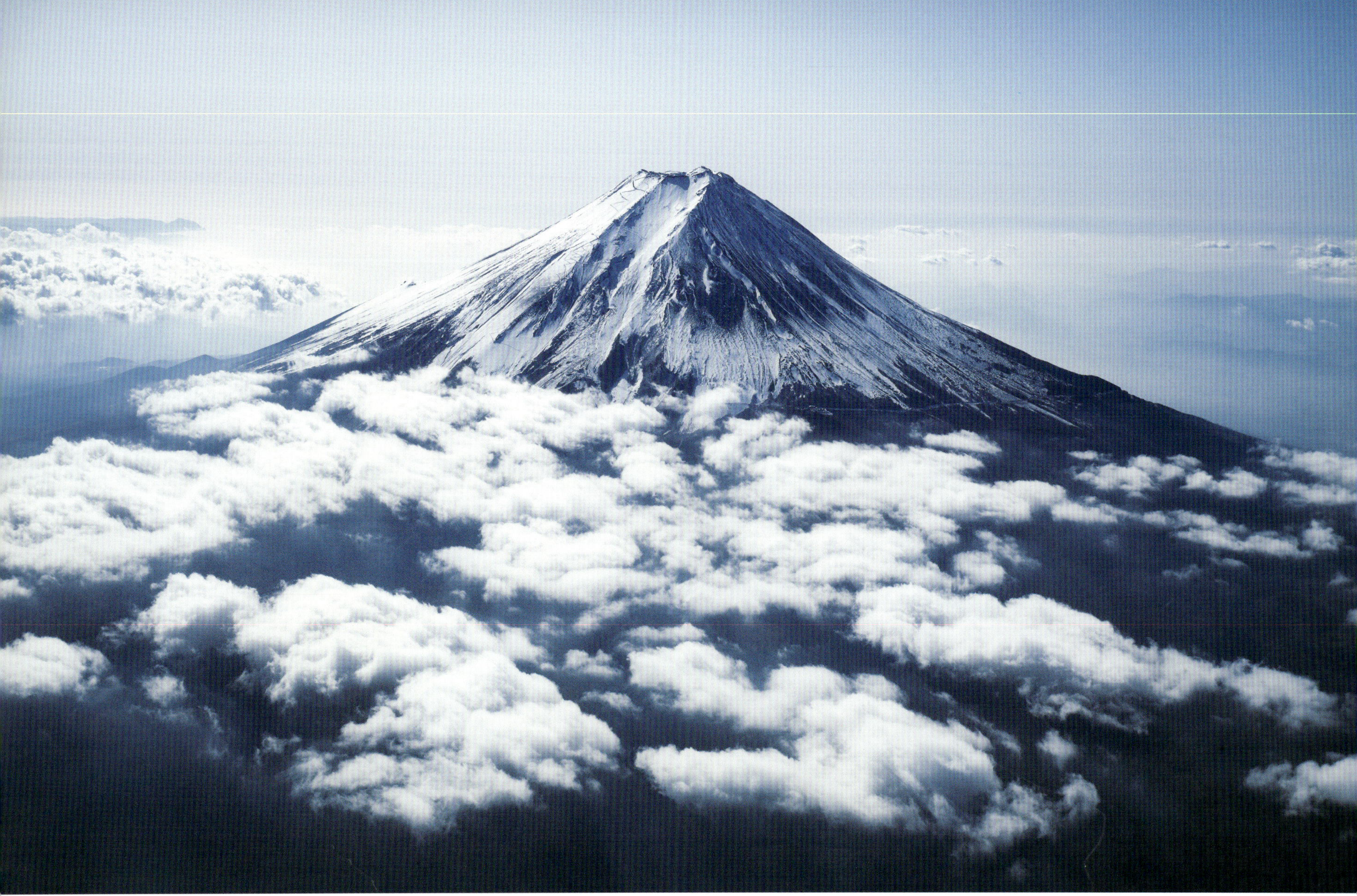

75 秀峰富士山

晴天の朝、セスナ機で富士山の周囲を旋回する。刻々と変化を遂げる朝の光と雲海の中、美しい裾野を広げそびえ立つその姿はとても優美であった。（山梨県南都留郡鳴沢村上空より）

Magnificent Mt. Fuji

Circling Mt. Fuji on a clear morning in a Cessna. In the ever-changing morning light above a sea of clouds, the form of the towering mountain, its slopes gently expanding towards its base, was ever so graceful. (From the sky above Narusawa, Yamanashi)

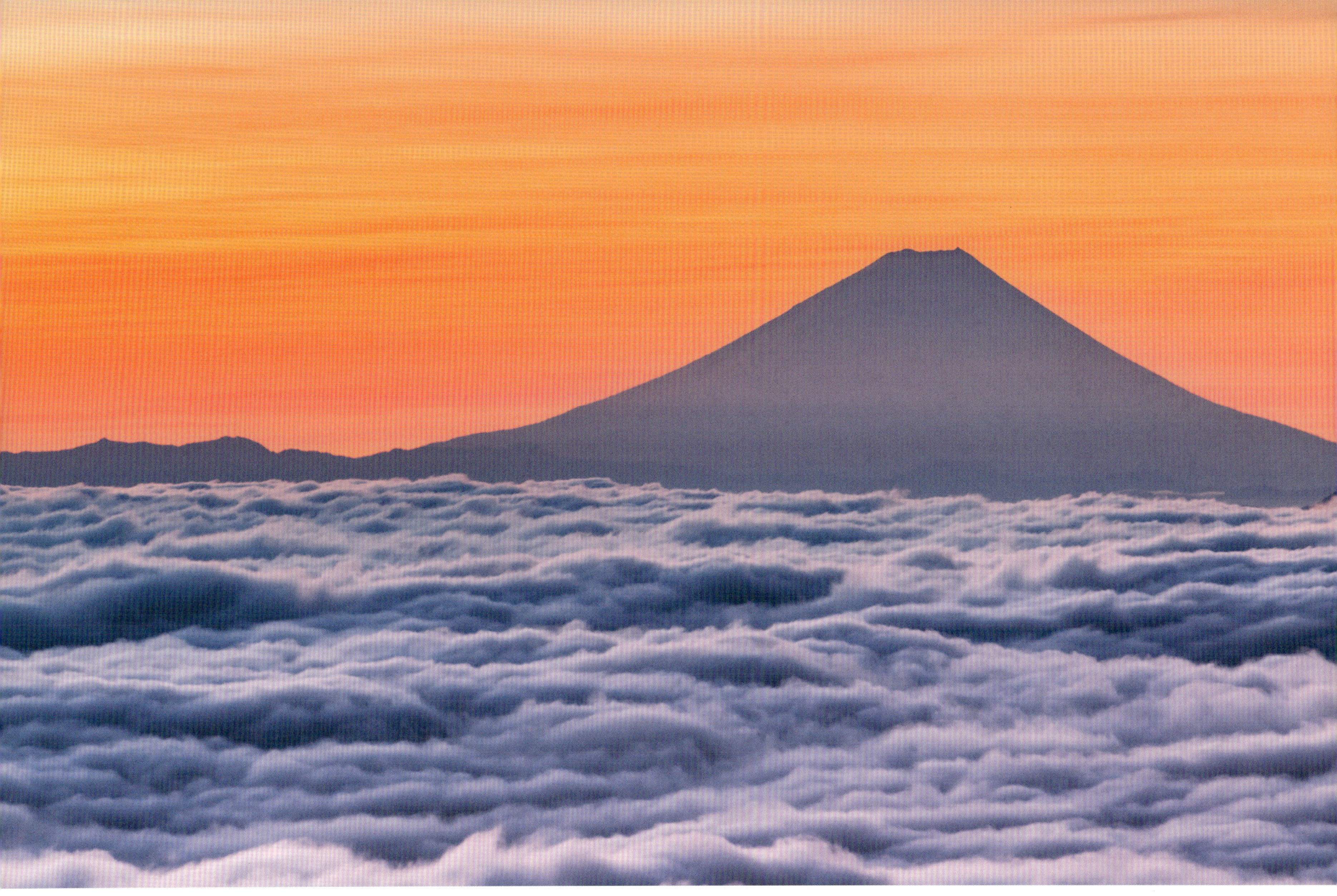

76　雲海越しにそびえる富士山　　　　山梨将典

諏訪盆地と南アルプス・八ヶ岳・富士山を望める高ボッチ山は、雲
海がよく見られる秋になると多くのカメラマンが訪れる。（長野県岡
谷市・塩尻市／高ボッチ山）

Mt. Fuji towering over a sea of clouds

With view of the Suwa Basin, the Southern Alps, Yatsugatake, and Mt.
Fuji, Mt. Takabocchi sees a great many photographers in autumn, when
a sea of clouds is most likely to be seen. (Shiojiri and Okaya, Nagano /
Mt.Takabocchi)

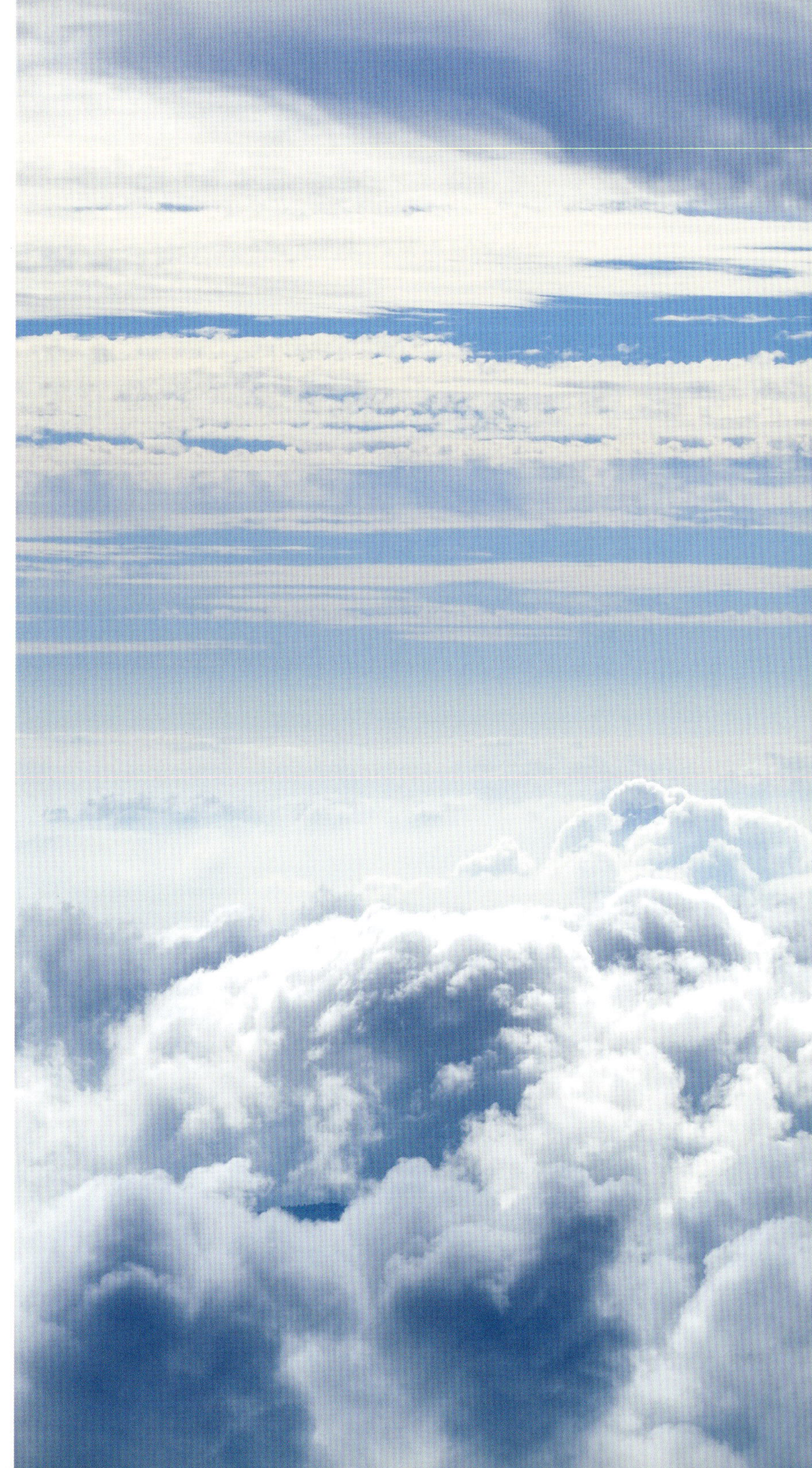

77　頭を雲の上に出し　　　　　富士山写真家 オイ

日本で富士山に次いで二番目に高い南アルプス北岳からの撮影。目の前に迫る高い雲海の先に、最高峰の富士山が堂々と頭を出している。（山梨県南アルプス市 / 北岳）

Head above the clouds

Taken from Kitadake, the second highest mountain in Japan, where the cloud cover had almost reached eye level. Mt. Fuji, however, Japan's highest peak, stood proudly, head thrust above the high sea of clouds. (Minami Alps, Yamanashi / Kitadake)

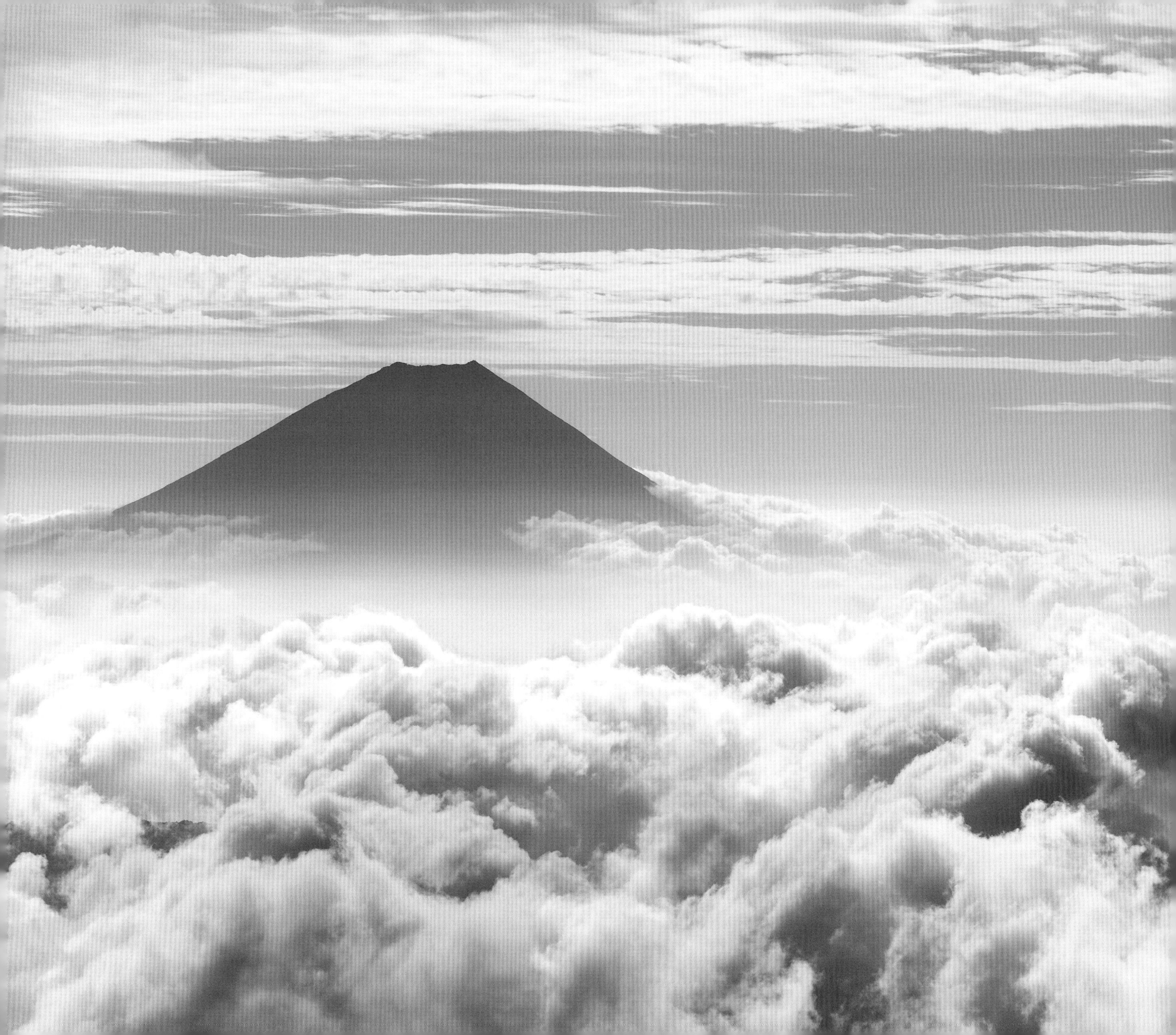

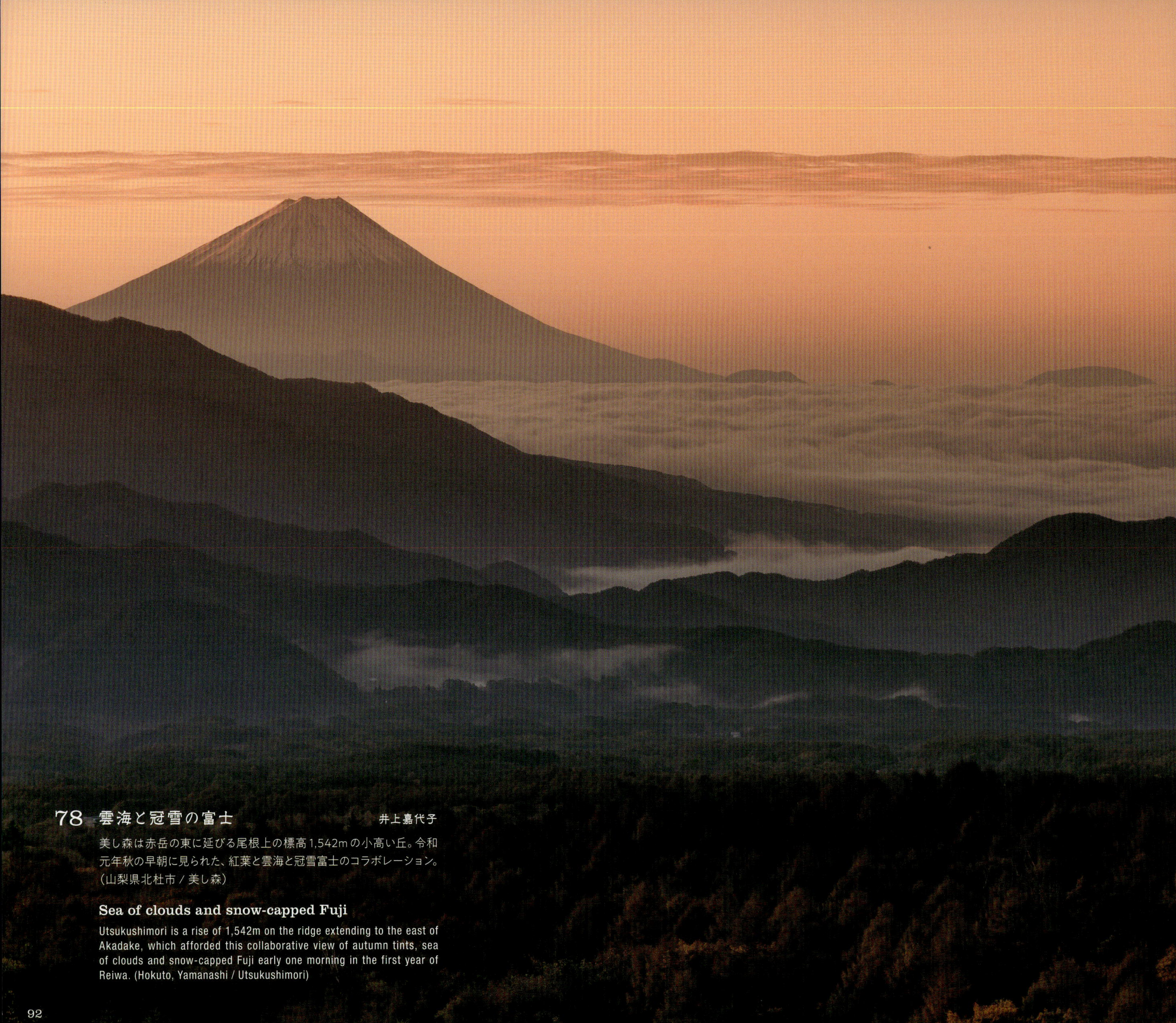

78　雲海と冠雪の富士

美し森は赤岳の東に延びる尾根上の標高1,542mの小高い丘。令和
元年秋の早朝に見られた、紅葉と雲海と冠雪富士のコラボレーション。
（山梨県北杜市／美し森）

Sea of clouds and snow-capped Fuji

Utsukushimori is a rise of 1,542m on the ridge extending to the east of
Akadake, which afforded this collaborative view of autumn tints, sea
of clouds and snow-capped Fuji early one morning in the first year of
Reiwa. (Hokuto, Yamanashi / Utsukushimori)

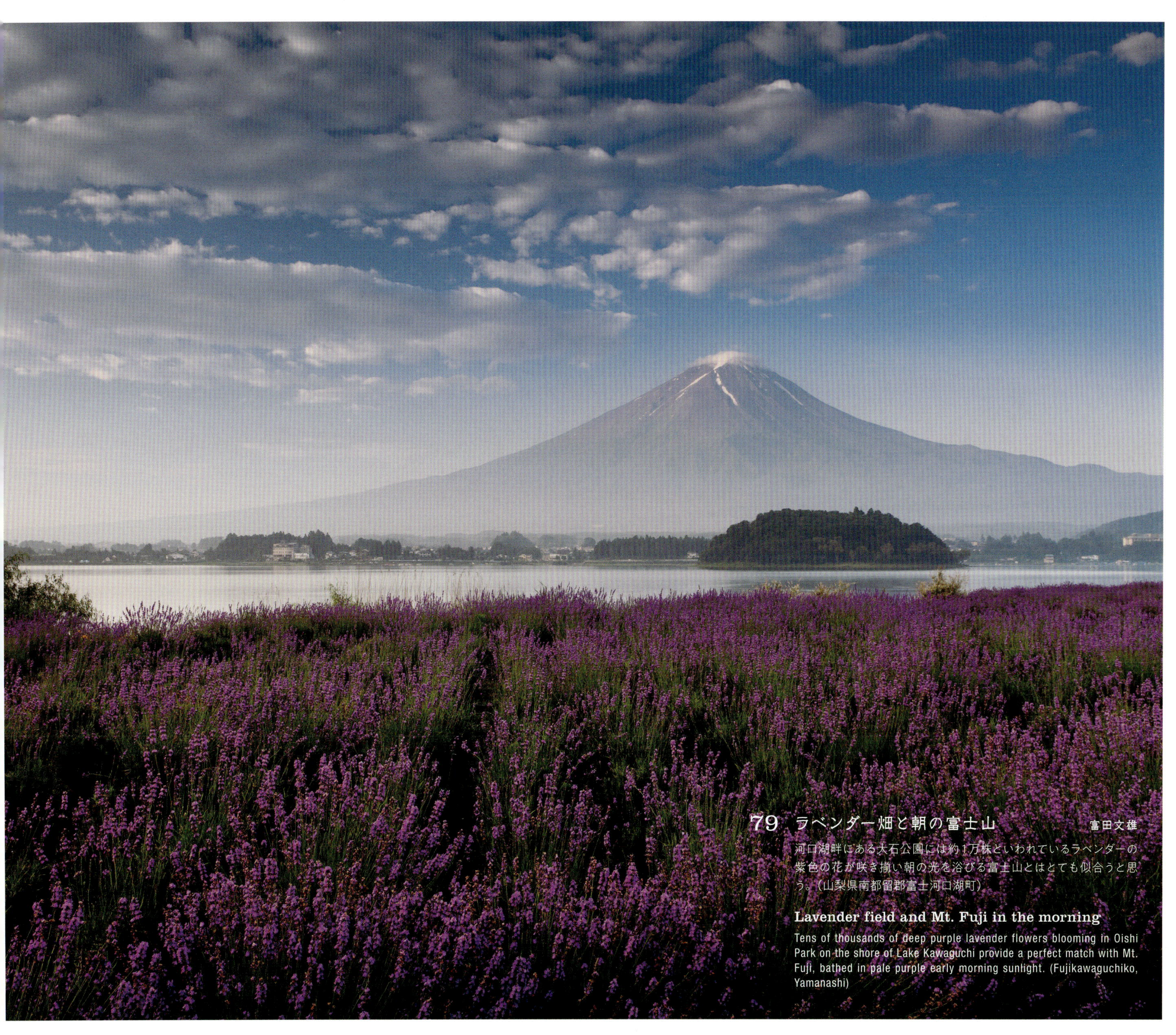

79 ラベンダー畑と朝の富士山　富田文雄

河口湖畔にある大石公園には約1万株といわれているラベンダーの紫色の花が咲き揃い朝の光を浴びる富士山とはとても似合うと思う。（山梨県南都留郡富士河口湖町）

Lavender field and Mt. Fuji in the morning

Tens of thousands of deep purple lavender flowers blooming in Oishi Park on the shore of Lake Kawaguchi provide a perfect match with Mt. Fuji, bathed in pale purple early morning sunlight. (Fujikawaguchiko, Yamanashi)

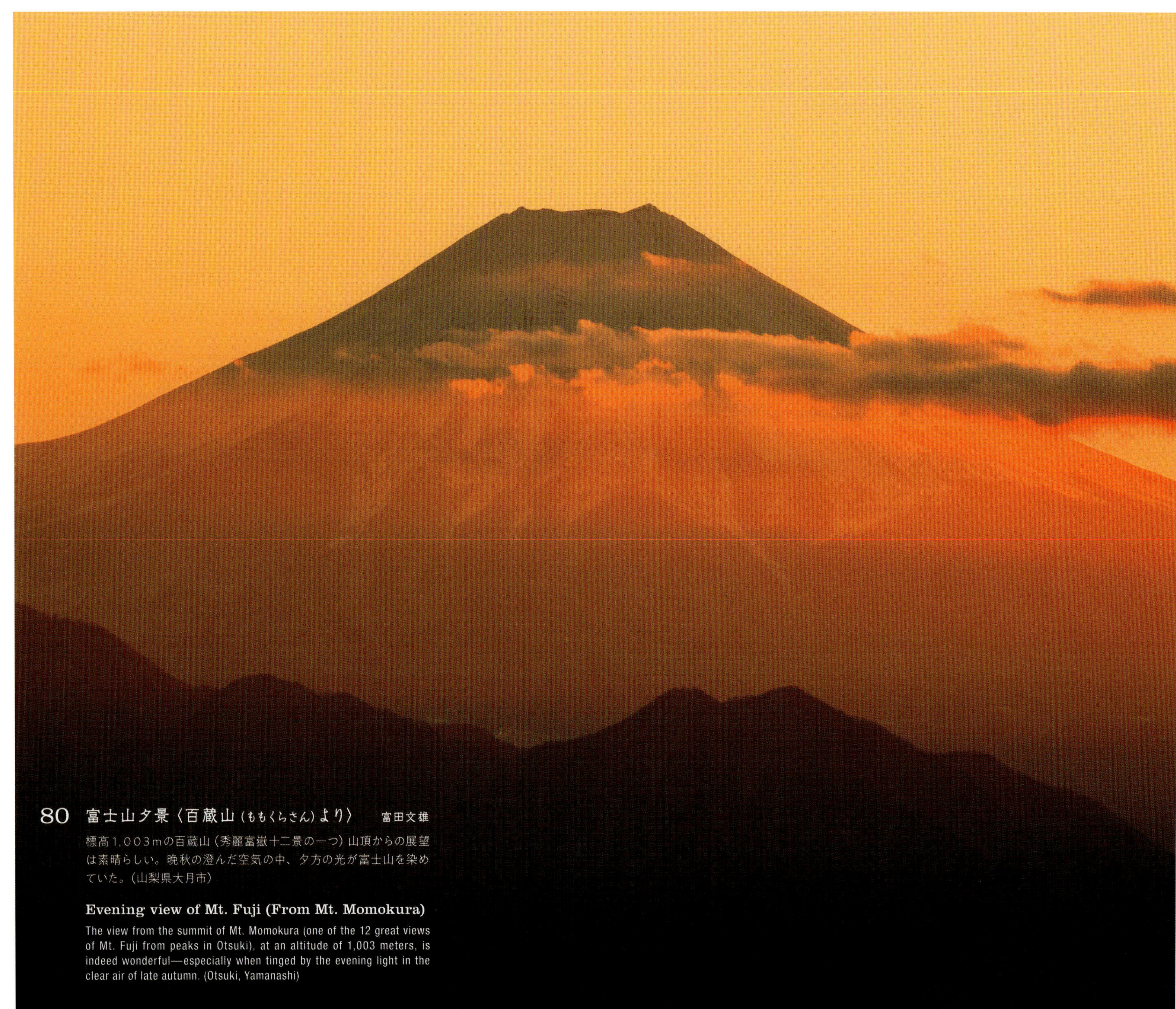

80 富士山夕景 〈百蔵山 (ももくらさん) より〉　富田文雄

標高1,003mの百蔵山 (秀麗富嶽十二景の一つ) 山頂からの展望
は素晴らしい。晩秋の澄んだ空気の中、夕方の光が富士山を染め
ていた。(山梨県大月市)

Evening view of Mt. Fuji (From Mt. Momokura)

The view from the summit of Mt. Momokura (one of the 12 great views
of Mt. Fuji from peaks in Otsuki), at an altitude of 1,003 meters, is
indeed wonderful—especially when tinged by the evening light in the
clear air of late autumn. (Otsuki, Yamanashi)

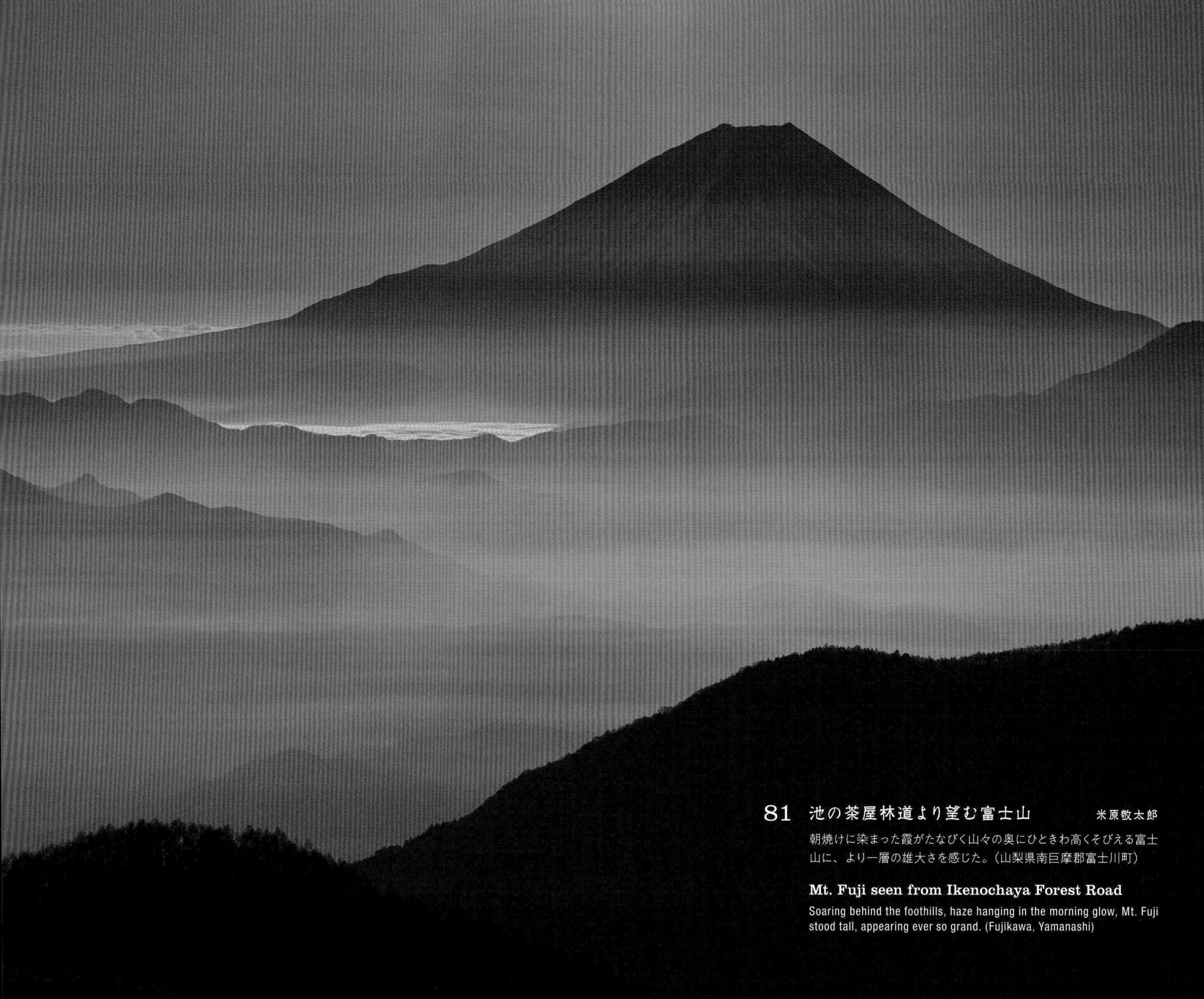

81　池の茶屋林道より望む富士山　　　　米原敬太郎

朝焼けに染まった霞がたなびく山々の奥にひときわ高くそびえる富士山に、より一層の雄大さを感じた。（山梨県南巨摩郡富士川町）

Mt. Fuji seen from Ikenochaya Forest Road

Soaring behind the foothills, haze hanging in the morning glow, Mt. Fuji stood tall, appearing ever so grand. (Fujikawa, Yamanashi)

　精進湖から黎明の富士山　　　　　　　　山梨勝弘

冬期、本栖湖と精進湖からは朝日と富士山を絡ませて撮影ができ
る。無風で冷え込んだ朝には、湖面から靄が立ち幻想的な朝となる。
（山梨県南都留郡富士河口湖町／精進湖）

Mt. Fuji from the Lake Shoji Lake at dawn

Winter affords views of the rising sun and Mt. Fuji from Lake Motosu
and Lake Shoji. On this cold, windless morning, mist rising from the
surface of the lake gave the scene an air of fantasy. (Fujikawaguchiko,
Yamanashi / Lake Shoji)

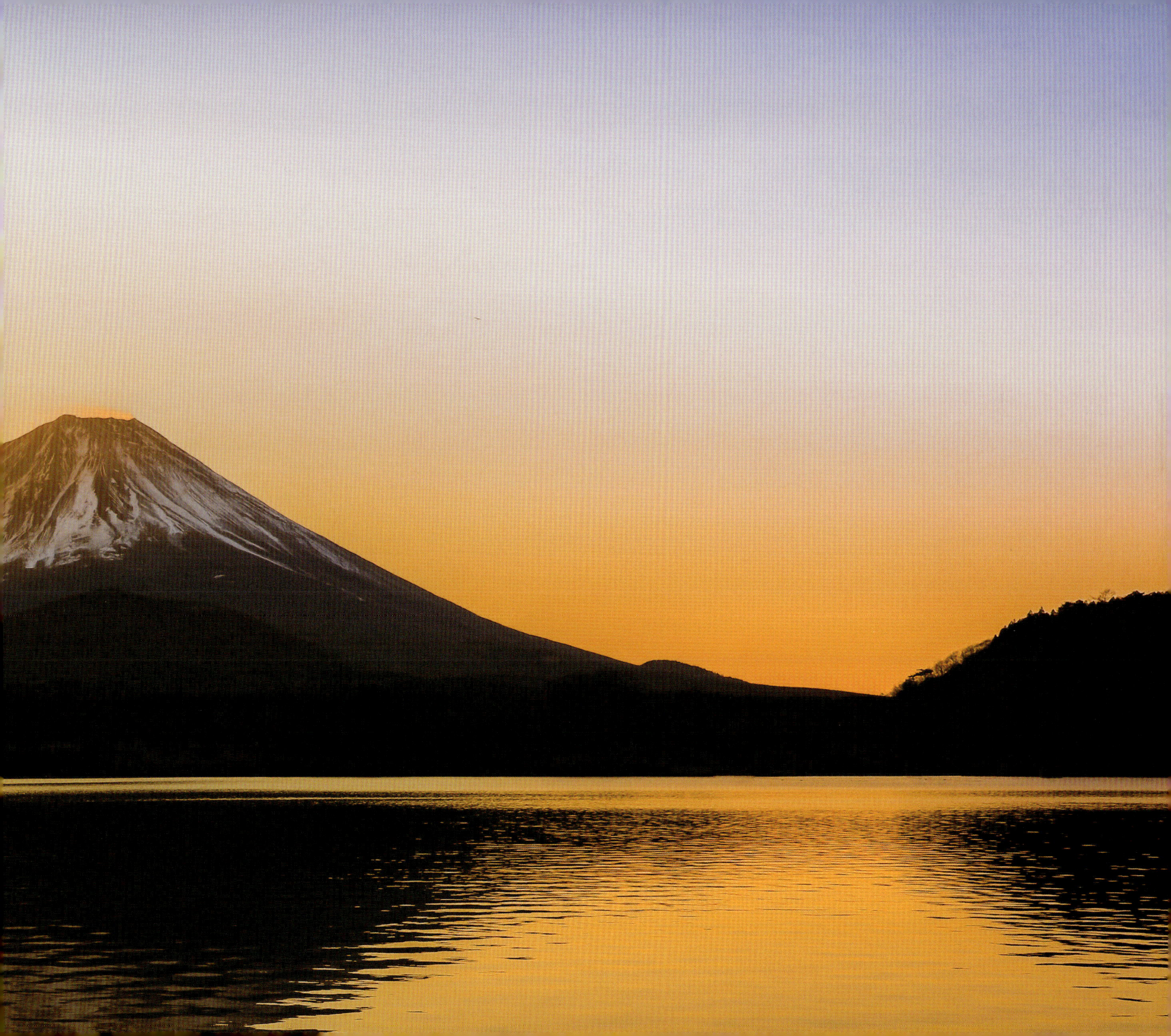

　夕焼けに浮かぶ富士山　　　　館野二朗

夕暮れ時の大観山から望む富士山。空は濃い夕焼け色にならず金色
系の淡いグラデーションが美しかった。（神奈川県足柄下郡箱根町）

Mt. Fuji floating in the sky after sunset

Mt. Fuji seen from Mt. Taikan at dusk. The sky turned not the vibrant
hues typical of sunset, but a gradation of pale golden tints that were
simply beautiful. (Hakone, Kanagawa)

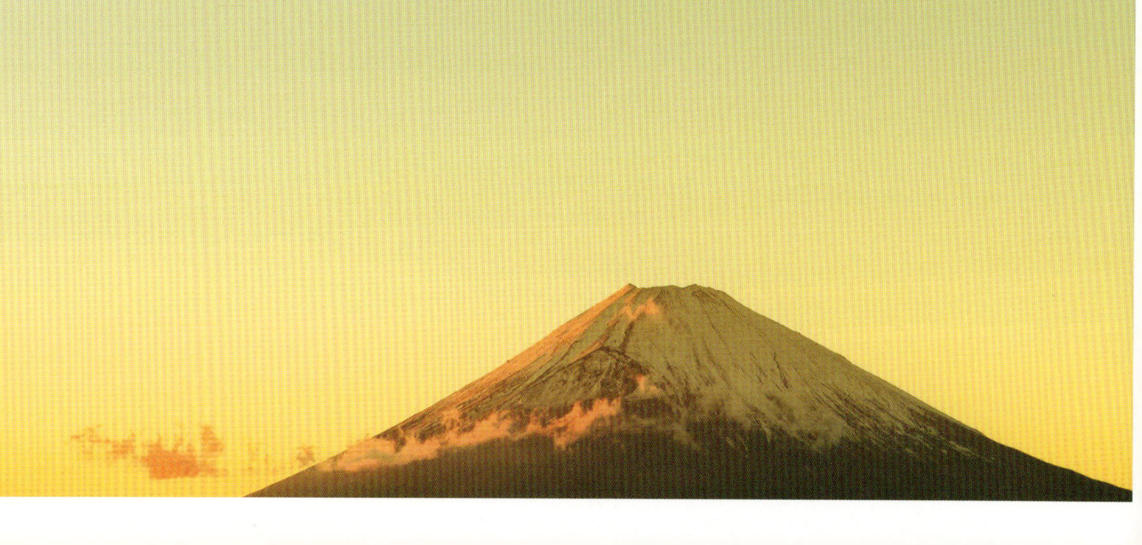

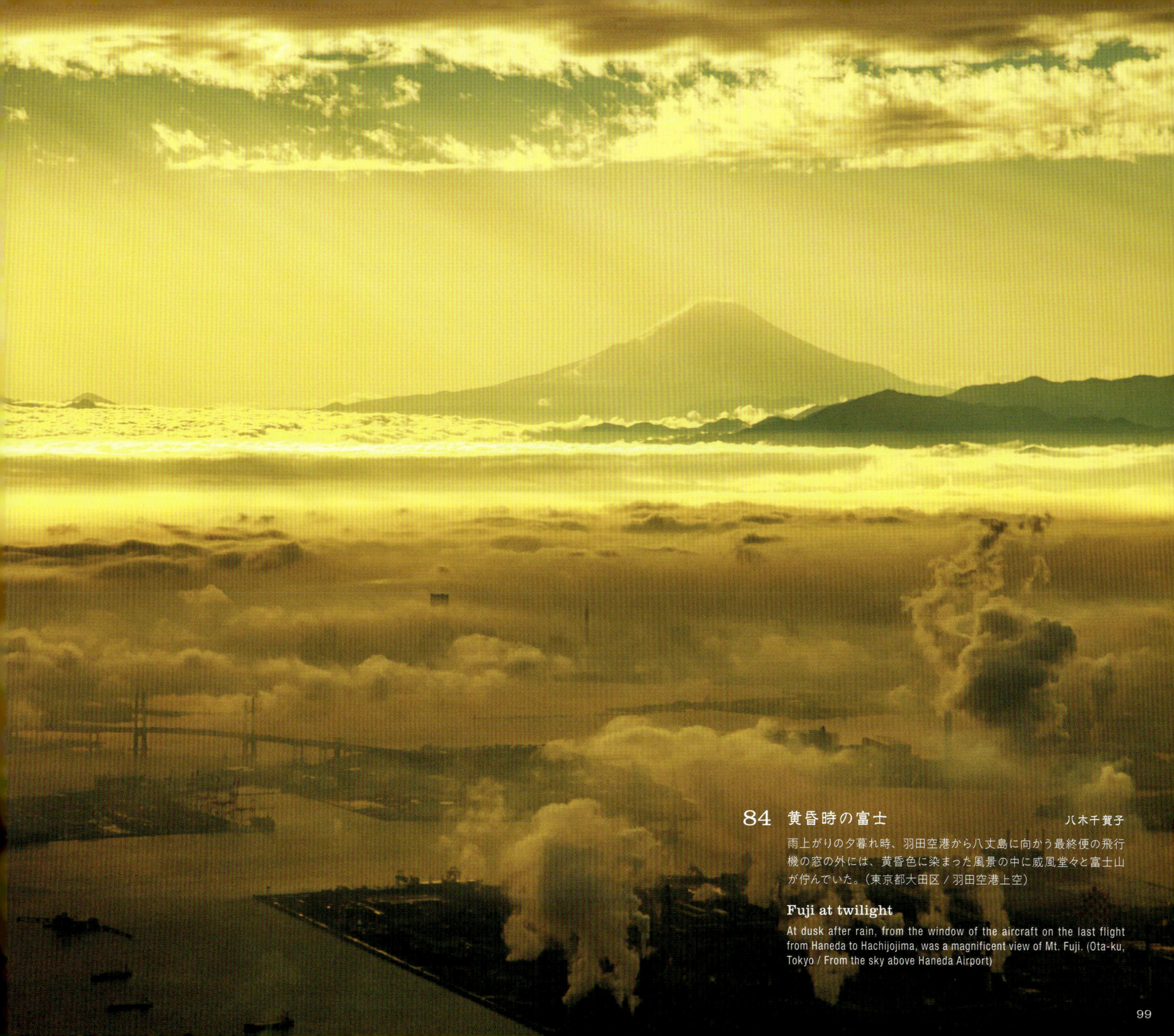

84　黄昏時の富士　　　　　　　　　　　　八木千賀子

雨上がりの夕暮れ時、羽田空港から八丈島に向かう最終便の飛行
機の窓の外には、黄昏色に染まった風景の中に威風堂々と富士山
が佇んでいた。（東京都大田区 / 羽田空港上空）

Fuji at twilight

At dusk after rain, from the window of the aircraft on the last flight
from Haneda to Hachijojima, was a magnificent view of Mt. Fuji. (Ota-ku,
Tokyo / From the sky above Haneda Airport)

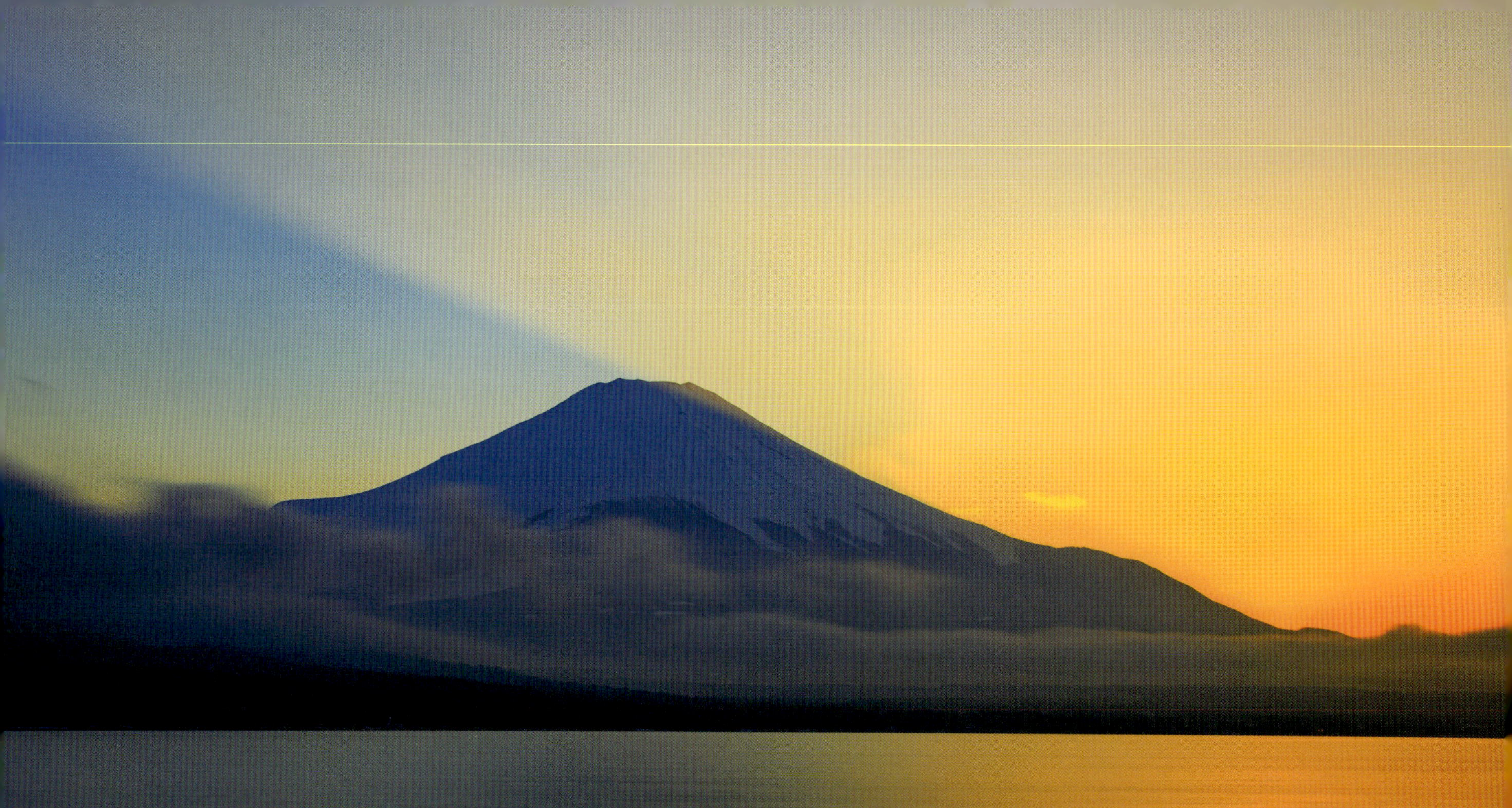

85 トワイライト富士　　　　　　八木千賀子

富士五湖の一つである山中湖畔にて、日没後太陽の光線が富士山
によって遮られ夕暮れのオレンジ色と夜のとばりへと向かう藍色の2
色に分けられた。（山梨県南都留郡山中湖村 / 山中湖）

Twilight Fuji

At the shore of Lake Yamanaka, one of the Fuji Five Lakes, the sun's
rays blocked by Mt. Fuji after sunset divided the sky into two colors:
orange of dusk and indigo heading to the edge of night. (Yamanakako,

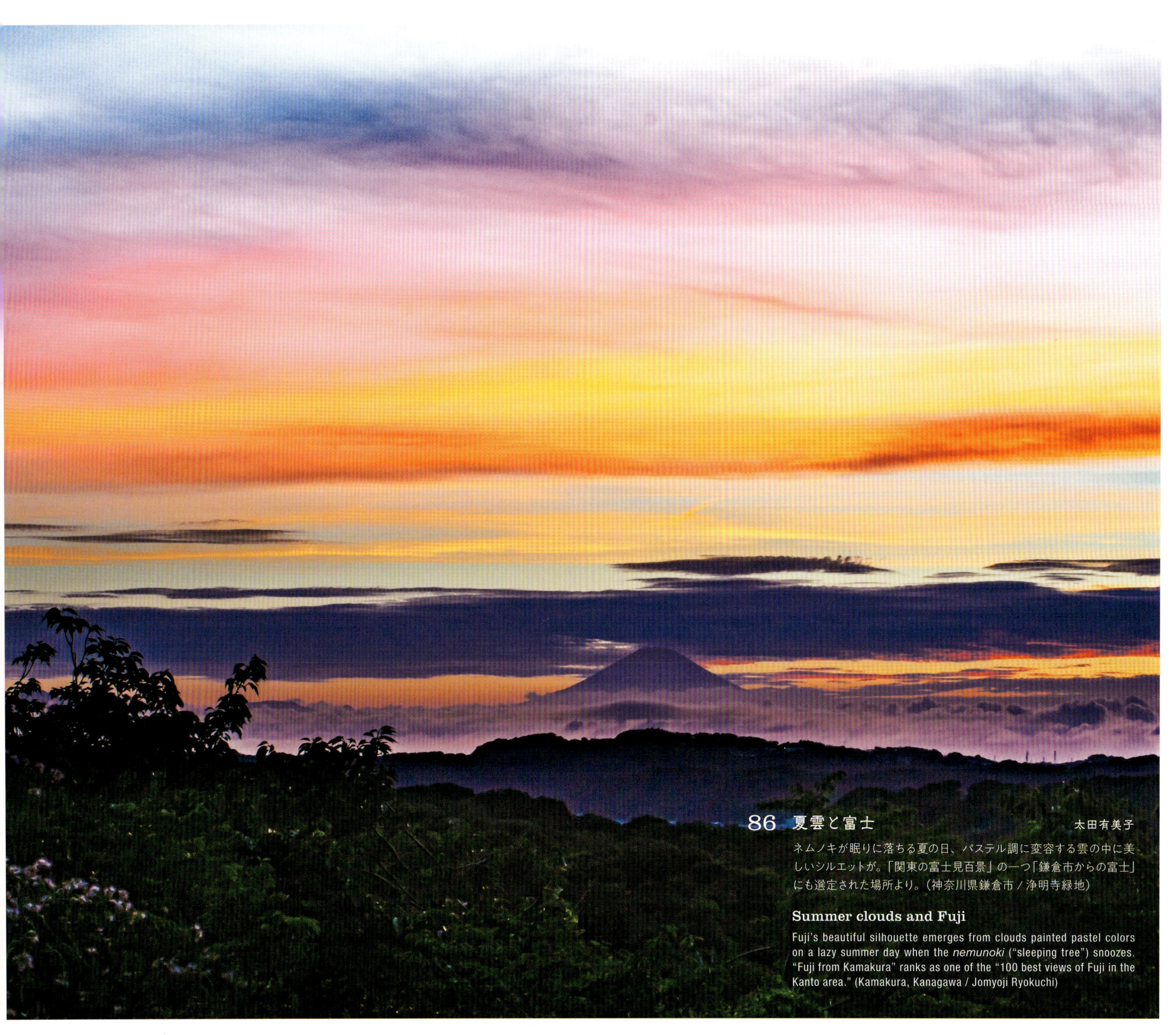

86 夏雲と富士 太田有美子

ネムノキが眠りに落ちる夏の日、パステル調に変容する雲の中に美しいシルエットが。「関東の富士見百景」の一つ「鎌倉市からの富士」にも選定された場所より。（神奈川県鎌倉市／浄明寺緑地）

Summer clouds and Fuji

Fuji's beautiful silhouette emerges from clouds painted pastel colors on a lazy summer day when the *nemunoki* ("sleeping tree") snoozes. "Fuji from Kamakura" ranks as one of the "100 best views of Fuji in the Kanto area." (Kamakura, Kanagawa / Jomyoji Ryokuchi)

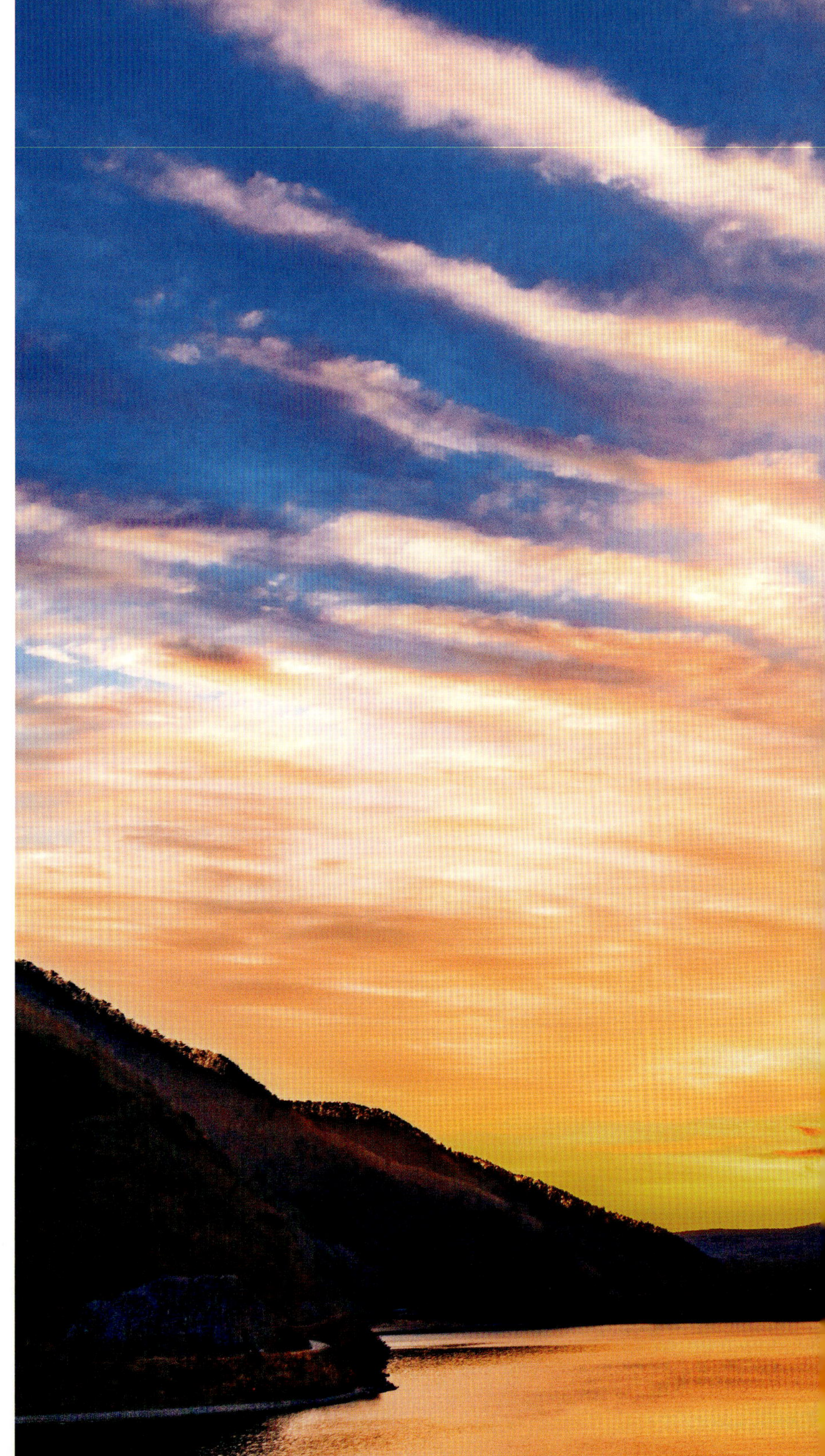

87 　本栖湖から朝焼けの富士　　　　　　　　高椋俊樹

夜明けと共に姿を現した富士山。本栖湖に映る空の色彩と雲の表
情がとても印象的であった。（山梨県南巨摩郡身延町／本栖湖）

Fuji in the morning glow from Lake Motosu

With the break of dawn Mt. Fuji burst into sight, and together with
the expressions of the clouds and colors of the sky reflected in Lake
Motosu, the scene was majestic. (Minobu, Yamanashi / Lake Motosu)

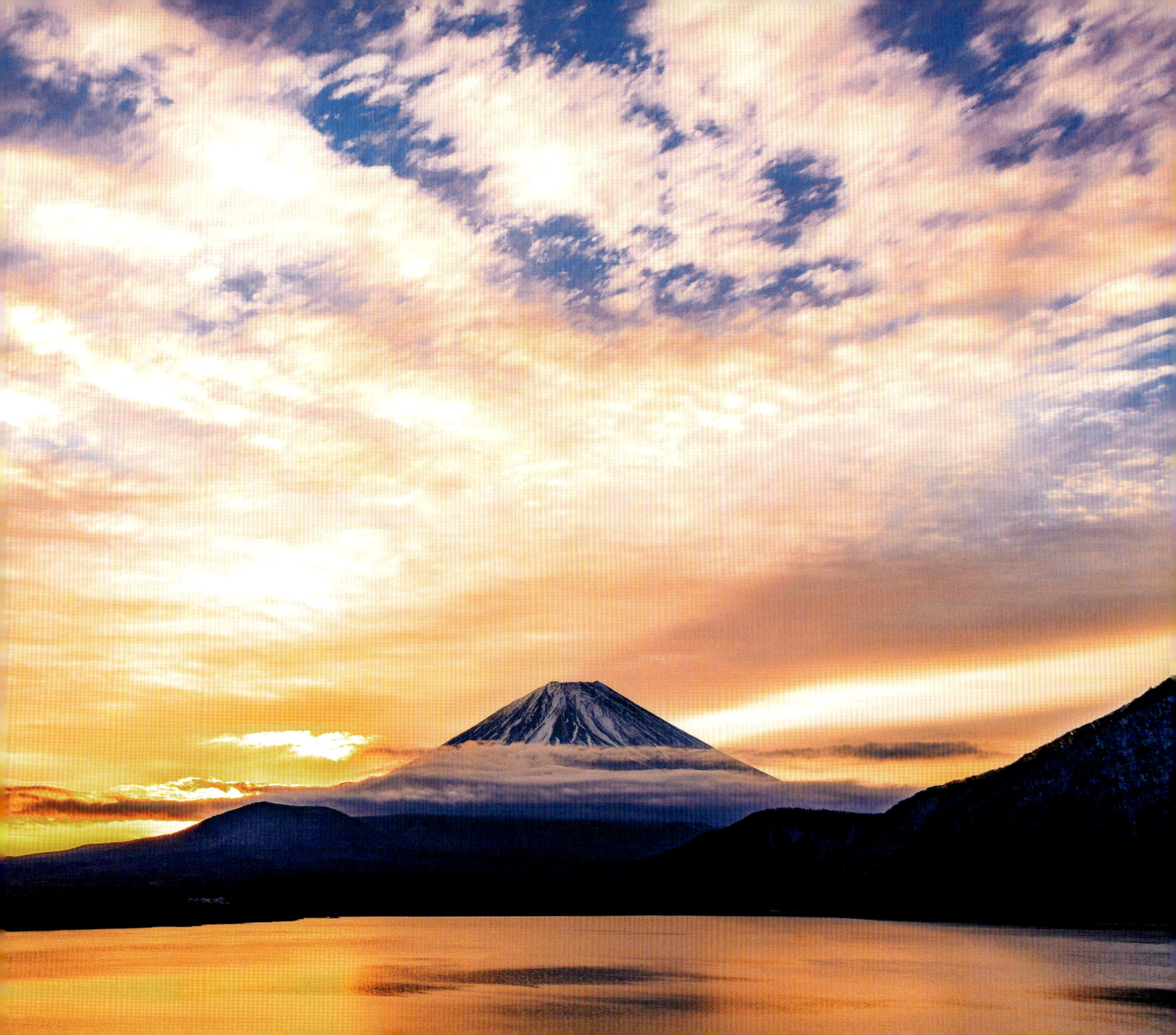

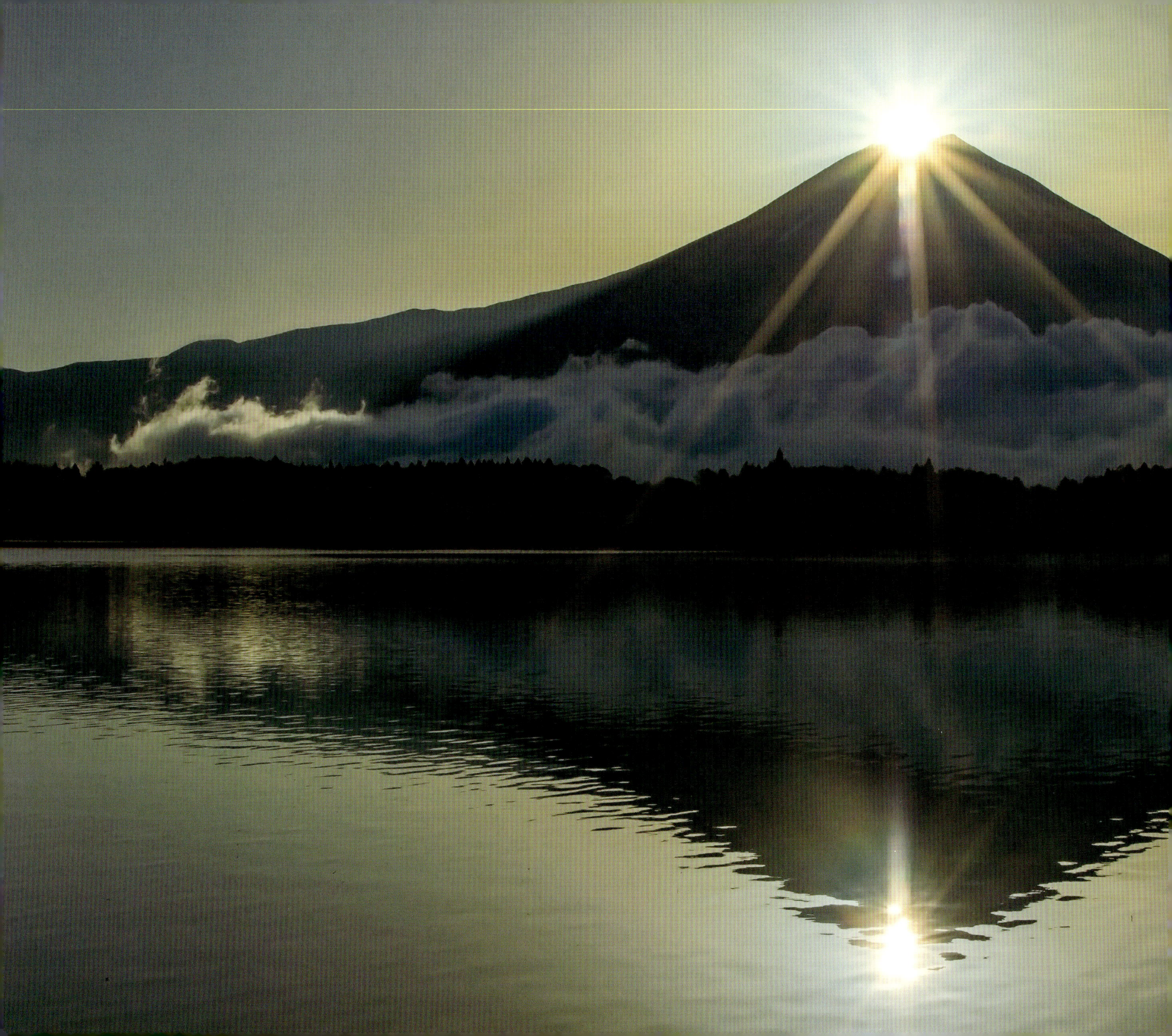

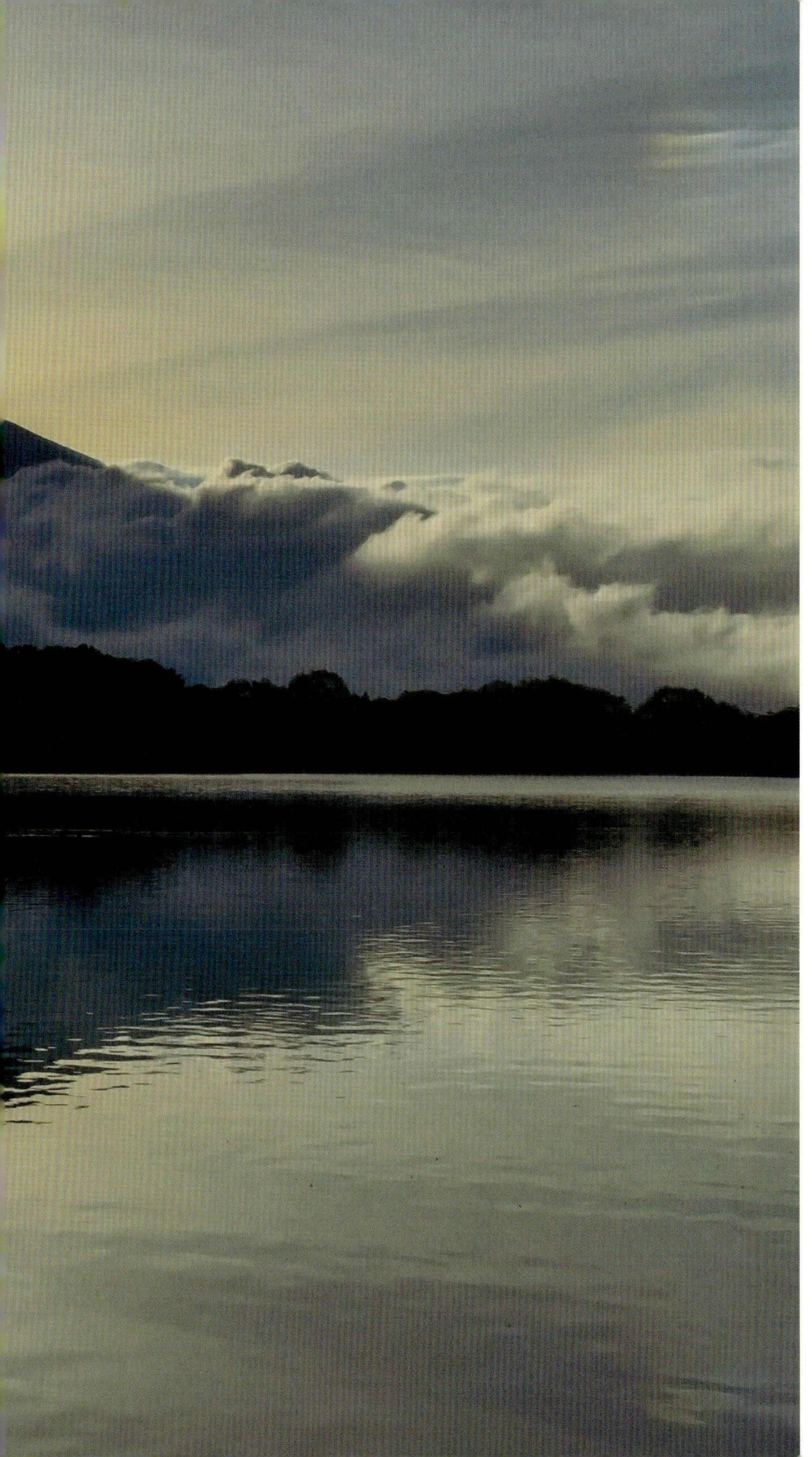

88 ダブルダイヤモンド富士

鎌形 久

富士山頂に太陽が重なり輝く「ダイヤモンド富士」。田貫湖では湖面に
富士山が映る「ダブルダイヤモンド富士」が見られる。裾野に湧く
雲海が一層ダイナミックさを演出していた。(静岡県富士宮市／田貫湖)

Double Diamond Fuji

The radiating sun perched on the peak of Mt. Fuji is known as "Diamond
Fuji." Lake Tanuki, where Fuji's image is reflected on the water's
surface, afforded this view of a "Double Diamond Fuji," the sea of
clouds skirting the foot of the mountain creating an even more dynamic
atmosphere.

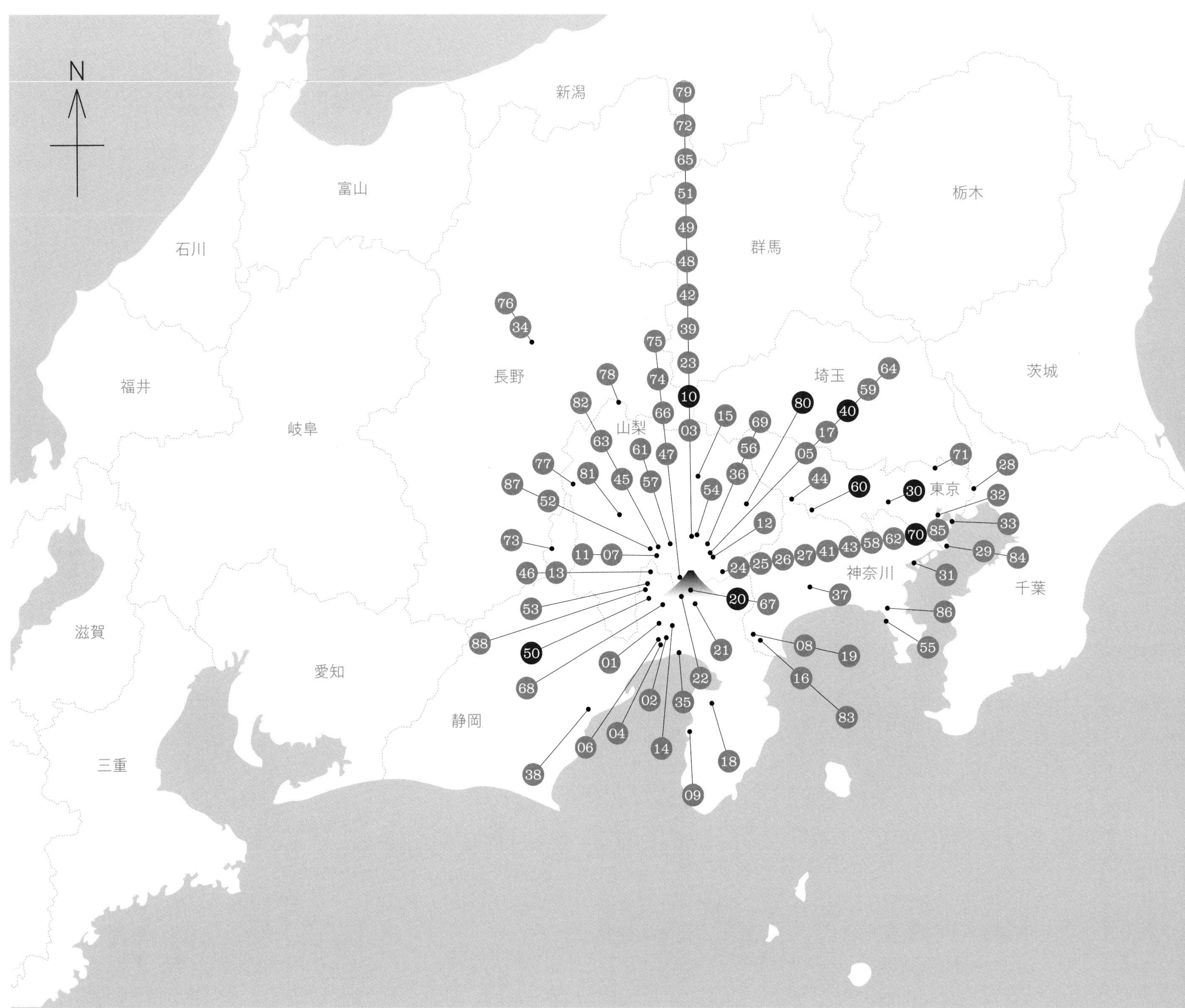

N
新潟
富山
栃木
石川
群馬
福井
岐阜
長野
山梨
埼玉
茨城
東京
神奈川
千葉
滋賀
愛知
静岡
三重

01 朝焼けの富士山と桜 — 2
02 夕日を浴びる龍巌淵の桜と富士山 — 4
03 河口湖の桜と富士山 — 5
04 かりがね堤の桜と富士山 — 6
05 新名庄川の桜並木と富士山 — 7
06 岩本山公園の桜と富士山 — 8
07 富士本栖湖リゾートのシバザクラ — 10
08 ツツジと富士山 — 11
09 菜の花畑と富士山 — 12
10 河口湖のコスモスと富士山 — 13
11 シバザクラと富士山 — 14
12 百日草咲く花の都公園と富士山 — 15
13 放し飼いの乳牛 — 16
14 茶畑から望む富士山 — 17
15 新緑に覆われた甲州の山並み — 18
16 芦ノ湖より望む富士 — 19
17 水田に映える富士 — 20
18 だるま山高原より駿河湾と富士山 — 22
19 芦ノ湖と富士山 — 23
20 春の富士山宝永火口(ほうえいかこう) — 24
21 水ヶ塚公園より富士山宝永火口を望む — 25
22 夏の午後の富士山 — 26
23 河口湖から望む赤富士 — 27
24 朝霧の山中湖と富士山 — 28
25 赤富士山中湖 — 29
26 紅富士 — 30
27 パール富士 — 31
28 夕暮れの東京スカイツリーと富士山 — 32
29 夕焼けの富士山と渡り鳥 — 34
30 東京郊外から夕暮れの富士山 — 35

31 朝の横浜から見た富士山 — 36
32 夕暮れのレインボーブリッジ — 38
33 薄暮に浮かぶ東京ゲートブリッジ — 39
34 朝の諏訪湖と富士山 — 40
35 田子の浦港と富士山の夕景 — 41
36 街明かりと山開きした富士山 — 42
37 雪晴れの街 — 43
38 朝鮮岩から望む夜明けの富士山 — 44
39 河口湖冬花火 — 46
40 忍野村の桜と富士山(ライトアップ) — 47
41 異様な吊るし雲と富士山夜景 — 48
42 月夜のラベンダー畑と富士山 — 49
43 満月に浮かぶ富士山 — 50
44 富士山暮色〈陣馬山(じんばさん)より〉 — 52
45 精進湖より望む赤富士 — 53
46 夜明け前の富士山 — 54
47 黄葉と新雪の富士山 — 56
48 錦秋の富士 — 57
49 真紅のコキアと赤富士 — 58
50 白糸ノ滝からの富士山 — 59
51 河口湖からの紅葉と富士山 — 60
52 紅葉と富士山 — 62
53 柿の実と白い富士 — 63
54 朝の富士と河口浅間神社の遥拝所 — 64
55 森戸海岸より富士山を望む — 65
56 雪化粧の五重塔と富士山 — 66
57 茅葺き民家越しの初夏の富士山 — 67
58 冬晴れの富士山 — 68
59 凍てつく朝 — 70
60 高尾山より望む富士山 — 71

61 樹氷と富士山 — 72
62 氷漂う山中湖と富士山 — 73
63 精進湖の結氷と子抱き富士 — 74
64 朝日を浴びる新雪の富士山 — 75
65 雲海と富士山 — 76
66 夜明けの富士山 — 78
67 宝永火口と影富士 — 79
68 雲海と富士 — 80
69 虹笠 — 82
70 夕暮れの彩雲と富士山 — 83
71 ダイヤモンド富士 — 84
72 ダイヤモンドの輝き — 85
73 焼雲の襲来 — 86
74 夕照の笠雲 — 87
75 秀峰富士山 — 88
76 雲海越しにそびえる富士山 — 89
77 頭を雲の上に出し — 90
78 雲海と冠雪の富士 — 92
79 ラベンダー畑と朝の富士山 — 93
80 富士山夕景〈百蔵山(ももくらさん)より〉 — 94
81 池の茶屋林道より望む富士山 — 95
82 精進湖から黎明の富士山 — 96
83 夕焼けに浮かぶ富士山 — 98
84 黄昏時の富士 — 99
85 トワイライト富士 — 100
86 夏雲と富士 — 101
87 本栖湖から朝焼けの富士 — 102
88 ダブルダイヤモンド富士 — 104

写真家プロフィール

井上嘉代子 (いのうえ かよこ)
1967 年岐阜市生まれ。インテリア業界・デザイン業界で撮影業務に従事の後独立。八ヶ岳と北海道を愛し、八ヶ岳暮らしを始める。風景や野生動物等をテーマに撮影、各種媒体に作品を提供。事故の後遺症により現在左手のみで撮影を行う。日本写真家協会会員、日本風景写真家協会会員、NACS−J 自然観察指導員。

太田有美子 (おおた ゆみこ)
1969 年兵庫県生まれ。写真家・丹地敏明氏の主宰するフォト・パダライスアカデミーにて本格的に写真を学ぶ。2014 年よりフリーランスの写真家。身近な植物や自然をテーマに撮り続けている。神奈川県逗子市在住。日本写真協会会員、日本写真家協会会員。

片岡 巖 (かたおか いわお)
1944 年新潟県生まれ。写真家佐藤昭五氏に師事後フリーランスとなる。自然が季節ごとに見せる輝きの瞬間、それに出会えたときの感動を求めて撮影を続け、作品をカレンダーや雑誌等に提供している。日本風景写真家協会会員。

鎌形 久 (かまがた ひさし)
1949 年千葉県生まれ。ライフワークである東北地方、北海道の白鳥を撮影するのと並行し、全国の自然風景とそこに宿る生き物たちの姿を撮影。写真展、写真集、各種媒体に作品を発表。主な著書に『Swan』『ニッポンの美しい自然と「四字熟語」』がある。

五島健司 (ごしま けんじ)
1960 年福島県生まれ、在住。20 歳頃より独学で写真を始める。年間 200 日以上キャンピングカーで日本全国を旅し、四季の景観を追い続けている。作品は写真展、出版物などに多数発表。主な写真集に『SILENCE - 移ろう季節の中で』『櫻酔い HANA-YOI』などがある。日本写真家協会会員。

佐藤哲郎 (さとう てつろう)
大学卒業後大手自動車メーカー勤務の後、米国ロサンゼルスのピアス大学に留学し写真を学ぶ。1991 年同大学を卒業後帰国しフリーの写真家に。都会の風景から大自然まで幅広く撮影し、カレンダー、ポスター等に写真を提供している。日本風景写真家協会会員。

新海良夫（しんかい よしお）

1953 年長野県生まれ。1979 年より日本各地の風景写真の撮影を始める。「自然が持つ色彩と光で日本の美を表現する」ことをコンセプトに撮影活動を続ける。写真展開催の他、各種媒体に作品を多数提供している。日本風景写真家協会会員。

杉本英男（すぎもと ひでお）

1942 年東京都生まれ。山岳写真家・白簱史朗氏に師事。美しい四季が織り成すドラマに魅了され、刻々と変わる自然の姿との出会いを求め撮影を続ける。企業カレンダー、パンフレット等に作品を提供。羽田フォトクラブ水曜会会長。

高椋俊樹（たかむく としき）

1960 年福井県生まれ。フォトコンテストで優勝、入選多数。カメラ雑誌や出版物に作品を提供、カレンダーやパンフレット等にも、数多く作品を提供している。鑑賞者の心にその場を想起させるような、臨場感のある作品を目指し、精力的に撮影を続けている。

竹内トキ子（たけうち ときこ）

東京都生まれ。現像所勤務で写真の面白さを知り、写真家・竹内敏信氏に師事。1989 年より本格的に富士山を撮り始めてから、現在まで富士山一筋に撮影。写真展写真集多数。主な写真集に『富士雪月花』『富士山 雲の変幻 II』がある。日本写真家協会会員。

館野二朗（たての じろう）

1975 年東京都生まれ。趣味の渓流釣りを通して、人の手の加えられていない自然の美しさを知り写真を始める。日本各地の自然風景と奄美大島を主なテーマに精力的に撮影活動を続け、カレンダーや雑誌等の媒体に作品を提供している。

富田文雄（とみた ふみお）

東京都生まれ。東京写真専門学校卒業。山岳写真家に師事の後フリーの写真家に。日本各地の自然風景、里の風景を中心に撮影。著書に『日本の里』『日本の美しい里』『日本の美しい里の絶景』(すべてパイ インターナショナル) 他がある。日本風景写真家協会会員。

豊高隆三（とよたか りゅうぞう）

1947 年東京都生まれ。大阪万国博覧会の取材ではじめて小型飛行機に同乗、航空写真に魅せられる。1970 年スカイフォト（株）設立。アサイメント撮影の傍ら創作活動にも尽力。写真展写真集多数。主な写真集に『空遊録』『Skyview』『空撮日本の自然』がある。日本写真家協会会員。

縄手英樹（なわて ひでき）

1965 年新潟県生まれ。大学卒業後オーストラリアに一年半滞在し、バイクで同地一周の撮影旅行をする。帰国後、写真家・清水誠司氏に師事の後フリーに。現在は日本全国の風景を中心に撮影活動を行い、作品を多数媒体に提供している。日本風景写真家協会会員。

温井和俊（ぬくい かずとし）

1938 年東京都生まれ。1962 年早稲田大学卒業。商社勤務の後、1995 年日本写真芸術専門学校に入学。富士山に魅せられ、年間を通じて富士山の撮影を続けている。雲や光を存分に生かした作風は幽玄で、海外での人気も高い。写真展多数。日本写真家協会会員。

深澤 武（ふかざわ たけし）

1974 年埼玉県生まれ。1998 年東京理科大学工学部卒。在学中より北アルプスの山々に憧れ信州をメインに撮影を始める。その後、日本各地へエリアを広げ風景や生き物の撮影を続け、各種媒体に作品を多数提供。主な写真集に『沖縄・八重山諸島』『奄美・琉球』がある。日本写真家協会会員。

富士山写真家 オイ

1985 年神奈川県生まれ。富士登山をきっかけに富士山の魅力に取り憑かれ、2011 年頃から撮影活動を開始する。2017 年には山梨県の富士山麓へ移住し、日々変化する富士山の表情と向き合いながら撮影を続けている。

八木千賀子（やぎ ちかこ）

1977 年愛知県生まれ。1997 年頃から写真を独学で始めた後、写真家・辰野清氏、栄馬智太郎氏に師事。東京カメラ部 10 選 2013 に選出される。2016 年に会社を退職しフリーの写真家に。日本全国の風景、八丈島をテーマに、撮影活動を行う。八丈島ふるさと観光大使。

山梨勝弘 (やまなし かつひろ)

1945 年東京都生まれ。東京写真短期大学 (現・東京工芸大学) 卒。1989 年
山梨写真事務所設立。四季折々の自然風景や街など幅広い被写体を対象とし
て日本全国を精力的に撮影。企業カレンダーや出版物に作品を提供、写真集
写真展も多数。日本風景写真家協会会員。

山梨将典 (やまなし まさのり)

1975 年東京都生まれ。東京工芸大学芸術学部写真学科卒業。広告デザイン
会社に勤務の後、2000 年にフリーの写真家となる。日本全国の風景、星景・
月光の景色をメインテーマに撮影活動をし、作品を写真集や雑誌、カレンダー
等に提供している。

米原敬太郎 (よねはら けいたろう)

1974 年京都府生まれ。1997 年多摩美術大学卒業、1999 年京都市立芸術大
学大学院修了。デザイン事務所勤務を経て独立。東京を拠点に、ファッション
を中心とした広告写真など幅広く活躍する一方、数年前より富士山の撮影に力
を入れている。

富士山八十八景

Eighty-eight views of Mt. Fuji

2020年6月21日　初版第1刷発行

編著	パイ インターナショナル
翻訳	伏原玲子　髙橋奈穂子　パメラ・ミキ
デザイン	淡海季史子
協力	株式会社アイノア　イメージナビ株式会社
編集	諸隈宏明
発行人	三芳寛要

発行元：株式会社パイ インターナショナル
〒170-0005 東京都豊島区南大塚 2-32-4
TEL 03-3944-3981　FAX 03-5395-4830
sales@pie.co.jp

印刷・製本：日本写真印刷コミュニケーションズ株式会社

© 2020 PIE International
ISBN 978-4-7562-5328-6 C 0072

Printed in Japan

本書の収録内容の無断転載・複写・複製等を禁じます。
ご注文、乱丁・落丁本の交換等に関するお問い合わせは、小社までご連絡ください。

Eighty-eight views of Mt. Fuji

Editorial Design: Kishiko Oomi
Translation: Reiko Fushihara / Nahoko Takahashi / Pamela Miki
Cooperation: ainoa Inc. / Image navi corporation
Editor: Hiroaki Morokuma
Publisher: Hiromoto Miyoshi
Printer: Nissha Printing Communications, Inc.

© 2020 PIE International
All rights reserved. No part of this publication may be reproduced, stored in a retrieval system,
or transmitted in any form or by any means, graphic, electronic or mechanical, including photocopying
and recording, or otherwise, without prior permission in writing from the publisher.

PIE International Inc.
2-32-4 Minami-Otsuka, Toshima-ku, Tokyo 170-0005 JAPAN
international@pie.co.jp
www.pie.co.jp/english

ISBN978-4-7562-5328-6

Printed in Japan